D0592278

ENGENDERED LIVES

ENGENDERED LIVES

A NEW
PSYCHOLOGY
OF WOMEN'S EXPERIENCE

Ellyn Kaschak, PH.D.

BasicBooks
A Division of HarperCollins*Publishers*

Poetry excerpt on page v reprinted from *Loving in the War Years* by Cherríe Moraga with permission from the publisher, South End Press, 116 Saint Botolph St., Boston, MA 02115 U.S.A.

Parts of chapters 5 and 6 were first published in *Women and Therapy* (Winter 1989); reprinted with permission.

Epigraph, chapter 6, reprinted from *Borderlands/La Frontera, The New Mestiza*, copyright 1987 Gloria Anzaldúa, with permission of Aunt Lute Books (415) 558-8116.

Poetry extract on pp. 101–2 from *Monster* by Robin Morgan. Copyright © 1972 by Robin Morgan. Reprinted by permission of Random House, Inc.

Library of Congress Cataloging-in-Publication Data
Kaschak, Ellyn, 1943–
    Engendered lives: a new psychology of women's experience/by Ellyn Kaschak.
      p. cm.
    Includes bibliographical references and index.
    ISBN 0-465-01347-3
    1. Women—Psychology. 2. Feminist psychology. 3. Feminist psychotherapy.   I. Title.
    HQ1206.K37 1992   91–58602
    155.6′33—dc20   CIP

Copyright © 1992 by BasicBooks, A Division of HarperCollins Publishers, Inc.

All rights reserved. Printed in the United States of America. No part of this book may be reproduced in any manner whatsoever without written permission except in the case of brief quotations embodied in critical articles and reviews. For information address BasicBooks, 10 East 53rd Street, New York, NY 10022–5299.

Designed by Ellen Levine

92 93 94 95 CC/RRD 9 8 7 6 5 4 3 2 1

Later, she met Joyce
and after they had been friends for a whole
school year, formed their own
girls' gang with code words and rhymes
that played itself cooly
on this *side of trouble*
they got separated by the summer.
—Cherríe Moraga
Loving in the War Years

To all the girl gang members along the way.
And especially for
ARLENE RABINOWITZ GOLDSON—
separated by summer

Contents

ACKNOWLEDGMENTS   *ix*

INTRODUCTION   *1*

1
Making Meaning   *9*

2
Gender Embodied   *37*

3
Oedipus and Antigone Revisited:
The Family Drama   *55*

4
Identity Embodied   *89*

5
Relationships: His and Hers   *114*

Contents

6
Limits and Boundaries   131

7
Self and Esteem   148

8
Order Out of Disorder: Disorderly Conduct   165

9
Eating   190

10
A New Model for Feminist Psychotherapy   210

REFERENCES   227

INDEX   253

Acknowledgments

The ideas in this book have developed within the context of feminist thought and action of the past two decades, in which I have found my intellectual and political home. Feminist theory and practice have been an endlessly rich source of ideas for me, and I have incurred a debt that I hope I have repaid, at least in part, with my own work. I cannot imagine my work and my life outside of feminist thought and practice or away from the women who make these ideas a way of life.

In addition to this general indebtedness, I owe a particular debt to certain colleagues and friends, without whom my work could not have taken its current form. First and foremost, Sara Sharratt and Sheila Bienenfeld provided a dual perspective, consistently different from each other and contrapuntal to my own. Each read and reread every word in this book until she knew my thoughts as well as I did. Sara Sharratt gave me the benefit of her deep understanding of feminist thought, as well as her support and friendship. She has been a true *compañera* in all the struggles and triumphs of my adult life. I thank Sheila Bienenfeld for her unfailing honesty, her intellectual and verbal acuity, her wit, and, most of all, the generosity with which she offered them. Her belief in my ability to do this work helped make it so.

Hannah Lerman gave the manuscript more than one careful reading and was both encouraging and critical, in the best sense of the word. Marny Hall read several versions of the manuscript and enthusiastically encouraged the work in progress. Natalie Porter and Kay Trimberger also read part or all of the manuscript and gave me the benefit of their perspectives. I thank Marcia Freedman for the final naming.

The members of the Feminist Therapy Institute have provided a context for my work. My women clients, students, colleagues, and friends have also served as my teachers. I also want to thank my parents, Celia and Bernard Uram, who first taught me never to compromise my beliefs or myself.

Jo Ann Miller, my editor at Basic Books, envisioned this book early on and, in a manner both skillful and respectful of the work, helped it take form, while Linda Carbone offered careful, yet enthusiastic, attention to the details of that form. Anna Lorenzi proved herself an intrepid and indefatigable research assistant, often pursuing an elusive fact or quotation across continents of unyielding data bases and answering machines until she came upon just the right study or reference or expert.

A sabbatical year from San Jose State University allowed me to write a first draft in as uninterrupted a form as my life ever takes. Finally, this book would never have come into being but for the various cafés in the Berkeley-Oakland area, in Paris, and in San José, Costa Rica, in which much of my writing and many of my observations took place. And, at last, Sandra Butler has been responsible for some crucial last-minute changes that make all the difference.

ENGENDERED LIVES

Introduction

Τhis book is about the lived and ordinary experiences of women. It is about the relationship between the social construction of gender and the most intimate feelings and thoughts, joys and sorrows, of each woman and every woman. It is about growing up, becoming a girl and then a woman, and the problems and solutions that accompany this course of development.

Engendered Lives has evolved from my own experiences as a feminist, a psychologist, and an educator. Some twenty years ago, I completed the academic part of my graduate training as a clinical psychologist and began a two-year internship at a major Veterans Administration hospital. There I would be trained clinically in an array of models and techniques, ranging from behavior modification to group therapy to family therapy, in a well-respected program that reflected and contributed to the most current thinking in the field.

At the same time, the influence of the women's movement was beginning to be felt and, where only a few years before there had been few or no women in most doctoral programs, we were now well represented—or so it seemed. As it turned out, we were represented in number only. Our perspectives remained absent from the models and practices of psychotherapy. I did not realize this at the time, believing that I was being trained in approaches to psychotherapy that were unrelated to and unbiased by the gender of the participants.

For example, as an intern, I was requested by my supervisor to go to a local porn shop and purchase literature that depicted sex between adult

1

men and young children. This material was to be used in the treatment of an adult man incarcerated for repeatedly molesting young children. As his therapist, I was then to supervise his program of masturbation and attempt to get him to transfer his interest from these images of children to images of women in *Playboy* magazine—a standard decontextualized behavioral therapy that is still very much in use. The new preference for *Playboy* models would then qualify him to be a normal, healthy adult male. At the same time, the patient was sent to local meetings of Parents Without Partners to find an "appropriate" woman to date. It occurred to no one that through this unsuspecting new dating partner, this man might be exposed to children. Nor did his effect on the women he might date seem to be of concern. He and he alone was the patient.

This was a somewhat awkward experience for me, to say the least, and my choice, at the time, seemed to be to decline and have a male colleague do it, thereby calling attention to my limits as a female member of the team, or to accept the assignment. At that time, I saw no other alternatives. My supervisor had offered me the assignment in an honest demonstration of his own lack of discrimination. I attributed my feeling of discomfort to being "uptight" about sexuality, a problem I would have to overcome if I were to become an effective psychotherapist. I later came to understand that what appeared to be lack of discrimination was really treating everyone like a man in a man's world and not questioning the appropriateness of that behavior. Certainly no thought was given to my predicament or to the possible danger to the women and children who might become unwitting participants in this man's treatment.

As a family therapy intern, I was taught to help families by removing so-called enmeshed mothers from their overly close interactions with their children and bringing in the uninvolved fathers as newly dubbed experts on child rearing. I was also taught to wonder what women who were being beaten repeatedly did to provoke and/or participate in maintaining the beatings. From a family systems perspective, they were as much a part of "the system" as their husbands and were thus considered to play an equal part in creating and sustaining the problem. Curiously, this principle of equal responsibility was invoked when a woman was being mistreated, but when a child appeared disturbed, the same therapists had no difficulty pointing to an enmeshed or even a "schizophrenogenic" mother as the cause. If the father had any responsibility at all, it was to become more involved as a way of diminishing the mother's influence.

My female colleagues and I got along fine as long as we played by the established male rules, which involved viewing psychological needs from a male perspective and ignoring or pathologizing those of females. Other female psychologists, most of whom had also been admitted recently to the field, were beginning to take note of the discrepancies. At the same time, we were questioning sexism and oppression in the personal spheres of our lives through the process of consciousness raising. We were beginning to make the kinds of discoveries after which nothing ever looks the same, but none of us had any idea how extensive the feminist social critique would become. It began to touch many of the traditional academic disciplines, psychology among them.

In 1972, Phyllis Chesler's *Women and Madness* appeared and spoke precisely to my and many other women's experiences as female psychologists in training. Her book, along with a variety of articles and chapters by other psychologists and sociologists, including Naomi Weisstein, Anne Koedt, Pauline Bart, Hannah Lerman, and Annette Brodsky (all reprinted in Cox 1976), had a profound impact on the nascent field of feminist therapy. A rapidly developing literature began criticizing the theories and practices of psychotherapy and proposing alternatives that might be helpful, rather than damaging, to women.

These alternatives were based upon the rapidly growing awareness that traditional therapeutic approaches reproduced the power differential between men and women, with mostly men setting themselves up as experts who diagnosed and treated mostly women patients and clients. As a result, these therapies had a multitude of built-in masculine biases, most prominent among which was a standard of mental health for women that differed from that for men; it largely involved helping women adjust to the prescribed feminine role. The definition of psychopathology in women was based on deviation from the prescribed into the territory of the proscribed: that is, mental health in women was measured by their adherence to traditional gender-role behavior.

Feminist therapists instead worked to eliminate exploitive power differentials between therapist and client and to enable women to overcome society's training through the development of such techniques as assertiveness training. As another example, psychotherapists had followed Freud's lead in assuming that women experienced two different kinds of orgasm. The clitoral, immature and imitative of masculinity, had to be replaced by the vaginal, phallocentric in mature, well-adjusted women. Based on the anatomical research of Masters and Johnson (1966), Koedt (1976) and other feminists led the way in documenting the fact that women experience only one kind of orgasm and that it is not focused on the penis or even most easily achieved in heterosexual intercourse. From this growing understanding emerged a treatment for pre-orgasmic women (previously known as "frigid"), which relied on simple behavioral techniques and had an almost

100 percent success rate for participants in a ten-week program. Before this remarkable innovation, treatment for orgasmic dysfunction in women typically took years and had a much lower success rate.

Groups involved in developing feminist therapy theory and practice sprang up almost simultaneously in several areas across the country, including San Francisco, New York, and Boston. It was both a grass roots and an academic/professional movement, as women began to question all aspects of their experience and as more female clients sought out female therapists. There was tremendous excitement about the new discoveries we were making in the field of therapy. We began a project no less ambitious than the dismantling and rebuilding of psychological theory and psychotherapeutic practice. It soon became clear to me what the problems were at the hospital where I had done my internship, although I alone did not have the power to change them. That power would accumulate as women joined together to change the face of the profession.

In 1972, I became a founding member of the Women's Counseling Service of San Francisco, a group that worked actively to develop a theory and practice for the new field of feminist therapy. I have continued this work ever since in private practice, through supervision, and through my position as a professor of psychology at San Jose State University, where, since 1974, I have been teaching clinically related courses, supervising therapists in training, and publishing related work.

In the intervening years, the field has become more complex and sophisticated in its theoretical analyses and therapeutic applications. The crucial importance of social context, complexity, and diversity of perspectives has become an integral part of feminist theory, as has the acknowledgment of the "value ladenness" of any research or therapeutic endeavor. There is a renewed interest in understanding the connections between sociopolitical phenomena and personal psychological experience and respect for the complexity of psychological experience and change.

All of the early collectives have long since disbanded and, for better or worse (some of both, in my opinion), the field has been highly professionalized. Most practitioners hold advanced degrees from recognized institutions, as well as licenses to practice psychotherapy. The Feminist Therapy Institute, an organization of which I am currently National Chair, was created about ten years ago. The members of this group work directly on the advancement of feminist psychological theory and practice. Feminist theory is a major and growing force at the cutting edge of the most exciting intellectual and therapeutic work being done. In this book, I present my work in this area.

Beginning from the proposition that every aspect of experience, from our

4

first moments, is gendered—our work, our relationships, our bodies, even our use of language—I will show how the abstract category of gender is embodied by and translated into everyday experience. This arrangement plays itself out in a variety of interesting and important psychological ways related, for women in particular, to physicality, sexuality, and sense of self and self-esteem, as well as to so-called psychological disorders such as depression, anxiety, and dissociative and eating disorders.

The most notable aspect of current gender arrangements is that the masculine always defines the feminine by naming, containing, engulfing, invading, and evaluating it. The feminine is never permitted to stand alone or to subsume the masculine. This arrangement leads, at best, to many paradoxes in women's lives. For example, women consistently provide sustenance to men and children and yet are considered weak and dependent. At worst, it is implicated in the unbridled violence against women and girls that is so much a part of our human landscape. Masculine meanings organize social and personal experience, so that women are consistently imbued with meanings not of their own making about appearance, sexuality, psychopathology, and many other crucial characteristics. Their most ordinary experiences often lead directly to what we then label psychological "disorders."

Although my approach is developmental, my focus is on the cultural context rather than on a narrow individual psychology. I consider social context to be part of the self just as the self always exists in context. I will attempt to expose some of the meanings by means of which sociocultural phenomena are translated into personal experience. I begin in chapter 1 with a discussion of traditional male-centered epistemologies and their influence in the fields of psychology and psychotherapy. This is followed by a discussion of certain feminist psychotherapies and the underlying epistemologies upon which they are based. In chapter 2, I trace the development and embodiment of gender in all people in this society. Chapter 3 presents the myth of Antigone and Oedipus and looks at how their relationship can serve as a template for understanding male-female relations in a patriarchal society. I take a closer look at the oedipal myth than did Freud and the Freudians, recognizing that it is a family drama and not just a story about a favored/cursed son. In particular, I try to resurrect and represent Antigone's lost perspective and even that of Jocasta, the mother of both. Based on this myth, I develop a model for the sociopsychological development of women and men in this society that emphasizes their eyes, vision, and blindness rather than the male genitals and castration. The development of a self based upon seeing and knowing rather than on sexuality makes more sense from this viewpoint.

In chapter 4, I consider some of the ramifications of this model. These include the male (oedipal) sin of looking, the necessity for feminine appearance to satisfy masculine desire and its implications for the formation of a female identity. In this way, the most ordinary meanings concerning women and appearance determine who women become. Chapters 5 and 6 pursue some further ramifications of the oedipal-antigonal relationship in the development of the female and male sense of self—that is, the placing of physical and psychological limits and their translation into psychological boundaries. Chapter 7 deals with the social-psychological development of the female self in general and of women's self-esteem in particular. In chapter 8, I discuss specific disorders in women and trace their sociocultural base to their most personal psychological manifestations in each individual. In chapter 9, I do the same with a specific problem of our times, women and eating. I end, in chapter 10, with some suggestions for working with the natural outcomes of learning to be a woman, such as depression, phobias, eating disorders, and dissociative disorders, which lead women into the psychotherapist's office.

In writing this book, I have become painfully aware of the limits of language to express new perspectives. That of women is often invisible not simply because it is unrepresented but because it is unrepresentable in our current language. Once one is aware of the biases of language itself, everything from the use of the pronoun *I*, which can seem overly personal and intrusive, or *we*, which may be too general and presumptuous, or even the presumably neutral *one*,* which cloaks value and opinion in the garb of neutrality and objectivity, becomes problematic. Referring to fields of study as *academic disciplines* implies a formality of structure, separateness, and boundedness that is deceptive. Often when I speak of psychology, I am aware of the overlap with sociology, psychiatry, social work, physiology, neurology, philosophy, and other so-called disciplines. In fact, the very act of naming must, by necessity, simplify complex reality, and one aspect of my writing has been to attempt to achieve clarity of expression without sacrificing the complexity of meanings. Women are compromised even as we speak. We have to invent simultaneously new ways to make meanings and new ways to speak them. Along with other feminists, I try to make my contribution here, sometimes with success but often limited by current language.

Another difficulty in terminology that has not been satisfactorily resolved is the use of the term *patient* or *client*. I am satisfied with neither,

*This third-person neutral pronoun is always used to signal objectivity. It is neutral by virtue of being indeterminate, not identified with anybody, as if not being able to locate the gendered perspective of the speaker or writer means there isn't one.

the former reflecting too closely the medical model of treatment, the latter a bit too reminiscent of customers of a business establishment. While I am aware of alternatives that have been suggested along the way by various feminist therapists, I am satisfied with none of these and, thus, continue the common use the term *client* except when I specifically want to reflect a medical approach to treatment. Having said this, let now me explain that, while not all the women whom I discuss in this book are clients, any descriptions of clients are actually composites. Having practiced for some twenty years, I have the luxury of a richness of client material upon which to draw. I have done this to protect the privacy of my own and my colleagues' clients, but it also serves to indicate the commonalities of women's problems. I have also included many nonclients (civilians) in my examples and analyses, again to illustrate the point that the issues I discuss are not confined, by any means, to a clinical population—nor is a clinical population different in kind from a so-called normal one.

The difficulty in finding a language to describe an integrated experience will become apparent to the reader, as it has to me. Any given experience must currently be described as either physical or psychological, either emotional or cognitive, and the perspectives from which it may be understood as physical, psychological, or perhaps sociological. In order to describe experience without fragmenting it, one must often use all these terms, by that very act acknowledging their conceptual separateness. The Chinese character *hsin,* much like the French word *conscience,* must be translated in English as "heart-mind." These foreign terms signify both cognitive and affective aspects of consciousness, both intellectual and moral awakening (Wei-ming 1989). The limits of the English language force me, from time to time, to string together, like strands of pearls in a necklace, aspects of experience that I wish to integrate into one complexity. While I use the term *complexity* to describe such a constellation of influences, I will also at times use a combined strand of the traditional terms in order to convey more clearly just what constellation I have in mind. The very difficulty in representing these perspectives speaks to their absence from our conceptual systems. American feminists have viewed women as oppressed, their voices not heard within the dominant culture. For the French, women are repressed, or culturally equivalent to the unconscious, and therefore unrepresentable in current language (Marks and de Courtivron 1981); they are invisible.

As the novelist and screenwriter Toni Cade Bambara has put it,

There have been a lot of things in . . . the Black experience for which there are no terms, certainly not in English at this moment. There are a lot of aspects of consciousness for which there is no vocabulary, no structure in the English language which would allow people to validate that experience through language. I'm trying to find a way to do that. . . . I'm trying to break open and get at the bones, deal with symbols as though they were atoms. I'm trying to find out not only how a word gains meaning, but how a word gains power. [Salaam 1980, p. 48]

As a clinician, I am aware of the dangers of generalization. In a very real sense, each woman's story is her own. As a feminist, I am equally aware that no woman's story is just her own. I try to write from this dual perspective. Each woman leads a particular life determined by her own talents and proclivities, her abilities and experiences, her ethnic and class membership. Yet all these experiences, I maintain, are organized by gender, so that each woman's story is also every woman's story.

1

Making Meaning

There are more things in heaven and earth, Horatio,
Than are dreamt of in your philosophy.

—Shakespeare
Hamlet, I, v

Many of the systems for understanding ourselves and our worlds are currently balanced precariously on the edge of a paradigm shift. This shift involves acknowledging the interconnectedness and reciprocal influence of the observer and the observed, mind and nature, and the impossibility of objectivity or control of all variables deemed irrelevant in an experiment. The Heisenberg Uncertainty Principle and the sciences of complexity represent this perspective in the field of physics, as does psychoneuroimmunology in the fields of psychology, neurology, and immunology.

Feminist thought has been a crucial part of this intellectual revolution. In the last two decades, feminist thought and analysis have been able to breathe new life into many traditional academic and professional disciplines, from the humanities to the sciences to the social sciences, to name them in the ways that they are currently and artificially divided. Many feminist writers have demonstrated and documented the patriarchal nature of our society and the variety of ways in which patriarchal values serve masculine needs (de Beauvoir 1968; Friedan 1963; Millett 1970), even in such arenas as science (Bleier 1984; Keller 1985) and the clinical practice of psychology (Broverman, I. K., et al. 1970; Chesler 1972; Miller 1976; Irigaray 1985), previously believed to be, or at least presented as, evaluatively

9

neutral and apolitical. In the most seemingly diverse fields, women's perspectives and ideas have been shown to be absent or buried or credited to men. It is always difficult, if not paradoxical, to take note of what is invisible, but it is precisely this paradoxical quest—to make the invisible female perspective visible—that has been undertaken by feminist scholarship.

A FEMINIST CRITIQUE OF MASCULINIST EPISTEMOLOGY

Scrutiny with a feminist eye has led to the development of a psychology that, for the first time, includes women's experiences and women's perspectives. The various prefeminist psychologies have spoken eloquently about how men socially construct and experience a unidimensional category named "woman," but have said little, if anything, about women's diverse experiences, about how women perceive themselves or others, about who women are, and especially about who and what women can be. While many of these theorists and practitioners have simply assumed that what they knew about men and mankind extended to women, others have filled volumes discussing and analyzing the construct "woman," but have failed to explain how they developed that construct or to acknowledge that it is a construct rather than an absolute reality, which would not need further explanation.

Epistemology is formally defined as the study of how knowledge is possible and how knowing is done (Bateson and Bateson 1987, p. 20). Prefeminist epistemologies were not only not objective or value-free but were based upon the world views and experiences of men, which appeared to *them* to be objective, evaluatively neutral, and universally applicable. Included among these so-called objective observations were men's experiences of women, along with a variety of androcentric psychological standards against which women were, and all too often still are, measured. Such biases could perhaps have been challenged sooner had the perspectives upon which they are based been explicitly acknowledged, that is, made visible. But the epistemology of a dominant group can be made to appear neutral, and its value base invisible, since it coincides perfectly with what appears to be society in some generic, universal form. Just as many sensory experiences depend upon the perception of contrast—so that, for example, a visual image that is made to move in unison with the eye's scanning

10

movement cannot be seen by that eye—masculinist epistemology in a patriarchal society may seem to define epistemology itself. A contrast had to
develop first in the mind's eye of a few women, and then of many, before
they could collectively make their perspectives visible. In this way, the
feminist critique began.

Thus feminist psychology had, as its first task, to expose this masculinist epistemology and challenge its use as the foundation of traditional
psychological thought. By *masculinist epistemology,* I mean systems of
knowledge that take the masculine perspective unself-consciously, as if it
were truly universal and objective. Despite claims to the contrary, masculinist epistemologies are built upon values that promote masculine
needs and desires, making all others invisible. It is important to note that
feminist thought sees its task not as promoting the needs and experiences
of women as normative or universal but as making visible the varying
experiences and perspectives that masculinist thought denies. Many
examples of this distinction will be considered in this and subsequent
chapters.

PREFEMINIST CLINICAL THEORIES AND METHODS

Over the last two decades, feminist psychology has moved through various stages of development. During its first decade, feminist scholars carefully considered and criticized clinical psychology and other related psychotherapeutic practices. Rather than undertaking a comprehensive
review of the substantial body of feminist criticism in this area, I will
consider some of the most basic and glaring epistemological blind spots
of prefeminist thought and their impact on the psychological and psychiatric professions.

The roots of many seemingly discrepant schools of thought and practice
are deeply embedded in the soil of masculinist thought, including those
schools that have most influenced clinical psychology and psychotherapeutic practice in the United States: behavior therapy, psychoanalytic
or psychodynamic therapy, and family therapy. I will consider each of
these approaches from the perspective of their shared epistemological
assumptions.

Behaviorism

Behaviorism has been presented as a scientifically based approach to an objective psychology. Derived from the logical positivist school of philosophy, it was translated into a uniquely American (pragmatic, control-oriented) form of empiricism originally by John Watson and B. F. Skinner, and eventually by a multitude of researchers and practitioners. It makes direct application of the same principles originally developed in controlled laboratory settings with animal subjects. Skinner's best-known work was conducted with pigeons and rats, Watson's with a white rat in the famous classical conditioning case of Albert, which he conducted with a little-known female co-investigator (Raynor and Watson 1921). The classical conditioning paradigm associated with Watson, involving the pairing of mutually exclusive responses, has been applied by Wolpe (1958) and other practitioners of behavior therapy or desensitization, in particular for the treatment of phobias (Wolpe 1970; Fodor 1974). For example, an individual who is afraid of open spaces will first be taught relaxation techniques and will then be asked to visualize an increasingly fearful series of situations involving open spaces. Each treatment will continue only as long as the client is able to remain relaxed. As soon as she signals that she is becoming anxious, the session is terminated. Eventually the individual passes through all the imaginary situations in a relaxed state and is ready to confront the actual feared situation.

The paradigm based upon the work of Skinner and many others with operant conditioning is known as behavior modification and has been applied extensively to work with children in school settings and with severely disturbed hospitalized or institutionalized patients. In these situations, contingent reinforcement is applied to increase or decrease the frequency of a desired or target behavior. For example, a child who does ten minutes of homework may immediately be rewarded with a period of play or may accrue tokens that can be exchanged for a desired activity or other reward. In its simplest form, this is a quid pro quo arrangement.

Most applications of these methods involve a mixture of both the classical and operant models. For example, an approach that grew directly from the early feminist therapy movement, assertiveness training, is based upon desensitization followed by active modification of behavior in the actual feared situation. That is, the individual may begin by visualizing a series of imagined situations in which she is able to behave assertively. The second step may involve rehearsal of these behaviors in the artificial setting of the therapy or training, followed by performing the desired behaviors in the actual settings that had previously been problematic for her.

Epistemologically, behaviorism is based upon the premise that every valid and interesting bit of information about persons is and must be, at least in principle, empirically knowable or verifiable. Universal behavioral principles, which apply not only to all people but across species, are sought and considered discoverable by controlled, objective, scientific observation, by identifying and manipulating the smallest possible separate or linked units of behavior. From this perspective, complex human psychology can be reduced to a set of fully knowable and determinate behavioral principles. Change occurs through the identification and manipulation of the smallest possible separate or linked units of behavior according to the same principles. Who and what is changed is considered a decision outside the boundaries of this method.

The feminist scholar Evelyn Fox Keller (1985) has noted that objectivity, control, individuality, and the advancement of science through competing and rising above ordinary life are the hallmarks of Western masculinity and Western masculinist science. The philosophical school of logical positivism translated to scientific empiricism within psychology falls squarely within this tradition. Adherents have claimed that this method defines both objectivity and the science of human behavior itself, by means of which one can learn to "understand, predict and control behavior" (Hassett 1984).

The method of this sort of science involves drawing rigid boundaries around minutiae, which can then be carefully controlled, observed, and manipulated, presumably without any undesired influence from the controller, observer, and manipulator or from the larger environment. This approach is obviously reductionist. It purports to be absent of values but in fact has its foundation in the value-based principles of objectivity, dispassionate and uninvolved rationality, control and manipulation, and separation of fact from value, experimenter from subject, and context from subject and experimenter. The psychological world, from this perspective, is both knowable and conquerable as an aspect of the material world.

Yet one achieves objectivity by ignoring a multiplicity of important, if not crucial, influences on the experiment that lie outside its narrow boundary as drawn. These include aspects of the physical context such as the experimental design and the setting in which it occurs, the time of day, the state of readiness of the subject, and whether participation is required for credit in an undergraduate psychology course. Additionally, aspects of the social context such as the effect of various qualities of the experimenter/behavior modifier (Rosenthal 1968), including race, gender, and even disposition, are "controlled for" or ignored. Not only are results in laboratories generalized to the natural environment but laboratory subjects are considered to be under the influence only of those variables the experimenter wishes to study, the rest being "controlled." The gender, class, race, and personal history of the subject, along with the very effect of being an experimental or a therapeutic subject, are all too often considered extraneous variables unless they are the object of study.

The behavioral approach tends to be individually or, at best, dyadically focused. For example, in working with a child who is having problems, the reinforcement contingent upon the child's behavior and applied by the mother or teacher may be altered. Contingencies maintaining the mother's or teacher's behavior are rarely considered. Mothers are given responsibility for their children's contingencies much more often in this so-called value-free literature than are children for their mothers' or are fathers for anyone's. Yet implicit in the very principle of reinforcement is its universality. The behaviorist model considers it possible, both in principle and certainly in practice, to ascertain, manipulate, and control the multiplicity of influences that affect a child at any given time.

Imagine a female child who perceives her father's hostile feelings toward his own mother. Additionally, she is aware of her mother's despair over a difficult marriage and an interrupted career at a time when women are gaining access to better jobs. Do these complex experiences affect the child only in observable and manipulable ways? What if we then add to the picture the meanings that the child attributes to these factors, in particular, her own diminished sense of self-worth? Are these aspects reducible to fragments of observable behavior whose combination is only quantitative and does not create a qualitatively different psychological constellation? Indeed, new, complex, and subjectively organized meanings will come to permeate this child's psychological experiences in an untold variety of situations.

Psychoanalysis

The psychoanalytic approach has already been the subject of serious criticism (Millett 1970; Chesler 1972; Koedt 1976; Lerman 1986) as well as attempts at revision (Mitchell 1974; Alpert 1986; Bernay and Cantor 1986) by feminist scholars. Its development has not proceeded according to the tenets of logical positivism; rather, this approach is based upon introspection and the analysis of intrapsychic events, such as transference and countertransference, manifested interpersonally in the therapeutic relationship. Nevertheless, Freud and various psychoanalytic theorists who have followed him have sought to discover natural psychological laws that are objective and universal. Psychological phenomena are divided into two realms of experience, the conscious and the unconscious, movement from the latter to the former being a primary goal within the process of analytic therapy, along with the recapitulation of early experience in the therapeutic relationship. The approach is reductionist in that it traces all human behavior to a few basic drives and/or early childhood experiences. It is deterministic in believing that all mental functioning is caused by identifiable factors already in existence. It is materialist in that it explains "higher" levels of functioning in terms of "lower" ones.

Inherent in the analytic perspective is a gender analysis based upon unalterable anatomical and biological differences between the sexes. As the behaviorists' approach has been judged as too narrow, so the Freudian approach has been criticized by feminists for being phallocentric. Its epistemology takes male experience as the universal norm, considering possession or lack of a penis the central element in the psychological makeup of all people (Cixous 1980; Kristeva 1982; Irigaray 1985). Those without penises are forever relegated, by definition, to inferior status and are unable fully to resolve important developmental tasks. Even women's essential role in childbirth is viewed, in part or fully, as a consolation prize, a substitute for the coveted first prize. Psychological makeup is determined by biology and by early childhood experience in the oedipal triangle formed by the child and parents. Woman is considered an *homme manqué* to be understood primarily and throughout her psychological development (or lack thereof) by her lack of a penis.* Unlike the behaviorist approach, the psychoanalytic clearly distinguishes between two types of people, the haves and the have-nots, the latter being forever doomed to second-class status.

According to the Freudian psychoanalytic perspective, all individuals pass through predictable and definable stages of psychosexual development, which must be successfully negotiated to become mature adults. All human experience is reducible to and explained by these stages of development, which are all completed in childhood and early adolescence and in relation primarily to the parents.

The same client I mentioned in the behavioral example, the woman afraid of open spaces, would be approached very differently by the analytically oriented therapist. The etiology of this fear, diagnosed as agoraphobia, would be sought in early childhood memories, dreams, associations, and transference in the therapeutic relationship. Undoubtedly it would be

---

*A male student once explained to me that he thought it is men who have penis envy: he admitted that he himself certainly envied his penis. This comment speaks of some men's relationship with their sexual organ, which they apparently believe has a life of its own.

sought in the psychosexual history in general and the oedipal or family drama in particular. Undoubtedly penis envy and castration anxiety would figure prominently. Only through uncovering the memory of the early traumatic event(s) that led to this fear, along with the accompanying affects, can a catharsis be accomplished and the anxiety discharged: that is, the underlying intrapsychic conflict must come to awareness and be resolved in the therapeutic relationship.

The analyst is viewed not as a particular person of a particular gender, class, or race with its concomitant values and perspectives but as a relatively dispassionate, neutral figure upon whom projection can occur. The analyst thereby becomes the current representation of the parent(s) of early child-hood and is, in this sense, both decontextualized and disembodied. Although more modern approaches, such as that of Harold Searles (1979), make explicit use of countertransference, it is still considered to be uniquely developed in response to the analysand. This takes place, most importantly, through the defense of projective identification, whereby the analyst is included in the picture but as a finely tuned instrument for receiving and interpreting the patient's projections and distortions and, second, through intrusion of the analyst's unresolved intrapsychic and familial conflicts stripped of any cultural meanings.

I will not, at this point, undertake a criticism from a feminist perspective of all the latter-day revisions, adaptations, and schools of psychotherapy derived from the original Freudian school, which can be broadly subsumed under the aegis of analytically oriented approaches, those emphasizing ego functioning being most prominent. Some of this work has already been begun (Westkott 1986), as have attempts to revise or adapt the original Freudian approach in a manner relevant to women's psychology (Miller 1973; Alpert 1986; Bernay and Cantor 1986). The object-relations approach, adapted to feminist psychology by Nancy Chodorow (1978) and others, will be considered at length in later chapters.

Family Therapy

The third school of therapy to be considered, the family systems approach, also reflects masculinist perspective and values in its inception and outlook. Introduced as an objective, meta-mathematical approach (Watzlawick 1967) that closely approximates technological systems thinking, it deals with observable behavior or communication based on a presumably neutral cybernetic model—that is, families function according to the same principles as do computers. Yet the major theorists have clearly interjected their own world views. Of the founders of family systems therapy, all but Virginia Satir were men, and they have typically approached families as regulated, rule-governed systems, like computers, or as hierarchical, executive-run systems, like businesses. Satir neither endorsed nor made use of either of these models.

The male theorists have also viewed parenting by mothers and fathers as necessarily differing, just as the culture at large does, without questioning this assumption. They trace the source of problems all too frequently to the *over*involvement, or enmeshment, of the mother with her children, neither acknowledging the bias inherent in the use of these terms nor understanding the patriarchal basis for this circumstance, but locating the problem within individual women (Hare-Mustin 1978, 1987). They blame women for being just what the culture prescribes: intensely involved with their families and children.

The family systems approach was introduced in the 1950s, the decade that saw the rise of the modern, white, middle-class, nuclear family, and took the familial configuration of the father in the executive role and the mother in the affective role as the norm and the normal—objectively, of course. In fact, these families were "more nuclear, more socially isolated, and more gender dichotomized than any in previous history" (Goldner 1985, p. 44). Although Jay Haley (1969) and others have recognized power maneuvers as a factor in developing symptoms, the basic power inequity of gender difference and the influence of larger social systems such as gender arrangements have been deemed irrelevant and thus steadfastly ignored by mainstream family systems theorists.

The systems approach, as a result, turns out to be a closed system that does not provide a means to assess differential power or to attribute responsibility to different parts of a system or to allow for external influences. For example, if a woman is being battered by her husband, the systems theorist is required to look at how this behavior is both serving and being maintained equally by both partners. Far from being value-free, this approach is misogynist and victim blaming (Bograd 1984). It also values the family more highly than any of its individual members and, in practice, often sacrifices the welfare of the individual to that of the group. For example, in a well-known, typical intervention by Salvador Minuchin, a family member, usually the adolescent daughter, is anorectic. Minuchin's strategy involves introducing the distant father into parenting as an expert who can teach the "overly enmeshed" mother a few things about parenting an adolescent. An outcome is considered successful when the anorectic symptoms are removed. I have yet to hear what happens to the mothers, who have implicitly been informed by an expert not only that they have not done their jobs correctly but that their relatively uninvolved husbands have the necessary expertise to correct the situation. How many of these mothers wind up quietly depressed after this "successful" family outcome?

The client fearful of open spaces would be approached with her partner or spouse and perhaps her whole family. Were she not currently in a partner or family relationship, her family of origin would be the focus of the therapy. The function of her symptom would be sought within these relationships. A typical analysis would consider her fear as a means to exercise power in a primary relationship, for example, to keep her husband or partner by her side. The couple relationship would be more finely calibrated so that closeness could be achieved more openly and the symptom would no longer need to serve the function of creating closeness. This might occur through open negotiation or by manipulating the situation so that the woman would back off and her husband or partner would then presumably come forward in a well-calibrated dance. She would see that she had actually been participating in preventing closeness by the very act of seeking it. The work of the therapist is to recalibrate the cybernetic system, all parts being assumed to exercise equal power. As in behavioral therapy, removal of the symptom would be the goal and an indication of a successful outcome. The meaning or sources of this fear in other spheres of her life as a woman would not be considered, nor would its relationship to other fears, feelings, or experiences.

Ironically, this approach was developed in order to consider the larger system in which an individual functions, namely, the family. However, the leaders in the field, as well as the multitude of other nonfeminist practitioners, have, by and large, chosen to ignore both the historical roots of the patriarchal family and its relationship with larger social systems, and instead to focus narrowly on the current organization of the family as the best and only means of understanding it. Feminist critics have insisted that competent and consistent application of systems theory must necessarily include formulations about the effect of larger systems such as class, race, ethnicity, and gender on the family and its members (Goldner 1985; Luepnitz 1988; Kaschak 1990). It must also include acknowledgment of the values, perspective, and gender of the theorist or therapist. Only after the development of a feminist critique of the field have feminist critics been able to begin to develop a perspective that is consistent with and explicit about feminist principles (McGoldrick, Anderson, and Walsh 1989; Walters et al. 1988; Luepnitz 1988). These are certainly not widely accepted among more traditional family therapists; they are passionately repudiated by some and dispassionately ignored by others who persist in applying misogynist and ethnocentric principles to their work with families.

Clinical Psychology

Psychologists have tried to divorce themselves from an early marriage with philosophy in order to make a more respectable union with value-free science. Even the second marriage, however, must prove a disappointment, for as Keller has noted, "Science is the name we give to a set of practices and a body of knowledge delineated by a community, not simply defined by the exigencies of logical proof and experimental verification" (1985, p. 4). Fact and value cannot be so easily separated, Descartes notwithstanding. Psychology is always based on subjective decisions from a particular perspective. Philosophy and epistemology are traveling companions on every scientific journey. It has been rightfully said that whoever claims to have no epistemology has a bad one (Bateson and Bateson 1987).

Nevertheless, generations of students have been taught about value-free science and, more surprisingly perhaps, value-free psychotherapy, which is based upon either observation or reflection and introspection (of men). In both cases, however, the theorist/practitioner defines the appropriate method of study and draws the boundary around what is to be studied. These perspectives and values have not only been institutionalized but have come to define reality and normality itself. Women are thus rendered invisible (unreal) or, by definition, abnormal. The absence of the diverse perspectives of women of all classes and colors from psychology limits its applicability to less than half of humankind. Add to this the exclusion of the perspectives of other people of color and the relevance of traditional psychology is further reduced.

Just as classification in chemistry is an artifact, an act of the chemist, not of nature (Bateson and Bateson 1987, p. 153), psychological classification and explanation are artifacts of the psychologist. The very definitions of *woman* and *man* are not real, independently existing entities but functions of the viewer, the definer, the categorizer, the namer and *his* values, *his* needs, *his* experience, and *his* physical instrument. That is, the knowledge to which one has access, or, better said, the knowledge that one creates, is a function of one's epistemology, one's manner of knowing, and what one defines as worth being known.

The categories *man* and *woman* are examples of a system of classification based upon the dualistic thought inherited in the Western world from Descartes, renowned among us for having validated his own existence by the "fact" that he thought. And indeed he did, but he thought in opposites, in dichotomies, seeking verifiable facts, passing down to his sons the notion that facts are only waiting to be discovered. The old adage that there are two kinds of people in the world, those who believe that there are two kinds of people and those who don't, points up the impossibility of criticizing this paradigm from within its own confines.

THE NATURE OF (WO)MAN

Consider the Nature of Man, that age-old puzzle that has been addressed by every important male philosopher and psychologist. Note just how the question is formulated, for embedded within the question itself are its potential answers. If one undertakes to study a category of being known as man, whose members are made up of men and "of-men" and "not-men," certain decisions and results are predetermined.

Bertrand Russell and Alfred North Whitehead have demonstrated that "[a] class cannot be a member of itself" (Watzlawick 1967) without creating an error of logical typing—that is, an error that results in the creation of a paradox, an undigestible piece of communication. Such an error occurs in the use of the word *man* to describe an individual member of the category "man." Is *man* an individual or the category of which "man" is a member? Not to experience consciously this paradoxical concept requires a distortion in perception and cognition that has been well accomplished in our culture and that creates a scotoma of all the senses, a denial of others for men, a virtual denial of self for women.

The trick involved in making sense out of this nonsensical proposition is to render woman either a subset of man or totally invisible, that is, either "of-man" or "not-man." Thus, if she exists at all, a woman becomes a kind of man. From that conceptually flawed starting point, it is a natural step for psychologists to ponder their inability to understand her, for they must wonder, "What kind of man is this anyway?" The answer, of course, follows from the nature of the question and the psychological perspective of the questioner: an abnormal one, a castrated one, a more emotional one, a less morally developed one, *un homme manqué*. It is from this epistemological framework that prefeminist clinical theories concerning women, whom they define as highly deviant, abnormal, or, at best, inferior men, were developed.

Freud, no doubt, understood something about the fantasies and fears of little boys and perhaps adult men when he postulated the presence of castration anxiety, but had no basis for transferring the existence of this fear to little girls, except through the mechanism of projection. To do so was to believe, as Freud apparently did, that little girls, at all times and in all places, upon becoming aware of the difference between their own and the male body, immediately and necessarily experience their own as an

20

inferior, mutilated form of the other. For this to be so, the little girl must be asking herself the question, "What kind of man (boy) am I?"

Could not a female psychologist equivalently project that the male child, upon experiencing the difference between his own body and that of the female, particularly his mother, must immediately and necessarily experience a sense of horror at the presence of an external and highly vulnerable growth? This would be the gynocentric mirror image of the Freudian castration theory, understanding the experience of a little boy from the perspective of an adult female. His question to himself would be, "What kind of woman am I?"

In fact, either or neither might occur, *depending*. Depending on the perspective of the viewer, of course, but also on the valuing context within which the hypothetical little girl or boy has developed and the meaning and values by means of which she or he has learned to interpret experience— that is, the valuing of the socially constructed differences between males and females by anyone who makes up part of the *meaningful* context of experience of that child, including parents, siblings, other family members, peers, other adults, media representations, and so on. Thus a gynocentric mirror image, to work as an analogy, requires a world that values the female as our own values the male, and degrades the male as ours does the female. The term *womankind* would include all humanity, both female and male. Only in such a world would the male child be prone to experience himself as a deformed female, would he be considered abnormal insofar as he differed from the female form and norm. It would take a remarkable leap, much like Alice's through the looking glass, for a male child in our culture to experience himself as an inferior female.

Feminist psychologists have had to point out to themselves and to a not-always-receptive community of nonfeminist psychologists that women can*not* be understood by superimposing on them either the experiences of men in general or the ideas of individual men concerning what it must be like to be a woman. Examples of this bias in clinical psychology abound and not only among its founding fathers. Consider the now well known and oft-quoted studies by Broverman et al. (1970, 1972), in which both male and female clinicians described the adult female as virtually opposite to both the adult male and the healthy adult. Both the methodology and the results of this study reflect the acceptance of the dichotomous nature of gender-related variables.

Other examples are all too easy to find. Psychoanalysts, in treating rape victims, have searched for the woman's unconscious masochism or desire to be raped. As we have seen, family therapists have analyzed the function of battering both for the batterer and the victim, whom they consider to have an equal stake in perpetuating her own victimization. For years, psychiatric journals have touted the salutary effects of antidepressants by printing "before" and "after" pictures showing a woman leaning on a mop looking despondently at her kitchen floor, and then happily mopping it after taking her medication. Case studies in which improvement *for women only* is inferred from changes in grooming and the application of makeup are common in the literature and in practice.

EMPIRICISM REVISITED

The empirical literature in psychology also provides abundant examples of research projects that use only male subjects but generalize to all people. Frieze et al. list the following common errors in methodology that "reflect and result in biases in the study of women":

1. Use of only male subjects in the experiment.
2. Not testing for sex differences.
3. Building theories by eliminating data from females that do not correspond to data from males.
4. Lack of knowledge of sex roles and how they influence behavior.
5. Exclusive use of male experimenters and investigators.
6. Ignoring important experimental and situational influences, including the use of male-biased tasks.
7. Viewing behaviors as dichotomous rather than integrated, especially conceptualizing masculinity and femininity as mutually exclusive.
8. Incorporating the value system prevalent in this culture (1978, pp. 16–17).

These are not potential, but actual, methodological errors that have been made over and over again and were accepted uncritically before the advent of feminist psychology. In fact, many of these errors continue to be made by masculinist and androcentrically based researchers.

THE MEANING OF MEANING

Current masculinist epistemologies are based upon the drawing of boundaries around fact and value and between man and woman, psychological and physical, psychological and sociological, intrapsychic and interpersonal. Categories, taxonomies, things, subjects, and verbs are created. A truth is posited that is independent of the observer, be he scientist or therapist, and that is general rather than relative (Harding 1987). Just as men in our society can appear independent if the cadre of female support (wives, mothers, secretaries) is not seen or is defined not as support of the male but as dependence on the part of the female, so can the observer appear independent only if the physical and relational context is made invisible. A slice of experience can be viewed as if it were experience itself.

Aside from its meaning as the study of the "rules" of knowing, *epistemology* also refers to the attribution of meaning, to the origins, limits, and sources of knowledge. Logical empiricists, for example, seek to set up an impregnable boundary within which reality is contained (Taggart 1985). The rest then becomes context or ground to the figure of observable behavior. These theorists err in considering themselves to be unaffected by that very context, for it is only by drawing an arbitrary boundary that anything can be considered only a context, only a modifier. As modern physics has amply shown, "the subject (perceiving apparatus) and object (the reality measured) form one seamless whole" (Berman 1984, p. 138). Logical empiricists, Freudians, family therapists, and other makers of boundaries are constantly seeking seams in a seamless tapestry. While it is probably impossible to work without some sort of boundary by means of which to organize experience, it must be acknowledged that any distinction between figure and ground is arbitrary and a function of the epistemology of the maker of that boundary. The narrower the focus, the more information is hidden from view.

To illustrate, Gregory Bateson (1987) spoke of his initial foray into Hawaii to study the communication of dolphins. The animals were, at the time, engaged in a behavior that was annoying the behavioral psychologists who were attempting to conduct certain conditioning experiments. According to the psychologists' perspective, the dolphins were interfering with their study. Bateson, who did not draw the boundary where these behavioral scientists did, took particular note of the dolphins' so-called annoying behavior rather than considering it noise to be eliminated. He realized that the dolphins were communicating about the very behavior being studied—meta-communications about the nature of the behavior, messages that

"This is play" embedded in the rest and the sine qua non of the successful interaction among these creatures. To ignore these messages was to eliminate a crucial aspect of communication, which always involves multiple events.

Unfortunately Bateson remained steadfastly unwilling or unable to apply this principle to an understanding of the development or treatment of women in society, judging from his discussion with his daughter in his last publication, edited and published by her after his death. As she notes, "after all these pages in which 'man' has meant human, perhaps readers will be able to generalize 'woman' to the same degree" (Bateson and Bateson 1987, p. 197). He was apparently more easily able to see things from the perspective of a dolphin than from that of a woman.

A FEMINIST CRITIQUE OF EARLY
FEMINIST EPISTEMOLOGY

As Ernest Gellner (1974) has aptly noted, epistemology is never the product of comfortable times. Having reached the limits of a prior epistemology, scholars are plunged into the uncertainty from which either fear and retrenching or creativity and intellectual revolution can ensue. Both forces are certainly now at work. Since methodology derives directly from epistemology, the many abuses and oversights of psychology in relation to women led feminist psychologists since the early 1970s to question the epistemology upon which the enterprise was based. In the 1980s and 1990s feminists have begun to refute and re-envision such systems. Feminist approaches themselves are not exempt from the same concerns; to the extent that we separate and reduce experience or consider as universal only one perspective or reality (such as white, middle class, and heterosexual), we are trapped in the same snares. The seeds of alternative perspectives lie dormant in any viewpoint. Making meaning is a process, never an endpoint in itself.

At the inception of the current feminist movement in the early 1970s, the discovery, stated simply, that each woman's problems were every woman's problems broadened and altered our perspectives. The invisible was made startlingly visible. Beginning to acknowledge the interrelatedness of various aspects of experience, feminist psychological thought of the time recognized that the personal is political and the political personal (a seamless web) and strove to include what are traditionally considered the psychological and sociological levels of experience and analysis. The private domain, the daily and the ordinary, the irrelevant "noise" in the system, were discovered to be where women's perspectives had been buried. The consciousness-raising group was considered a model for feminist psychotherapy (Brodsky 1973), a forum to counteract the consciousness-lowering aspect of women's socialization. The new model of psychology and psychotherapy focused on women's common problems in this society, and often sought collective rather than individual remedies.

This early aspect of feminist psychological revision succeeded in identifying unnamed and untreated issues and in changing the content and the focus of treatment, no mean feat in a society that either ignored or denied the validity of women's voices. Yet it has had relatively little effect upon the masculinist context of psychology itself. As the issues identified by feminists were adopted by the mainstream, they were sanitized of their feminist and societal implications. In this way, the focus of treatment and change is still on women. Male participation in these problems—problems still viewed through the masculinist filter—thus remains unseen. By defining them non-contextually as women's issues, however, even therapists who adhere to the most traditional values can conscientiously work with clients who have survived rape or abuse, who struggle with problems with sexuality or food or substance abuse without any societal, and certainly no feminist, understanding of why the problems even exist or what meanings inhere in them.

This approach makes a place for women within existing societal structures, but just what is that place? As mainstream theorists and therapists see it, women now have still more individual problems on which they can focus, resulting in a proliferation of specially designed treatment and self-help programs and literature for women. Women, already the major consumers of psychotherapy, have become a greatly expanded market.

A second consequence of the resilience of the sexist system is that a few privileged (mostly white, educated, well behaved, and well dressed) and highly visible women are these days being permitted to share some of society's rewards, while droves of others are being driven into poverty. Looking only at the first slice of experience, one can infer that great progress has been made, the sort of progress that leaves the masculinist psychologist less perplexed. The dressed-for-success woman looks more like a man; one can begin to discern just what sort of man she is after all. As this seeming change occurs, the larger context again fades from conscious view, and even many feminist psychologists are beginning to turn back to the narrower field of vision, to the individual problem and the individual solution.

In the field of psychotherapy, professional programs for treating the problems of modern women spring up everywhere as the societal context and feminist concerns recede and psychology absorbs these issues as individual and appropriate for treatment. The professionalization of the treatment of "women's problems" is not an ally of social change; rather, it creates a group of nonfeminist experts whose investment lies in developing and retaining their expertise and their programs. Traditional professional psychology is, in this way, strengthened, while the potential for the development of more useful and complex psychological models of change is weakened.

During the second decade of feminist psychology, roughly the 1980s, several influences converged to lead feminist clinical psychology and psychiatry, in particular, from an emphasis on a societal level of analysis to an almost full swing of the pendulum back to the intrapsychic or the purely personal interpersonal. A well-developed psychosocial analysis of the status of women in our society had been accomplished without an accompanying understanding of its translation to the personal psychological level. Instead of searching for the interstices of the two, many feminist psychologists began to focus narrowly on the latter in a search for complexity and depth in theory, along with professional legitimacy. For women to begin to be believed when they spoke was, in itself, revolutionary. But for the revolution to continue, we must be able to draw a more complete picture of the source of women's problems and the most useful and appropriate loci for intervention and change. As an obvious example, it might be more useful to deal directly with men's violence toward women and children rather than eternally treating the casualities.

Clinical psychology, in general, is now being strongly influenced by object-relations psychology, and feminist psychotherapy, interestingly enough, is following suit. The very term *object relations,* used to describe relationships with people or *parts* of people, ought to be anathema to feminists, but instead has been adopted by many feminists without so much as a call to revise the terminology. In a sense, this branch of feminist psychological thought is very much in keeping with mainstream clinical psychology and has used the principles of the object-relations perspective in the service of gender analysis rather than develop a qualitatively different feminist paradigm. This perspective is itself reductionist and revisionist, looking to the pre-oedipal childhood phase of Freudian theory for the source of gender differences.

A significant number of feminist psychologists have looked to the object-relations approach for help in understanding the complexity and tenacity of gender differences and misogyny. The work of Nancy Chodorow (1978), a psychoanalytically oriented sociologist, has been extremely influential in

26

this development. The model she proposes appears to hold promise for the development of an alternative explanation for the traditional distinctions between the psychological styles, if you will, of females and males in our culture and all cultures in which women mother. She attributes gender differences to traditional parenting arrangements in the nuclear family, which she treats as if they were universal. This perspective does not judge women as inferior, but as different.

In fact, many feminist proponents of this approach have come close to judging the female relational style as psychologically superior or more functional for the needs of the human race as a whole than the more rational style they attribute to men in general (Chodorow 1978; Gilligan 1982; Miller 1984; Dinnerstein 1976). To do so, of course, is to adopt a mirror image of prior claims of masculine superiority and is identically based on the post-Cartesian construct of separate, dichotomous gender categories and decontextualized universal attributes. Although offering a pro- rather than an anti-female sentiment, this perspective is still dualistic and universal rather than particular, separating human qualities and choices from the larger social context. For example, is it always better for everyone to be relationally oriented? Is it even better for women and, if so, why? A relational orientation is not just one thing consistently fueled by the same forces and the same consequences, but differs situationally and motivationally in complex ways, some of which strengthen and some of which damage women.

TOWARD A FEMINIST EPISTEMOLOGY

During the second decade of feminist thought, roughly coinciding with the 1980s, another feminist psychological approach considered models of female development and functioning that more accurately reflect the complexity of women's experience, beginning with the epistemological base rather than the masculinist infrastructure built upon it. These theorists have asked important questions concerning epistemology. Rhoda Unger (1983), for example, has pointed out that epistemology is not and cannot be the knowing of absolute truths, but must be relative, contextual, complex, and subjective. As Morris Taggart (1985) and others have noted, truth is not independent of its location and function within the social context. Rather than creating rigid categories and discrete boundaries, feminist epistemologies can allow for interrelated, embedded aspects of the same experience, as well as for the inclusion of different kinds and aspects of information.

A feminist epistemology must take as its starting place the experience of women and, in the individual case, the experience of each woman within the complex personal, interpersonal, cultural, and evaluative context. In a lifetime of scholarly work, the phenomenological world of even one woman could not be completely mapped in all its complexity, but only approximated. Nevertheless, to begin means to acknowledge that every aspect of experience is complexly intertwined with and embedded in all the others, that the personal and interpersonal do not stand alone, that categories of cognition are not separate from the experiencer's physical body, feelings, and abilities to organize the raw flux of sensory information impinging at any time.

At an earlier time in human experience, there was no separation between the observer and the observed. One learned of the world through immersion in it, through participation. The Greek word *psyche,* from which derives our word for mental processes, originally meant "blood" or "soul." But masculine values judge a lack of separateness as seriously problematic, nonobjective, or, even worse, feminine in nature. Contemporary approaches have instead divided experience into levels ranging from the individual physical or biological to the intrapsychic to the interpersonal to the societal or cultural, and divided psychology into cognitive, affective, or behavioral levels of experience. Depending on the perspective, one of these aspects is typically considered to be prior to and causative of the others. For example, the Gestalt approach considers feelings as fundamental; the cognitive and rational-emotive take thoughts as the starting place for psychological experience. These are all chicken-and-egg disputes and cannot be resolved from within the confines of an epistemology that subscribes to linear causality.

Psychology, sociology, history, economics, and philosophy have been separated into different "disciplines," although a feminist understanding clearly involves them all, along with other related disciplines. Psychology itself has also tended to separate cognition, affect, behavior, and the physical body of the individual. Most of our clinical models focus on one or the other of these aspects of human experience, which, while perhaps pragmatically more manageable, reflects a narrow, often reductionist and linear epistemology. A new feminist discipline that does not make this artificial division in women's experience but views these aspects as inextricably intertwined would be a giant step forward.

A catalog of separate treatments for discrete disorders or even categories of people, such as survivors of abuse or adult children of a variety of family dysfunctions, ignores the complexity of human experience and its inter-relatedness. It is not simply external experience internalized, but inter-twined with personal meaning, feeling, and fantasy, that contributes to sameness as well as allowing for differences in functioning among females or males. This dividing and fragmenting of human experience is yet another inheritance of the Cartesian viewpoint. Many of our recently spawned treatment programs for these narrowly defined problems, as well as the media, have popularized this kind of fragmented thought by discussing problems as if they were discrete categories of people, such as Adult Children of Alcoholics, Adults Molested as Children, or Co-Dependents.

The task of the third decade lies before us: to continue to develop more complex and integrated feminist models of epistemology and change. We must not look for one correct way to describe or explain all women's experience. We must seek instead the interstices of the complex influences that make up psychological experience within a particular context.

It is difficult even to think this way without the language to do so. I am left to talk about combining levels and aspects, still the language of parts rather than of a complexly integrated whole. Attempted explanations must stress that physical, intrapsychic, interpersonal, and cultural-evaluative in-fluences are intertwined with interpersonal communication and behavior, which are intertwined with physical representations of all of these, which are in turn intertwined with sociocultural prescriptions and proscriptions. Embedded within each intrapsychic event and interpersonal act are also influences of culture, class, race, and ethnicity and the meanings and evalua-tions attributed to any characteristic or behavior of the individual by these systems. All these elements are implicate in any particular act-thought-feeling.

There are only imaginary boundaries. Each aspect of experience contains all the others. The physical aspect of experience may be thought of as including the genetic, the biological, and all aspects of the body and its environment in its current state. The body, as it grows and develops from the embryonic stage, contains, embedded within each of its cells, the result of genetic programming, biological makeup. In addition, every experience at each of the other levels is embedded within the physical being of each person. These all become part of the musculature, the development of bone structure, and so on. One learns what is natural. As Bateson (Bateson and Bateson 1987, p. 35) has pointed out, "the shell has the narrative of its individual growth pickled within its geometric form as well as the story of its evolution." Abraham Lincoln remarked that one can read in a man's face, by the time he reaches middle age, the sort of life he has lived.

Embedded within the intrapsychic aspect of experience are influences of the physical, the interpersonal, the cultural, and the societal. The interpersonal aspect also encompasses and includes aspects of the physical and the intrapsychic, including cognitive, affective, behavioral, and existential levels. Perhaps even more important, no aspect of experience escapes being gendered and assigned meaning.

Context

Culture may be defined as a framework of values and beliefs and a means of organizing experience. It includes the rules by which interpersonal events are perceived and punctuated. Even private thought is conducted in socially constructed language and, thus, cannot be purely personal and self-contained. The culture of the society in which one is raised and lives defines what can and cannot be conscious or, viewed slightly differently, what must remain unconscious.

The unconscious itself and its contents are largely determined by the rules of the culture in which it has developed and are not just a consequence of any presumably natural personal development of the infant in the family, as suggested by intrapsychic approaches such as Freudian and object relations. No choices, acts, thoughts, or feelings are free from cultural dictates. While I am not proposing a discrete structure known as the unconscious, constellations of experience of which the individual is only potentially aware must include the effects of all the information to which that individual has been exposed—and not just that acquired within the family. Culture also dictates what is and is not remembered and how forgetting occurs.

For example, in Freud's time and place, repression of sexual thoughts and impulses was common. Becker (1973), in his male-centered treatise, *Denial of Death,* considered the knowledge of *his* own death to be the basic content and cause (structure and function) of repression, the essential piece of information that must, for the sake of man's survival, remain unconscious. At the time he wrote this work, Becker was facing his own imminent death and, as Freud had, based his theory on his own personal experience. Why didn't he make this explicit? Would it have destroyed some claim to universality?

Sexual thoughts/feelings, fear of death—indeed, all the aspects of experience are incorporated in a condensed and often symbolic manner organized by and accessible through meaning. They can be separated artificially for study because our currently dominant epistemological system categorizes them. The unconscious is available or potentially available as emergent

30

psychological/physical constellations (or we might call them complexities) of meaning. These complexities are blended into more conscious constellations rather than being buried beneath another layer of consciousness. As a Stradivarius, through the process of hysteresis of resonance, is altered permanently by any tones played on it, so is the human being altered by experience. The location of the change or of unconscious material is not a meaningful question in either case.

Since women's experience differs in many crucial ways from that of men in this society, might not the essence (structure and function) of repression be different for women? Certainly women had forgotten many terrifying experiences, such as rape and childhood molestation, until the larger culture permitted awareness. Might not women of different racial, class, and other meaningful experience both develop and forget different meanings? This question will be considered at some length in this work.

The determination of what should be defined as context is an epistemological act in that it is one of punctuation, of the drawing, rather arbitrarily, of a boundary around experience. In a sense, that is, the observer must interrupt or define a situation in which there is a flux of information from the physical to the cultural, embedded and intertwined, and define figure and ground or context. In doing so, an artificial boundary is drawn between the figure and the context such that we come to believe that the figure exists separately from the context. Similarly, the context fades from awareness, for any culture relegates much of context to that hidden territory, the unconscious. As Marshall McLuhan once noted, not intentionally in defense of the masculinist perspective, if a fish could speak, water is the last thing it would identify as part of its environment (in Berman 1984, p. 131). Similarly, it has been said that it is not falling that hurts, but breaking the fall. That is, if you forget that the ground exists and consider only the figure, you will eventually be in real trouble.

Most important, perhaps, is that whoever gets to draw this line, to create the boundary, is the owner of the context and, as such, holds the power to define reality, to say what matters and what does not. Since the context of our culture is patriarchal, masculinist, and misogynist, it can and often must be unconscious in order for females to function, but it leads them to contain within themselves the pains and wounds to which they are subjected. For males, to whom it is not likely to be as jarring or debilitating, it can more comfortably remain outside of awareness.

In a man's world, women become the other, the unmentioned and unmentionable, indeed the derogated other, as aptly noted by de Beauvoir (1968) and others. Even more perniciously, women come to experience themselves as other, living in a split reality—their own and that of men.

Men experience no such split as they outgrow the childhood world of women. It would be a revealing social experiment to hire mostly males to teach elementary school and mostly females to teach the higher grades. The potential effects of this change might be considered by those who identify the traditional parenting arrangement as the sole or primary source of female and male psychologies. Constant cultural meta-messages inform females that their experience is not real, or that it is wrong or bad, or that it is wrong or bad for them to have their own separate perspectives. This is also part of what female children learn in and out of the family, and learn to forget.

The acknowledgment of the value ladenness of virtually every epistemological and psychological approach is at the core of feminist psychological thought. Feminist thought acknowledges multiple realities and, therefore, multiple, complex, and variable models of psychological functioning. It calls for consideration of the particular circumstances of each woman, of her reality informed by her individual history, her physical body, feelings, thoughts, acts, class, racial, ethnic, and cultural "context," and the values and judgments of herself and all meaningful others concerning all of these. These aspects are all embedded in any experience and must be included in a careful analysis of such experience. No two women exist in exactly the same particular circumstances and context, although all exist in the same circumstance as women.

Meaning-Symbolism

Epistemology's first expression is not in the answers, but in the questions it generates. What, then, are these questions from a feminist epistemological perspective? The first step must be to seek, as fully as possible, the common and diverse experiences of women with all their intertwined and embedded aspects. Of central importance is the meaning attributed to the thoughts-feelings-acts-characteristics of women individually and collectively. So we arrive at our questions: (1) How fully can the ordinary and quotidian experience of this woman and of women in this society be understood? and (2) What are the *multiple* meanings of these experiences?

The question of meaning mediates all other levels. As children we learn to learn; that is, we learn something about the task of learning as we are, in fact, learning. So do we all learn something contextual, something on the meta-level about every experience we have. This meta-level of meaning, embedded in every experience of every individual within every society or culture, actually serves to bind a community together and unconsciously regulate its everyday affairs. The meaning or evaluation of a given aspect of experience can be strengthening or debilitating for women, enervating or enabling for men, but in both cases it is the glue that binds together the rest of experience.

The very essence of being human is attributing meaning to events, which we do through symbolic thought and metaphor. The fundamental issues of each person's life are those of meaning—meaning of events, of relationships, of actions of the self and others, of life itself. These meanings are typically organized into a person's life story, which retrospectively makes sense of experience. The attribution of meaning is pervasive throughout, rather than divisive of, experience or perception. It is not the narrower question of cognitive approaches; it is not cognitive rather than affective, conscious rather than unconscious, factual rather than evaluative. Within a feminist epistemology, the question "Where does meaning reside?" is not a meaningful one; multiple meanings emanate from all levels of experience.

For example, let us reconsider Abraham Lincoln's statement that one could tell what a man's life had been from looking at his face. What might a woman infer about herself from this comment that is different from the possible inferences of a man? Perhaps any or all of the following. A woman's experience does not show in her face. A woman's experience should not show in her face. A woman's experience must not show in her face. A woman does not, should not, must not have experience. A woman's face has no meaning, but is just a thing of beauty. A woman's experience has no meaning. A woman's experience must/should be hidden, and not show, especially on her face. We all know what a woman's experience is because it is prescribed, it is natural, it is the same for all women. A woman's experience is not interesting enough to think about, much less to search out. A woman will tell you her experience. A woman is not worth thinking about. A woman is not worth a president's thought. A great man must/should/does understand things about other men, other great men, other men's faces. Lincoln was commenting on his own etched face. Lincoln was explaining his own perceived ugliness. It did not occur to Lincoln to think about women's faces. Women's faces are subsumed in the category of men's faces.

How might each and all of these implied meanings—and I have presented only those that occur to me at this time—affect a female listener? This one simple sentence brings up points concerning the physical, the intrapsychic, the interpersonal, the existential, and the cultural, all imbued with the evaluative. The female listener would not necessarily be aware of all these possible meanings, but, inasmuch as they affect her in any way, they are relevant.

To take a second example, several studies have revealed a differential effect of maternal employment on boys. In so-called lower-class (note the superior perspective from which this designation is made) families, maternal employment is associated with a reduction in the respect and admiration of sons for their fathers (Douvan 1963; Gold and Andres 1978; Hoffman 1974; Kappel and Lambert 1972; Propper 1972; Romer and Cherry 1978). No comparable effect has been reported in middle-class families. Apparently maternal employment has different meaning for these two groups of boys, or did at the times the studies were conducted. For the lower-class and presumably more traditional group, maternal employment was interpreted as paternal failure to support the family—that is, it was about their fathers, not their mothers. The deleterious effects on these sons are a function of attributed meanings.

The next question inherent in a feminist approach is "Who places the boundary that defines context and meaning?" Inherent in feminism and in feminist psychotherapy must be the making conscious of potentially conscious or emergent evaluative contextual material, because women live in a society whose meanings are constructed by men—and in industrialized Western society, by white men—and must be made aware of the two realities in which they live. For women of color, experience is yet more divided.*

Within every meaningful event are values. The feminist psychological thought presented here is in agreement with certain other approaches, such as that of von Bertalanffy (Davidson 1983), the founder of general systems theory, in considering everything to be imbued with values, which are expressed in relationship, thus giving symbolism or meaning an essential role in all our transactions. It is not in agreement with the narrow interpretation of systems of the family therapy approach.

For example, the very sense of self is a metaphor, that is, both an existential and meta-level concept. It involves a symbolic abstraction in order to attribute meaning and consistency to an aggregation of experiences and messages to the individual about those experiences. Even to experience oneself as an individual is the result of a particular set of cultural values in which separateness and individuality are taken as developmental goals. The sense of self and of a gendered self is always value-laden and complex, never as simple or situationally consistent as models of role theory would have it. Even studies of self-attribution of gender-appropriate behaviors have begun to demonstrate their variability in different circumstances. That is, people

---

*All people of color in a white-dominated society may have a related, but not identical, experience.

are never simply masculine, feminine, or androgynous, but display different combinations of the qualities that are subsumed under these rubrics in different situations, at different times, and with different participants (Kaschak and Sharratt 1989). The question that must be asked is, What does any experience mean in general and in particular for women, and is it different from the meaning of the very same experience in the case of a man or men?

If a woman says to a psychologist, "I want to be in a relationship," what can she mean? "I have no identity outside a relationship." "I feel worthwhile only when I am in a relationship." "I am afraid to be alone." "I am afraid no one will want me." "I want or need to be taken care of." "I need to take care of someone else." "I want to love and be loved." "I want to do the right thing." "I am acting out of fear." "I am acting out of a need for identity." "I am seeking approval." "I am seeking intimacy." "I am seeking support." "I am looking for a surrogate parent." "I am trying to be a good woman." "I value you and our relationship." "I am trying to please you." "I am trying to defy you." Does she mean all of these? How are these different meanings conveyed and manifested physically, intrapsychically, interpersonally, and culturally? How is each embedded in all the others? How are they valued by her, by society, and by the psychologist?

When a woman relates something to her, the feminist psychologist or therapist can attempt to understand in a complex way: What are the *various* meanings of this event or experience to or about this person? What can be understood from *all* of them rather than from choosing one correct insight? Within this feminist paradigm, the evaluative component is obviously of paramount importance, since it is frequently so debilitating to women and so destructive of the sense of self. Its alteration is central to constructive change. Thus, feminist psychotherapy cannot be narrowly personal and, at the same time, cannot exclude an understanding of the personal effect of misogynist evaluations of women in general and of each woman in particular.

The feminist methodology and epistemology offered in this book involve understanding multiple meanings, their sources, and the seamless web they make up, as well as identifying those that are enhancing and those that are damaging to an individual woman and to women in general. I will view gender as a way of organizing knowledge, that is, as an epistemological system. I will not have as a goal to distinguish between fact and value, between objectivity and subjectivity. I will not divide experience into separate, mutually exclusive categories. Instead I seek to begin to unfold, in full complexity, wholeness, and depth, the embedded meanings in ordinary experience, embodied and located in actual individuals and actual perspectives that are named. "Every reference to the 'real world,' even where the reference is to physical or biological events, is a reference to the organized activities of everyday life" (Garfinkel 1967, p. 36).

I will draw from clinical and nonclinical material and anecdotal, literary, and empirical sources. As I also am limited by my own perspective as a white, middle-class, feminist academic and psychotherapist, I will most certainly miss some aspects of experience and, I hope, will see some that others have missed. I attempt to include experiences of women of color and women from non-Western nations with which I am familiar. The particulars of the situations I describe, as well as the experiences of women of color and women from non-Western nations, will most certainly differ, but I believe that the general foundation I develop is applicable to them. In the following chapters, I begin this task.

2

Gender Embodied

We can tell you something of the life she lived. We can catalogue her being: tissue, bloodstream, cell, the shape of her experience to the least moment, skin, hair, try to see what she saw, to imagine what she felt, clitoris, vulva, womb, and we can tell you that despite each injury she survived. That she lived to an old age. (On all the parts of her body we see the years.) By the body of this old woman we are hushed. We are awed. We know that it was in her body that we began. And now we can see that it is from her body that we learn. That we see our past. We say from the body of the old woman, we can tell you something of the lives we lived.
                                                                —Susan Griffin
                                                          "The Anatomy Lesson"

I begin this chapter with a consideration of the interrelation of various aspects of women's experience that have been separated by prefeminist approaches, from the macrocosmic societal to the microcosmic texture of the personal, individual experience. This is a step in the feminist project of reintegrating the hidden or lost aspects of ordinary experience into our knowledge concerning the psychology of women.

37

THE ILLUSION OF GENDER DICHOTOMY

The consensual reality of Western culture has held that gender is a given, contained in or identical with the sex of the newborn. Gender and gender-linked attributes are viewed as natural rather than as socially and psychologically constructed. Paradoxically, then, all children must be taught what is natural and those who do not learn their lessons well are viewed as unnatural.

It has been one of the programs of feminist psychology to introduce and demonstrate the distinction between gender and sex. Many theoretical and empirical works have developed and established this distinction, introduced early on by Gayle Rubin (1975) and others. In addition, the work of John Money (1973) and John Money and Anke Erhardt (1972) has shown quite clearly that assigned gender rather than sex establishes a feminine or masculine identity. That is, children raised as boys or girls become boys and girls even when this identity is later discovered not to match genetic makeup. As Robert Stoller has suggested, the effects of "biological systems, organized prenatally in a masculine or feminine direction, are almost always . . . too gentle in humans to withstand the more powerful forces of environment in human development, the first and most powerful of which is mothering" (in Miller 1989, p. 253). In other words, it is not the possession of certain genitals or even chromosomes that establishes gender identity and related characteristics and behaviors, but whether meaningful others treat the individual as female or male and, in that way, teach the individual how to be a female or a male. Our culture has no human category more basic than this one and, in order to survive psychologically, each of us must be educated in how to be either female or male.

One of the two gender categories is assigned at birth based on external genital apparatus. In our society, these categories are considered to be invariant throughout life, with the exception of surgical intervention, by means of which the removal or addition of the appropriate genitals then permits a concomitant change in gender irrespective of chromosomal makeup.* Not all societies offer this democratic choice; in many, castrated men simply become eunuchs, as in the case of harem attendants. Even in our own society, both intentionality and adoption of a new gender identity are required for a man to be considered a transsexual rather than a castrated

---

*Garfinkel (1967) has done an interesting analysis of an individual who underwent a surgical change and the concomitant learnings that were required to adopt a new gender identity socially and not just surgically.

man. Obviously the change from female to male does not allow for as much ambiguity, nor do society's constructs provide as many gradations.

Although there is ample evidence (Money 1973) that gender-related physical characteristics are continuous, not dichotomous, attributes, they are, again by consensual agreement, culturally and *morally* divided into only two categories (Garfinkel 1967). There is considered to be something wrong with a person who does not fit neatly into one of the categories—not something just physically wrong, but a moral and even intentional transgression punishable by ridicule and humiliation, psychological and sometimes even physical violence. Failing all these modes of enforcement, or as a consequence of the damage caused by them, this problem is likely to be considered for psychotherapeutic treatment.

In order to create and maintain the illusion of dichotomy, any ambiguities must be eliminated or disguised. This is accomplished by means of a myriad of signals and markings indicating that one is female or male, including posture, manner of moving and speaking, dress, and voice tone (Frye 1983). These signals are physically based but they become psychologically pervasive as the individual develops, so that they are eventually both expressed and experienced in every realm simultaneously. Focusing for a moment on the physical, it is women who generally have to alter their bodies and restrict their movement to maintain the illusion of dichotomy. With the use of razors, depilatories, tweezers, hairstyling, makeup, nail polish, nylons, high heels, bras that lift, augment, or reduce, garments that tighten and reduce, women do not look anything like men. The differences are not only observable but often exaggerated. Gregory Zilboorg (1944) has suggested that this reversal of the more commonly observed pattern in other species—wherein it is the male who must appear decorative and attractive to the female—is a function of the extreme power differential between males and females in our culture. Women must make themselves pleasing to men.

Certainly men also participate actively in physically and psychologically signaling their gender appropriateness, but in less artificial and physically constricting ways: in our culture, they must consistently signal ways in which they take up more space and make a greater impact on the environment than do women. They must be more powerful in every way, from the personal to the institutional. As one example, on a recent radio talk show, the guest was an expert in vocal training. Several of the callers were distraught males who wanted to know what to do about their voices, which were relatively high in comparison with the acceptable range for men. The expert immediately trotted out a series of exercises designed to help these men practice lowering their voices. Why should this be deemed necessary?

Viewing the problem from the societal perspective, it is apparent that the illusion of dichotomy must be maintained. Translated to the personal, individual experience, these men were motivated to avoid the personal humiliation of not fitting into their assigned category. They were sure that something was wrong, not with the categories but with themselves, and were desperate to change it. George Bush was faced with this same problem during his campaign for the presidency. He was coached in how to alter his voice in order to avoid being seen as not masculine enough for the job. Some of his later actions in the Gulf War, however, put his masculinity beyond question.

In a society that emphasizes individuality to the extent that ours does, people attribute causality to individuals more than to characteristics of the environment or social context. This has repeatedly been shown to be so clinically, as well as in the extensive psychological attribution literature. Gender dichotomies are not questioned. Instead an individual who is unable to conform with their rigid distinctions thinks, "There is something wrong with me."

There is a distinction to be made here between the experience of females and males that is crucial to the psychology of each. Simply put, while males may be ridiculed and humiliated for behaving or sounding or looking like females, so may females. Women are subject to censure not only for behaving too much like men but for behaving too much like women. We can all easily conjure up examples of hurtful criticism of women for being masculine (pushy, castrating, dominating) as well as feminine (talking incessantly, nagging, gossiping, being concerned with appearance, driving poorly, dieting)—a form of misogyny that is a part of daily life. Even the Sunday comics, often standard fare for children as well as adults, are still filled with long-suffering husbands ridiculing their wives' obsession with appearance, shopping, and dieting and their poor housekeeping skills. A truly revolutionary moment will occur when people stop laughing, for example, at mother-in-law jokes.

This process starts early when young boys taunt girls and exclude them from their play, and culminates in "the normal male contempt for women" (Brunswick 1940). Such an aggressive and derisive attitude does not at all detract from, but adds to, traditional masculinity. A woman's hatred of men would certainly not be considered natural either by psychologists or by society at large; it would be defined not only as unfeminine but even as masculine, and undoubtedly as pathological. This important point in the psychology of women today cannot be overemphasized. While a man in our society can attain approval and avoid humiliation by behaving in socially prescribed masculine ways, a woman does not have this same uncomplicated alternative. She may be admired for responding in an appropriate (feminine) way, but she is also subject to social sanction for this behavior, just as she would be for responding in an inappropriate (masculine) way.

Enforcement of such gender adherence in Western society is largely psychological, based upon the extremely powerful mechanism of humiliation, which results in the experience of shame. Shame is one of the most potent of societal and individual psychological enforcers, putting nothing less than the basic sense of esteem and worth at stake. A person who is ridiculed feels a sense of shame or humiliation, a sense of being physically and, secondarily, psychologically so seriously flawed as to experience annihilation of the self, the desire not to exist. Something is so wrong with the very core of the self, both physically and psychologically, that it must dissolve.

It is particularly shameful not to fit clearly into a gender category, so that individual and interpersonal psychology are both based upon the need to fit. Herein lies the motivation of transsexuals, who must make themselves fit one or the other category. Even those who seem to desire not to fit, as would someone striving for an androgynous identity, often report a deep sense of shame when, in a minor public transaction, their gender is mistaken or cannot be discerned. I have heard clients and nonclients describe their sense of embarrassment or shame in such a situation, as well as the embarrassment of the person who was unable to categorize them and who is socially required and personally motivated either to apologize profusely or to sustain the ridicule.

As a classroom exercise in my graduate seminar on gender and ethnicity, I often ask a female and a male student to exchange gender roles in a role play of a dating situation; she takes the traditional male role as she views and experiences it, he the female role as he sees it. Although the students understand the importance of this exercise and usually participate in it good-naturedly, they consistently report a sense of humiliation and shame in enacting the other gender's role. Most important, this sense of shame is specifically related to the physically based psychological aspects of that role. The woman often reports that her manner of behavior, seating positions, and use of her body and space made her feel "lewd." She has displayed and used her body too openly and freely, which, if done by a male, would be considered natural and thus invisible. On the other hand, the man most often relates his sense of shame to feeling diminished both physically and fully as a human being by having to be so sensitive to cues from the other person and by having both to contain himself and to remain in a state of permeable readiness.

A major function of our heterosexual pairing arrangements involves maintaining the illusion of dichotomy of the prescribed gender differences themselves. Couples generally pair up with the male partner being taller, older, more educated, and so on, than the female. Certainly he is expected to have a deeper voice, a larger body, be more than she is in the ways that men are supposed to be. The couple who defies this arrangement risks ridicule and a sense of embarrassment or shame. In order not to diminish their sense of self, most people in our society do not violate this norm and, thus, participate in maintaining the societal and personal illusion of gender dichotomy. The small number of heterosexual couples who do defy these proscriptions usually have the approval of a subculture whose rules allow them to be praised and respected, not ridiculed. Less typically, some couples may redefine as personally meaningful not following society's mores in this sphere. If they feel humiliated, however, their rebelliousness will not be long-lived unless it becomes a means of counteracting the humiliation by denying or mastering it. The power of shame as a motivator should not be underestimated.

ANATOMY IS DESTINY

Freud was accurate in observing that anatomy is destiny, but erred in his explanation, in his level of analysis, which was both phallocentric and reductionist. Destiny is inherent not in biological anatomy but in anatomy gendered and meaningfully contextualized. Anatomy given meaning in our society becomes destiny, for this is the meaning that it is given. One of the most existentially profound and psychologically meaningful issues with which each of us must contend is the arbitrariness of anatomy and its assigned meanings, which then determine every individual's life path to an extraordinary extent. Once assigned, it is gender, as the basic psychological organizing principle in the family (along with age) and in larger society (along with race and class), that determines and organizes development and identity.

Research has indicated that gender identity is generally established somewhere between an infant's twelfth and eighteenth month (Person and Ovesey 1983) and is well in place by the third year (Money and Tucker 1975). By that time the child has developed an organized concept of itself as a girl or a boy, along with many of the associated meanings. That identity or template will then continue to grow in complexity and to incorporate new levels of meanings and behavior as the individual matures and is further educated by parents, teachers, and peers, or even as society permits the specific attributes identified with each gender to change.

The organizing principle of gender is general rather than specific. It does not involve, for example, whether one wears one's hair short or long, or dresses in skirts or pants; rather, it creates the illusion of being a girl or a boy, a woman or a man, by dictating what a female or a male in this society does. Gender is *achieved;* it would probably be more accurately expressed as a verb than as a noun. It is something that one *does* repeatedly, probably thousands of times a day. It is a higher-order abstraction whose actual content or referent is, in principle, irrelevant but, in practice, crucial and which is enforced by approval and acceptance if one conforms and ridicule and humiliation if one transgresses. As previously noted, if a smaller reference group, such as a feminist one, supports changes in the specifics, such as developing androgyny or more involved, sensitive fathering, then its members may receive approval for them, but this is not a change in the higher-order principle that one must comply with the gender prescriptions of meaningful others to gain approval and avoid humiliation.

In this way, physical attributes are tied to gender not by a natural attribution of meaning but by a rather arbitrary one. While the body is always gendered, it is also true that gender is always embodied. Stable meaning can be found in neither the particular attribute or act nor the gender with which it is associated, but in the division of attributes by gender, in the gender system itself. There is obviously a significant tendency in our culture for that division to be made by according males the more expansive and aggressive qualities and females the more vulnerable and confining ones. Many attributions don't fit these categories, however, and are much more arbitrary in content. Women, for example, were once not allowed to wear pants without violating the culture's system of confinement. Through much struggle and social upheaval, this stricture has loosened, although many subtle means of confining women are still with us.

Similarly, long hair on men, once considered effeminate (a special derogatory term for femininity displayed by males; note the need for such a word) or associated only with women, has come to be seen as macho by the same men who would once have ridiculed it. There is an old country-and-western song about a hippie who hides his long hair in his hat before entering a "down-home" sort of bar. His life is endangered when his hair begins to escape the confines of the hat and is noticed by the "good old boys" in the bar. These days, that same group of drinkers would most likely be sporting long hair themselves. The meaning given to long hair by the valuing context has changed.

In another example, the father of a young son pointed out to me that the boy's legs were smooth and well shaped "like a girl's." He could not conceive that they were "like a boy's" or that shapely legs could be anything but a gender-linked, dichotomous variable. Conversely, a woman who wore a bathing suit to the beach without shaving her legs was approached by a young boy who asked incredulously why she had legs "like a man's." He was asking her to fit herself into one of the two categories by shaving her legs. The perception of the physical ungendered in this dichotomous manner is impossible for most people.

Can the body exist ungendered? To adapt the old adage about the meaning of a cigar, Is the body ever just a body? In our society, for a human to exist ungendered would be to exist in a meaningless state. It has been repeatedly demonstrated that people notice instantly whether a person is male or female* (Bem 1981; Grady 1977; Kessler and McKenna 1978; Laws 1979). Without this knowledge, not only would interpersonal and intrapersonal development be interrupted but even physical development would be "unnatural." How would one stand, sit, walk, speak, think, feel, and act ungendered? How would others know how to think about, feel, and behave toward one?

From the moment of birth, if not sooner, given the modern technology available for ascertaining sex prior to birth, the body is gendered. Before the development of technology to determine sex *in utero,* a variety of superstitions were invoked to indicate the gender of the unborn child. Predictably, for example, if the fetus is active and moving a great deal, it is believed to be a male (Lewis 1972). No doubt, if it turns out to be a girl, it would be considered a bit unnatural or "active for a female." One can only speculate how this seemingly minor interpretation might become embedded and elaborated in the future physical and psychological development of this active girl. For example, she might feel that she is not quite like a girl whenever she is active. She might refuse to be too active in order not to feel like a boy. Chances are she will be unaware of having made this choice unless she continues to be described this way after birth and her parents continue to discuss it in her presence.

In any case, in the beginning is the question: Is it a boy or a girl? The answer is destiny itself and in one word establishes hundreds, thousands, of future life experiences. Everything from manner of dress, posture, appropriate seating positions, eating patterns, performance of household chores, sexual expression, and voice tone and inflection, to freedom of movement

---

*In fact, we do this not only with humans. On a recent visit to a zoo in Australia, I was part of a group that was curiously viewing a newborn koala cub. The first and virtually immediate question from the audience was, Is it a boy or a girl? Only after knowing to which gender group it belonged could people go on to comment on or respond to the cub.

in public, safety, educational path, career choice, self-esteem, and self-concept, flows from the gender one is assigned at birth as a function of anatomy. How much more directly tied to anatomy could destiny be?

There is no existence in our culture prior to and separate from gender. That such an existence is socially and psychologically constructed makes it no less real. As meaningful adults begin responding, it is embedded into the infant's most essential physical and preverbal self-concept as sensory-motor and kinesthetic knowledge. One cannot comment on a baby's existence—"Isn't he ———?"; "Isn't she ———?"—without access to information concerning that baby's gender. One cannot even speak of a baby in the English language without a third-person gendered referent. One of the main functions of a first name is to identify one's gender quickly (Miller and Swift 1976). It is almost impossible to find a greeting card congratulating parents on the birth of a baby that does not incorporate gender attributions. There is no concept, no identity, more basic than this.

As many empirical studies have demonstrated, beginning at birth, parents treat female and male children differently in a variety of ways that directly or indirectly influence or define the physical and the psychological. Jeffrey Rubin, Frank Provenzano, and Zella Luria (1974) found gender stereotyping to exist within the first twenty-four hours after birth. Although there were no significant gender-related differences in newborns themselves, both mothers and fathers rated female children as significantly softer, smaller, finer-featured, and less alert. Fathers were more extreme in stereotyping. They rated boys as more alert, stronger, firmer, hardier, and better coordinated than girls. Other studies (Alberle and Naegele 1952; Tasch 1952; Pedersen and Robson 1969) have found that fathers expected their newborn sons to be aggressive and athletic, their daughters pretty, sweet, fragile, and delicate. Mothers have been observed to be more physically responsive to male children than to female children (Cohen 1966) and to tolerate more aggression from sons than from daughters (Sears, Maccoby, and Levin 1957). Both fathers and mothers viewed infant daughters as in greater need than sons of nurturance (Pedersen and Robson 1969; Sears, Maccoby, and Levin 1957). Based on their own study, Rubin, Provenzano, and Luria concluded tentatively that "it is physical and constitutional factors that specially lend themselves to sex-typing at birth, at least in our culture" (1974, p. 140). From the beginning, then, females and males are set on different physically based psychological paths.

Under ordinary circumstances, to have a body means to be alive, to move, to act, and to interact. In this society, however, literally everything about *how, when,* and even *if* we do any of these activities is gendered. Any question about the physical is meaningless until it is gendered. Conversely, everything about it is meaningful once gendered. The meaning is located contextually, not in the act or attribute itself, and is communicated interpersonally, by the ideas, feelings, expectations, and behavior of significant adults; by how an infant is held, touched, talked to, talked about; by the kinds of toys considered appropriate; by the color coding of clothing and blankets. This emphasis on sex differentiation by both parents, fathers to a greater extent, increases with the age of the child and tends to reach a maximum in the adolescent years (Unger 1979), when the parents and family members are joined most vigorously by peers.

THE PSYCHOLOGY OF THE BODY

In the English language, as in many others, third-person referents are specifically gendered ("he" or "she," that is, a male or a female physically and psychologically). But unlike most other Western languages, in English the indeterminant third-person referent is embodied: *somebody, anybody, everybody,* even *nobody* (not embodied). Even "anonymous" has a body. Human existence of any kind is both gendered and embodied.

We cannot separate human life from the body. All our experiences in this world—sights, sounds, smells, tastes, touch, simple and complex feelings of all kinds, our sense of time (which defines history, among other things) and place, what we perceive and what we ignore—are brought to us courtesy of our physical selves. Senses, feelings, the mind itself, are all embedded in, coexistent with, our physical selves. Our bodies are sending and receiving devices engaged in the circular exchange of information with the environment and with others. They are also as much the repository of experience as are the realms of mind or feeling. Experience imprints itself on the face, the hands, the body, the musculature, and even the bone structure of every individual. These elements contain the residue, the evidence of experience, that makes us who we are in every sense, including the physical. From the most material to the most symbolic, the overt to the implicate, we are what we experience.

However, the psychological and the physical have been approached as separate realms in Western, post-Cartesian thought. In addition, thinking and feeling are considered not only separate and different but largely psychological in nature. While certain Reichian-based schools of psychotherapy do locate feelings in the body, cognition is generally considered not to be physically located or to be located only in the brain, separable from the body and from feeling. Although our language provides for these distinctions, it does not allow us to indicate that these systems—thought and feeling, the physical and the psychological, the intrapsychic, the interpersonal, and the sociocultural—are all present in any human activity, are all part of the same event. As part of gender training, each of us is taught selective awareness and selective expression. As part of early education in Western society, each of us is taught to split and categorize our experiences; thus dualism appears natural to us.

Let us consider some examples of the embeddedness of the psychological and the physical in each other. A manual laborer develops physically and psychologically in a much different manner than an office worker, not only with regard to musculature but in the degree of connectedness to the physical. In order to perform the required task, an office worker must learn not to experience many bodily sensations and needs, while a manual laborer must pay attention to the physical. An individual who tends to worry a lot eventually embeds anxiety into the musculature, posture, facial lines and expression, and into internal organs such as the heart, stomach, and intestines; and, in that way, is also physically disposed both to worry and to stress-induced illness. Many diseases have been shown to be induced by chronic stress, and even the healing of a simple wound can be slowed by certain emotions.

The relatively new field of psychoneuroimmunology is beginning to demonstrate that immune cells produce every kind of hormone that the brain produces, that our bodies and minds are not dualities at all but are inextricably intertwined. As another example, when individuals who suffer from multiple-personality disorder change from one self to another, such presumably stable physiological features as allergies or visual acuity change as well (Miller 1989; Kluft 1987). One personality may need glasses to see, another may have perfect vision; the actual shape and curvature of the eye undergo a physical/psychological change. The more habitual the psychological state, the more it inhabits the body. The more it inhabits the body, the more it may induce the psychological, or at least a predisposition thereto, so that the physical is also embedded in the psychological.

Paul Ekman (1983) has suggested, based on his cross-cultural research, that people experience the same physiological changes when they force themselves to make the facial expression characteristic of a particular feeling. Smiling, for example, can lead to a feeling of happiness. The physical movement seems to induce the physiological changes in the same way that the subjective state does.

I realize that I am coming dangerously close to resurrecting the James-Lange theory of emotion (Lange and James 1967), long out of fashion, which postulates that the physiological response precedes psychological awareness of an emotion, which is then actually deduced by the person experiencing it. For example, I feel afraid only after experiencing and making meaning of my pounding heart or some other physiological response to fear, or I register sadness after noticing my tears. I reject the linearity and unidirectionality of this model for the same reasons I would reject one that considered thoughts or emotions to take precedence over other aspects of human experience. I suggest instead that experience is both contained in and expressed by the body, as well as by the mind, and that each aspect is embedded in and constantly influenced by the other. Experience can emerge to awareness first in either of these realms, depending on the situation and the person's characteristic style of expression, but it is always expressed and experienced in both. Better said, there is no true "both," except insofar as we are taught to divide and categorize our experiences. Instead there is a unified, complex experience.

The physical self, then, receives, mediates, and is temporarily and permanently altered by all experience and information and, in turn, expresses to the surrounding people and environment various aspects of the individual's experience, feelings, and beliefs, all of which take root and are slowly, but firmly, planted in the body. A seemingly unlikely reference for a feminist analysis, Nietzsche once noted quite astutely that "every feeling is an embodiment attuned in this or that way, a mood that embodies in this or that way" (in Heidegger 1979, p. 218). Each of us develops his or her own body of knowledge, a living, breathing, moving understanding. While that body differs for each of us, it also contains general common elements. The most basic of these have to do with gender and organize the physical, as well as the psychological, experience from the first moments of life.

Once developed, they also predispose us to respond in certain ways to certain situations and to eliminate alternative responses. For example, a woman in danger on the streets may freeze or try to hide or be ingratiating. In fact, it has been shown that, in response to intrusion, women do freeze more (Mahoney 1974; Unger 1979) and also maintain a tenser posture at rest (Mehrabian 1968) than do men. Battered women may not fight back, and the masculinist viewpoint would see them as colluding or asking for it, since a man in the same situation would be expected to fight back. But a woman's body and mind are typically trained differently from a man's—to feel rather than to act, to be disarming rather than to disarm—and women cannot be blamed for being one way when a situation presumably calls for the other.

Every individual inhabits a body, and eventually habit sculpts its forms. This does not mean simply that different feelings or experiences are localized in different parts of the body—as certain somatically oriented therapies propose, dividing experience again into corporeal compartments—but that each experience is embedded in every aspect of the body and of the mind. Heinz Pagels (1988) offers the analogy of kneading food coloring into dough: after several rounds of kneading, the coloring becomes evenly distributed throughout the dough. Such is the case with gendered experience and the physical body. Thus, we all become the bearers of tradition, the keepers of the gender system. Memories are stored everywhere, not just in our minds. Or, better said, the mind's realm is not confined to the brain. Intelligence exists at all levels of experience.

In the highly gendered society in which we live, the nongendered question really has no meaning. Even the most basic question about the realm of the physical cannot be reduced or separated from the issue of gender and is instead transformed into "What does it mean to have a female or a male body?" As Carole Vance has pointed out, the task then becomes to "describe and analyze how cultural connections are made between female bodies and what comes to be understood as 'women' " (1984, p. 10). How does the experience of gender change the body and shape feelings, sensations, and thoughts?

A woman of some forty years enters my office. She moves very carefully and hesitantly, stopping at the door and waiting. Although she is just my height, she keeps her head lowered in such a way that she has to look up at me. She doesn't seem sure whether to close the door behind her or wait for me to do it. She waits. She asks where she should sit and I indicate which chair is for my clients, although it is obvious from the configuration of the room. She sits down, removes her shoes, and tucks her legs under her body. She wraps her arms around her body as if to hold herself in and silently waits.

This is my perspective, what I see. What information has been conveyed about her, her body, her self-concept, her relationships with others? What would this same scene look like from an androcentric perspective? From her own?

In those moments she has expressed, in a highly encoded manner, an enormous amount of information about herself. Perhaps she seems attractive and feminine, likable. She is being a good little girl, taking up little space, waiting for clues and cues. Perhaps she is afraid, uncomfortable, waiting to be judged. Perhaps she feels hopeful, angry, despairing, too small to be seen, too insignificant to be helped. Perhaps she is consciously aware only of a slight sense of discomfort. Perhaps she is so concerned about how she is being viewed that she does not know her own physical experiences and sensations. Perhaps she scarcely remembers to breathe, so intently is she anticipating my response. Perhaps her posture and musculature "naturally" fall into this position from years of doing so and she is not consciously aware of it.

Has she expressed and experienced all these varying emotions and sensations in gender-appropriate ways? Has she learned her lesson or defied it? What is the effect of my presence, my perspective, my gender on her physical presentation of self? How might her behavior differ in the presence of a male therapist (in general, and with a particular male therapist, since I am also a particular female therapist)? Most important, how much of what she experiences is habitual and unconscious, so well embedded in her body and her identity that they also influence her experience of herself? If her body has been trained to be hesitant and tense in new situations, does this lesson show? The answers to all these questions are encoded in the language of the body and must be considered by the therapist within a contextually complex feminist approach.

Now, what if I told you that she is a black woman? Were you picturing her as a generic (read white) woman? If you now think that you know something additional about her, something about the potential effect of racial identity, then you have missed the point. A white woman is of a particular race—and class—as well, both of which contextually locate her gendered attributes and behaviors. To consider gender and class relevant only when someone is not white or not middle class means that one is viewing all women as white and middle class, unless otherwise noted. This is no different from viewing all people as men.

Now what if our imaginary client were a man?

A man of some forty years enters my office. He moves very carefully and hesitantly, stopping at the door and waiting. Although he is just my height, he keeps his head lowered in such a way that he has to look up at me. He doesn't seem sure whether to close the door behind him or wait for me to do it. He waits. He asks where he should sit and I indicate which chair is for my clients, although it is obvious from the configuration of the room. He sits down, removes his shoes, and tucks his legs under his body. He wraps his arms around his body as if to hold himself in and silently waits.

What do I know about him, his body, his self-concept, his relationships? From this description, it would be easy to infer that he is either severely depressed and/or atypically feminine, depending perhaps upon whether this is a temporary or permanent demeanor for him. Was the woman depressed or feminine or both? These qualities are not as easily separated in her case because, for women, they are not necessarily independent qualities. We must consider the interstices of the social and the personal. Altering the gender of the client in this manner permits us to see how behaviors and attributes reflect the personal embedded in the culturally gendered. It is most instructive that a description of a depressed-sounding man makes him appear more like a woman.

A young man enters my office. He wants to impress me favorably, to please me, to communicate to me his sincerity, because I am in a position to recommend to the court concerning the custody of his young child. He is eager to gain custody. He moves carefully and in a contained manner. He waits for me to indicate which seat he should take, concerned that he not "accidentally" take my seat or offend me in any unconscious physical way. He also sits in a contained manner, looking at me directly, leaning forward. He asks how to address me and waits for me to control the interview. He is being careful not to exercise dominance.

Like a woman, he is concerned about my judgments, my perception of him before his own. In this case, however, he is consciously aware of this, while she is generally not. This attitude may be so embedded in her physical and psychological makeup that her body/mind takes charge in this situation. His use of the physical is a conscious attempt to manipulate my impression of him by making himself small, contained, and deferential. As this is not his body's custom, he wears it a bit awkwardly. He seeks my approval in a more feminine manner, which signals deference.

Is he acting like a woman? If so, how does he continue to signal that he is a man acting like a woman? How do his body and his mind incorporate this behavior? Does he leave with a sigh of relief or with a pain in his shoulders or with a slight headache from looking at me in a quizzical manner for the better part of an hour? Does he leave feeling in some way like a woman?

A meaningful understanding is based upon asking many questions about his experience from his, my, and the culture's perspectives. How does this temporary posture interact with his habitual one? How would the meaning of his behavior differ in the presence of a male therapist? Would he feel the need to signal deference or could he use a masculine approach, which with a male therapist might signal symmetry and not dominance?

Another person enters my office and sits. He addresses me deferentially as "Dr. Kaschak" and, with his words, attempts to please and charm me. He wants me to like him. He spots the footstool I sometimes use and pulls it

51

toward himself, placing his feet unself-consciously on it as he talks. He has carried a drink from the lobby's soda machine into my office and puts it on a nearby table. He reaches for it and sips periodically as we talk. From time to time, he absentmindedly scratches the inside of his upper leg.

What do I know about him? Much of his nonverbal behavior might go unnoticed since he is male and it is appropriately masculine, as that of the female client in the first example was appropriately feminine. He does not appear to be aware of what he is doing with his body, but is acutely aware of his words. There is nothing unusual about his behavior. He is expressing physical comfort, but using space and touching his body in ways that would call attention were a female to engage in them. They convey a sense of expansiveness and entitlement, with no expression of concern about whether his gestures might be considered inappropriate or "provocative," as they would be in a female.

Does he feel that he will be judged by his words, not by his physical presence or behavior? How does my gender affect his use of his body and the space between us? What is the phenomenology, or perspective, of the actor himself? How is his experience formed by the gender system to which he has been subjected, and by the class and ethnic system in which it is embedded and which is embedded in it? For example, does he feel more confident in this situation than the female client because his body has learned to feel more confident, is less threatened, is not violated? Let's try it with a female client and see what impressions are conveyed.

She enters my office and sits. She also addresses me deferentially as "Dr. Kaschak" and, with her words, attempts to please and charm me. She wants me to like her. She spots my footstool, pulls it toward her, and puts her feet unself-consciously on it as she talks. She has carried a drink into the office and puts it on the table nearby. She reaches for it and sips periodically as we talk. From time to time, she absentmindedly scratches the inside of her upper leg.

How does it read with a female in the same situation? Is she masculine, provocative, or lewd? How does the socially constructed physical behavior of each of these hypothetical clients interact with their immediate sensations and feelings, and mine? These questions and the others I have posed in each case are not abstract queries meant to be answered abstractly and noncontextually, but issues that must be considered in the particular situation and, thus, are intended to direct the attention of the therapist or theoretician. They are questions of meaning.

The Batesonian heuristic device that he called "double description" (1979) is helpful here in the development of a clinical strategy to understand the multiple meanings of these and other situations. It points to the usefulness of the difference between two viewpoints, like that of the parallax produced when a pair of eyes perceive depth in an image. Similarly, an examination of the three pertinent perspectives involved in understanding any woman's experience—the androcentric, the woman-centered, and her own phenomenology—can serve to highlight their differences and therein to construct a higher-order understanding. This is, of course, "triple description," at the very least. Perhaps "multiple description" would be more appropriate to a feminist approach, which always allows for multiple perspectives in the service of making visible points of tension or conflict.

For example, the phenomenology of the individual is both primary and crucial, but not sufficient for a complex understanding. Once the personal phenomenology is elicited, it becomes important to understand the various influences on and meanings of a particular experience. Points of tension or conflict lead us to overlapping or differing meanings, but in any meaningful situation or experience one must ask which perspectives and values contribute to the experience of the individual being described. If this is not done, they remain invisible, embedded in the individual's psychology to be defined and experienced as individual problems or even as women's problems.

In addition, the perspective of the reporter or therapist or describer must always be made explicit. For example, it was reported at a recent conference (International Congress of Psychology, Sydney, Australia, 1988) that in a particular institution the men behave better and are therefore more manageable in coed wards than in all-male wards. As a result, mixed-sex wards have been considered desirable. But apparently the better behavior of men has to do with their sexual access to women—frequently unwilling women, whom the men coerce or rape. Clearly, more than the researchers' report is necessary for a complex understanding of the situation. Whose perspective counts here? How is each participant and the gender system served?

Before this intervention was brought to the attention of feminists, these questions were not asked. The male researchers neither reported the effect on the behavior of the women patients nor even noted this drastic methodological and human error. Only by comparing overlapping descriptions of this situation from the perspectives of the institutionalized men and women, as well as from the masculinist and feminist positions of the investigators, did a fuller picture emerge. The question can then be reformulated as, To what degree are we willing to sacrifice female patients for the sake of the well-being of male patients? This is not unlike the question that must be asked in society in general, nor is the failure on the part of the male researchers to note that there was a female perspective in this situation anomalous.

The connection between anatomy and destiny is not inevitable, as Freud suggested, but socially/psychologically constructed and maintained. Human sexuality is largely socially and psychologically created (Foucault 1978; Money and Erhardt 1972; Money 1973; Money and Tucker 1975; Stoller 1968) and, in our society, defined by men and then taken as proof of the necessity of the same social/psychological system. Freud's focus on the oedipal relationship of the nuclear family, the stage upon which this destiny is played out, also deserves another look through a feminist eye to see what lies at the periphery of masculine vision. I will undertake this re-vision in the next chapter.

3

Oedipus and Antigone Revisited: The Family Drama

Moreover, the "dark continent" trick has been pulled on her: she has been made to see (= not see) woman on the basis of what man wants to see of her, which is to say, almost nothing.
                                                                —Hélène Cixous
                                                        The Newly Born Woman

What is sexuality? Toward whom is it permissible for it to be felt and expressed? Does it enhance or detract from one's sense of self? Is it safe or endangering? Is it associated with feelings of pain, pleasure, or numbness? Does one seek or demand satisfaction or hide sexual feelings and acts? Are they shameful? Do they enhance one's potency? One's desirability? One's vulnerability?

The learned expressions of sexuality give us another opportunity to consider gender embodied. Everyone is born with a genetically determined sexual potential. The means and direction of that expression, at least in our society, involve a narrowing of focus, a learning of what is possible, what is considered appropriate or inappropriate. While sexuality changes and develops throughout the life cycle, it does so only within a context of learned meanings.

From the masculine perspective, women are defined by their bodies. Everything about a woman is both grounded in and defined by her female body and, in particular, its sexuality, defined in masculinist society as the ability to arouse, rather than to experience, desire. The measure of woman's sexuality is man's tumescence. What about her is arousing, and even whether she intends to arouse, is also designated by the male. It may

55

be her legs for a "leg man," her breasts for a "breast man," her resistance or her nonresistance for a rapist. His feelings become hers, his desire her desirability, his admiration her measure of worth, his disdain her degradation, his ridicule her humiliation.

Most traditional psychological approaches distinguish between normal and pathological fragmentation, or fetishistic male desire. For example, it is considered perfectly normal for a man to be aroused by high-heeled shoes on a woman's feet. It is probably normal for him to be aroused by high heels just seen or about to be seen on someone's feet, or even fantasized on someone's feet. It is probably not normal for him to be aroused by the shoes alone or the feet alone—but the most current official diagnostic system permits even that, as long as the relationship is not repeatedly or exclusively preferred (American Psychiatric Association 1987). Only at this arbitrary point does modern psychological thought consider it fetishistic.

Women's sexuality is shaped by the indeterminate male observer, as well as by his more determinate representatives in her life, including her father and other significant male adults, as well as brothers and males from her peer group. It is also shaped by women: mothers or other female primary and secondary nurturers, and even daughters, both by example and by direct statement. It is influenced mightily by the messages of the culture communicated through movies and television and, in particular, through rock music and its purveyors. It is not absurd to ask whether children might learn more about sexuality from MTV than from their parents. These various influences typically do not contradict one another, but collude to instruct young girls that their sexuality is based on appearance and performance, on desirability rather than desire, on restraint rather than exploration. Sexuality is perhaps the most obviously gendered realm of functioning in this society.

Masculinist psychological theory, when it has explicitly dealt with sexuality as a core construct, has typically considered that of women by extrapolation from, or as a variation on, male sexuality. Freudian theory has given us the male and female oedipal complexes, identical up to the point of resolution: the oedipal complex can be fully resolved in the male, as a bearer of the penis, but can never be resolved in the female, who lacks the instrument of maturity. Once again, women are, in comparison with men, only partially formed human beings according to this theory; full adult maturity requires, by definition, a penis.

Object-relations theorists, both feminist and nonfeminist, have reconsidered the Freudian approach and, in keeping with the Kleinian tradition, have focused on the pre-oedipal stage as more determinative than the oedipal, particularly in female development (Chodorow 1978). Yet this approach still takes as its basis the oedipal, or male, model. Other approaches have simply considered this model irrelevant or less than useful in its overemphasis on sexuality—and male sexuality, at that—as the central organizing principle in human development. Certainly it is reductionist at best, simplistic and damaging to women at worst. It would thus seem that a feminist perspective must discard the myth of Oedipus as central to both male and female psychology.

Yet perhaps there is something to be learned from the myth of Oedipus that is neither reductionist nor misogynist. Perhaps it can be instructive in the development of a complex model of women's psychology. It has certainly captured the popular imagination through several hundred years and across different cultures as a family drama unmasked. And so it is, but what if we were to read it more fully than did Freud, and not only from the perspective of the son?

BEYOND FREUD'S VIEW OF THE OEDIPAL CONFLICT

The myth of Oedipus as representative of the sexual development of the universal male child and his incestuous desires toward the universal mother is a cornerstone of Freudian theory. Upon it rests the dynamic formulation of repression and the unconscious. The plight of the unfortunate Oedipus has been rendered so much a part of popular culture that it would seem we hardly need reminding of the sequence of events leading to the tragic fate of Oedipus the king. However, that very popularization from the perspective of the son only is what cries out for a retelling. Sophocles' trilogy of plays is, in fact, replete with complex family dilemmas. Second to Oedipus in importance is his daughter/sister, Antigone, for whom the third part of the trilogy is named. As Oedipus represents the dilemma of the son, so does Antigone personify that of the dutiful daughter in patriarchal society.

Freud turned consistently to the mythology of the most patriarchal and sexist of civilizations, the Greek and the Roman, for psychological understanding. This may not be problematic insofar as one applies them in turn to patriarchal cultures such as our own. Such an analysis, however, is not universal in any sense, but may be useful in understanding family dynamics and relationships within patriarchy. As such, the oedipal myth is far richer and more complex than is indicated by Freud's and subsequent readings of it. Certainly there are important characters other than Oedipus, and their dilemmas as members of the family and society must be considered. Even that of Oedipus should not be reduced only to the role of son and husband, as he is seen primarily as a father in two-thirds of the trilogy.

While the most famous play in the trilogy, *Oedipus Rex,* was written by Sophocles in about 425 B.C., *Antigone* was actually written first, somewhere around 442 B.C. *Oedipus at Colonus* was written last, in 406 B.C., shortly before Sophocles' death at the age of ninety. As Rudnytsky (1987) has noted, regardless of how one views the trilogy, *Antigone* must be considered the pivotal play, since it may be viewed as either a beginning or an ending. More to the feminist point, for the reader interested in the fate of the daughter and not just that of the son, *Antigone* must be considered as seriously as is *Oedipus Rex.*

In the familiar story, Oedipus ascends the throne as a result of solving the riddle of the Sphinx. Having murdered his father, King Laius, he can assume the paternal throne, whose spoils include the queen—his mother, Jocasta. For a period, the two incestuous partners rule Thebes happily and ignorantly as husband and wife. Two girls and two boys are born of their union: Antigone, Ismene, Polynices, and Eteocles. Only when Thebes falls upon hard times does Oedipus, in seeking the cause, discover the truth about his origins from the blind prophet Tiresias. True to his destiny, he had not avoided slaying his father and marrying his mother.

Upon learning his true identity, Oedipus puts out his eyes with Jocasta's brooch, and she commits suicide by hanging herself. Her purpose in the family apparently ends with her role as wife to two kings and mother to one. There is virtually no evidence of a bond between her and the four children she bore with Oedipus. They appear to be their father's children.

Although Freud's reading and the popular rendition end here, with Jocasta's death and Oedipus' self-inflicted blindness, a mere third of the play has unfolded at this point. The remainder involves the fate of Oedipus as well as his four children, particularly Antigone. As their lives continue, they will play out the destiny of their father/brother, Oedipus. While Jocasta is irrelevant to the next generation, so that her suicide does not impede but facilitates the course of events, Oedipus' life must and does continue.

In *Oedipus at Colonus,* the blind Oedipus wanders the land, accompanied by and completely dependent upon Antigone, who serves as his protector and his eyes. Betrothed to the son of Creon—brother of Jocasta and successor to Oedipus—she is unable to marry him because she must instead spend her days caring for her father. As Oedipus had his destiny, so is this hers, each determined by the acts of their fathers, as they are children of their fathers and not their mothers. Ismene, although less central than Antigone, also devotes herself to her father's welfare, while Oedipus' two sons have turned against him and each other and are contending for his lost throne. At the end of this section, Oedipus, guided by Antigone, returns to die a peaceful and honorable death. Before dying, Oedipus entrusts the welfare of his unprotected daughters to Theseus. He then orders the two away, since, as females and daughters, they are not entitled to "see what you should not see" (Roche 1958, p. 155). Only Theseus, as a man and a king, can be with Oedipus in his last moments on earth and can know the secret site (and sight) of his death.

In the third part, Antigone comes to the fore as a central character whose fate does or should concern us as much as does that of Oedipus. It is she who remains a faithful guide to her father and loyal to her brothers, thereby placing herself in peril. Her two brothers continue to battle, ultimately to the death, thus leaving Creon the undisputed master of Thebes. He orders that Polynices, who died fighting against his own city, be left unburied and dishonored on the battlefield. When Antigone decides to defy Creon's order and bury her dead brother, she is summarily condemned to death by Creon. Haemon, Creon's son, responds to this edict by pleading with his father for mercy toward his betrothed, which his father denies. Antigone is soon found hanging, a similar death her only tie (a noose) to her mother. Dead by her side and by his own hand is Haemon.

Reading the Oedipus myth only from the masculine perspective renders the female characters minor, if not invisible. If it is read through a Freudian lens as a parable of sexual development, then one error of which we are quite aware is the resultant holding of female sexuality to a male standard, since the latter becomes the only standard. Sophocles' drama, as well as Freud's reading of it, is from the perspective of the son. In fact, according to mythological tradition prior to Sophocles, it was the sin of Laius, father of Oedipus, in abducting and raping the son of King Pelops that brought the curse upon his house. The sins of the father were visited upon the son and (tangentially, in the eyes of the ancient Greeks and of Freud) upon the wife/mother. Sophocles, however, "anticipated Freud's rejection of the seduction theory in favor of the Oedipus complex" (Rudnytsky 1987, p. 255). The deeds of the father are replaced by the desires of the daughter (or son). As the hypothesis of seduction as a mere fantasy of the child has been repudiated by recent feminist clinical and empirical work, which has conclusively established and documented the prevalence of molestation by fathers and other adult male relatives, so does this reading of the oedipal and Antigone myths demand another look. The deeds of the father and husband must be considered along with the perspective of the wife/mother and the daughter herself in order more fully to glean the dynamics of the family in patriarchal society.

It now seems apparent to us that Freud, in repudiating the seduction hypothesis, was psychologically impelled to reject the notion that his respected colleagues and friends could be sexually molesting their daughters, or that he himself had a psychologically incestuous relationship with his own daughter, helpmeet, and analysand, Anna. There is also evidence, via a reported dream, of unrecognized feelings toward another of his daughters, Mathilde (Lerman 1986). Additionally, Balmary (1979) has suggested that Freud's failure to recognize in the Oedipus myth the culpability of the father was tied to his failure to recognize his own father's reputation as a Don Juan. By means of a psychological transfer that Freud himself would have labeled projection, the transgression of the father becomes the wish of the child. He never again dealt with sexuality of the adult male directed toward children (Lerman 1986). Instead, it became children who sexually desired adults. Laius' sin becomes that of his son, and Oedipus' that of his children. As Freud's version imposes childhood sexuality upon adults, so does it attribute the depth and complexity of adult sexuality to children. It assigns to women and children the embodiment of and responsibility for adult male sexuality. Instead let's look at adult sexuality as located not in children but where it belongs, in adults.

As Oedipus' dilemma became a symbol for the dilemma of the son, so might that of Antigone be considered representative of the inevitable fate of the good daughter in the patriarchal family. While Freud (1975, pp. 382, 424) was aware that he had his own Antigone in the person of Anna, he failed to consider her dilemma from her perspective, and dynamically oriented psychology has, to this day, followed suit. Oedipus was a son and a husband, as was Freud, but both were also fathers. The fathers of psychology have all but ignored the psychology of fathers. In *Antigone*, Oedipus' fate is represented by his children, externalized representations of himself. The sons battle for his lost power, while the issue for his daughters is one of loyalty to him and to their brothers. He remains the focal point. So if Sophocles ignores the inherited curse of Laius, he does not omit the inherited curse of Oedipus, as the son is also the father. There is a great deal more to be understood about masculine psychology through reconsidering the myth of Oedipus, the father, and about the feminine through understanding his daughter Antigone.

Anna Freud (see Masson 1984) took the position that if oedipal theory were removed from psychoanalytic theory, the importance of both conscious and unconscious fantasy would disappear with it. Freud's "discovery" of the Oedipus complex was applied to male children and later extended to females with a sleight of hand so clumsy that it captivated almost no one, least of all Freud himself. Even he eventually repudiated this construct, saying, "We have an impression here that what we have said about the Oedipus complex applies with complete strictness to the male child only, and that we are right in rejecting the term 'Electra complex' which seeks to emphasize the analogy between the attitude of the two sexes" (in Strachey 1953–74, pp. 228–29).

The Electra terminology was not adopted, but a symmetrical model of female and male psychosexual development is still with us. The oedipal conflict and Freud's reading of the Oedipus myth have influenced the views of generations of psychotherapists concerning childhood sexuality, including many feminist theorists, who accept the basic model while focusing on the pre-oedipal years as crucial for the development of females. According to Freud himself, "The phase of exclusive attachment to the mother, which may be called the pre-Oedipus phase, possesses a far greater importance in women than it can have in men" (in Strachey 1953–74, p. 230). Nancy Chodorow and many contemporary feminist object-relations theorists have returned to an emphasis on this stage of development for the female:

There is analytic agreement that the preoedipal period is of different length in girls and boys. There is also an agreed on, if undeveloped, formulation concerning those gender differences in the nature and quality of the preoedipal mother-child relationship. . . . As a boy moves into oedipal attachment . . . , his father does become an object of his ambivalence. At this time, the girl's intense ambivalent attachment remains with her mother. [Chodorow 1978, p. 97]

Yet even such a focus accepts the different stages of the basic oedipal model as appropriate for both genders, and it is this very model that merits reexamination. While some of the best-known male thinkers throughout history, from Hegel to Nietzsche, have concerned themselves with the plight of Oedipus, the son, it remains for us to consider the myth through female eyes.

OEDIPAL PSYCHOLOGY OF THE SON/FATHER: A FEMINIST INTERPRETATION

For a boy or man in patriarchal culture, women are often not experienced as individuals separate from himself. First his mother, then his wife, and finally his daughters are experienced as extensions of himself and his own

needs. While he must experience the frustration of inevitably partial gratification of his needs by his mother or her substitute, he is instructed by her,
by his father, and by society that he continues to have the right to expect
caretaking and gratification from females. The male child fails to resolve
this infantile grandiosity, but only transfers it from his mother to other
women. He is the king of his domain, as was Oedipus, saved by his mother,
although her own life and that of his father were thereby put in peril.
Oedipus eventually loses her, along with his throne and his eyesight; however, he does not even pause to mourn her loss, so concerned is he with his
own fate as a man and a king. Oedipus simply transfers his sense of
entitlement to Antigone, who takes over from Jocasta as an extension of
him and his fate. His fate becomes hers. Her mission is to serve him, to
provide both sight and sustenance, yet still she is viewed as weaker than he.
"For who would borrow eyes to walk or lean his weight on weakness?"
(Roche 1958, p. 92).

The oedipal complex in men rarely reaches resolution in a patriarchal
society, as adult men typically continue to experience themselves in this
grandiose manner, which includes a sense of entitlement to women. Thus,
it is a complex neither of childhood nor of sexuality narrowly defined, but
one that applies more generally to masculine psychology in a patriarchal
system. It is characterized by extensive boundaries that subsume others,
particularly females, who are considered to contain the feelings, conflicts,
and meanings that men attribute to them. For Freud, this meant that the
transgressions of the fathers were really the desires of the daughters. For
fathers, this means that their daughters exist to meet their (the fathers')
needs. It is the right of the fathers to train their daughters to please them
in all ways, including sexually, the latter all too frequently through incest
and through the father's perceived right to view and comment upon his
daughter in a sexualized manner. This right is extended to all men in a
patriarchal society, who have the right to view and evaluate, to sexualize
any woman who falls within the range of their sight.

Gregory Zilboorg (1944) noted, as did Freud, that father-daughter incest
was the last incest taboo to be introduced. According to Zilboorg, ma-
trilineal inheritance made a mother and children one class and the father
and children another. Since this taboo had to do with the preservation of
property, it evolved as necessary. This analysis misses the obvious: if the
inheritance or property of the father includes the daughter, then this is not
as likely to be considered a necessary taboo and will be the most frequently
violated. In a pamphlet published by Barbara Bodichon in 1854, she noted:
"The legal custody of children belongs to the father. During the lifetime of
a sane father, the mother has no rights over her children, except a limited

power over infants, and the father may take them from her and dispose of them as he thinks fit" (in Heilbrun 1988, p. 85). Psychologically, if not legally, the contemporary father may not consider his sexual right to his daughter to be a violation at all.

It is by virtue of their gaze that men sin against women, that they objectify them, make them prisoners of appearance, of age and color, of physical beauty, of their shape and size. Only through blindness can such sight cease to oppress. Oedipus rips off Jocasta's brooches and destroys his eyes, not his genitals, in an act of self-mutilation. No one is castrated or even threatened with castration. Blindness and not castration is the appropriate punishment for Oedipus' sin. The prophet Tiresias, who revealed his fate to Oedipus, was also blind. Perhaps to be a wise man he must be blind, just as, in order not to continue to sin, Oedipus must also be blinded. Freud considered this blindness to describe the "strange state of mind in which one knows and does not know a thing at the same time" (Rudnytsky 1987, p. 21, from Strachey 1953–74, p. 117)—that is, repression.

Some time after his self-mutilation, Oedipus reconsiders and decides that he may have punished himself too harshly:

> *And yet, how was I the sinner?*
> *I provoked to self-defense in such a way*
> *that even had I acted with full knowledge,*
> *even then, it never could be called a sin.* [Roche 1958, p. 97]

Jocasta, dead by her own hand, is never viewed in this light nor is her death lamented. In fact, Oedipus eventually manages to deposit his own shame into Jocasta, saying to her brother, Creon, who succeeds Oedipus as king: "And to her shame she gave me children" (Roche 1958, p. 97). Later, his explanation for this transfer of blame continues:

> *Neither in this marriage then*
> *shall I be called to blame*
> *nor in the way my father died—*
> *on which you harp with so much spite.*
>
> *Let me ask you this, one simple thing:*
> *if at this moment someone should*
> *step up to murder you,*
> *would you, godly creature that you are,*
> *stop and say: Excuse me, sir, are you my father?* [Roche 1958, p. 128]

In fact, Oedipus does continue to commit a related, but not explicitly sexual, sin by treating Antigone as an extension of himself and his eyes. He gets another chance to resolve his Oedipus complex, but does not use it wisely. Jocasta is given no such option. A woman has a chance at engulfment only once with her children, who must eventually leave her and forget their profound ties to her. She is dead to them in this sense, as was Jocasta to her children. She should not stand in their way. A man continues on once his days with his mother are done. All his women are extensions of him; he gets many more chances to engulf them, as well as to be mothered.

As the oedipal son passes through the stage of relinquishing his mother, he begins to look at other women. Through adolescence and adulthood, he retains the prerogative to evaluate and sexualize all women but his mother, including his own daughters. In total blindness he loses the sexualized gaze, yet even then does not lose his kingly sense of entitlement.

Oedipus, the son, was fated by the gods to become Oedipus, the husband of his mother. Jocasta herself comments that many men, if only in their dreams, have married their mothers. She speaks for masculine entitlement to their mothers and to their dreams and fantasies. She is part of the spoils of the king, the chosen one. She is a medium of exchange between Oedipus and Creon, Oedipus and Laius. It is not she who calls for the punishment of Oedipus. Instead she comes quite close to acknowledging his entitlement to her. In the traditional arrangement, wives are also mothers to their husbands, supplying emotional and physical sustenance in the form of caring, feeding, cleaning, and the like. So Jocasta is Oedipus' wife/mother. She is neither threatening nor castrating in any way. He is blinded, but it is she who dies for the sin. While she could be passed along to the next king, her brother, Creon, this would undoubtedly turn a tragedy into a comedy in men's eyes.

Jocasta is certainly not a person in her own right, but a wife, a prize to the king, someone from whom her children must separate. The connection between her and her children must be rendered invisible as they pass from childhood to the masculine world of the father. As children carry their father's name, they are his and not hers. In inquiring after Oedipus' identity upon his return, the chorus requests of him, "Sir, your ancestry? Your father's name?" (Roche 1958, p. 95). They are his route to immortality. As the chorus states, "we are mortals born of men" (Roche 1958, p. 192). In oedipal society, we are all our fathers' children.

A mother's relationship with her daughter often centers on caring for men or children. The invisible bond between Jocasta and Antigone is almost one of identity, as Antigone takes up Jocasta's task of caring for Oedipus much as a wife/mother would. He is their connection and their downfall, and this parallel is underscored by the identity in their form of death. As a result, Antigone is considered primarily his daughter rather than his sister. Her relationship to her mother is rendered invisible in oedipal psychology. Oedipus himself refers to his daughters as just what they are, "Dear props of my life" (Roche 1958, p. 133).

Jocasta bears no resemblance to the castrating mother of Freudian theory, and indeed it is the father who is the threatening castrator of his son, even in Freudian theory. It is fear of castration by the father that leads to repression and sublimation of the desire for the mother; it is men who are dangerous to one another. Oedipus slays his own father, although unknowingly, and, as a result, gains access to his throne and to his queen, who comes with the post. Her only act of violence is appropriately feminine, an "acting in"—turning aggression or other unacceptable feelings against herself—by means of which she destroys herself. The parallel holds in the next generation: the brothers are slain in battle; Antigone is dead by her own hand.

For men, sex is power in oedipal psychology. The two sons of Oedipus fight each other to the death for possession of his throne, although the unfortunate Jocasta is, by this time, no longer available to the victor as part of the spoils. Even if she were, the point of the tale and of Freud's theory is that she is the one woman who is not available to them, at least sexually, nor, being their mother, would she be desired. The mixture of sex and power in oedipal psychology requires that men be bigger and stronger and more central than their partners, leading them to young girls and daughters and not to a bigger and more powerful mother. Incest is most commonly committed by fathers or stepfathers against their daughters, rarely between mothers and sons.

The feminine psychology of women is characterized neither by the sex/power mixture nor by a grandiose extension of themselves into others and thus does not lead them characteristically to approach erotically smaller and more helpless people. A woman is more likely to experience her child's needs as her own than the reverse, and the child's need is not for sex with an adult. Only since the feminist movement has encouraged women to reclaim their own vision has the startling incidence of rape and sexual molestation of daughters by their fathers or other adult male relatives become known and believed. This was not an accomplishment of the fathers, but of the mothers and daughters, who questioned the property laws of men.

In order to do so, they first had to be able to question the masculine psychological rule of entitlement. It has been asked quite seriously by masculinist jurors, If a man can't rape his own wife, whom can he rape? Similarly, if his own daughter is not his property, an extension of himself to do with as he wishes, then who is? The problem for many fathers, then, becomes not so much the incest taboo itself as that of getting caught violating it and accepting that they have done something wrong or damaging. Certainly the incidence of molestation and rape of female children makes it almost common enough to be normative and, as such, to demand an analysis in terms of the "normal" psychology of the oedipal father. That is, how does a sense of entitlement, combined with a weak sense of limits and of the self, come to be expressed through sexuality in a patriarchal society?

Extrapolating from this model, we would have the concept of the "castrating father," a term I have never heard used in either professional or popular jargon. Somehow instead we have the "castrating mother." How does the threat of the father get deposited into the mother? The "natural masculine hatred of women" is made deserving, is located in women rather than in the dangerous father—for he might retaliate. He is the true threat. He must be murdered, as Laius was, or he will castrate or murder. Even brothers are a danger to each other as they vie for power. It is power that all these men seek, not sexuality per se. René Girard has noted that "at the core of the Oedipus myth . . . is the proposition that all masculine relationships are based on reciprocal acts of violence" (1972 p. 48). This violence is related to the father, not the mother.

Male sexuality, then, is an expression of male dominance and power, with woman as the spoils. Power and sexuality cannot, in oedipal psychology, be separated. Their extreme expression is rape. The currently accepted principle in rape treatment programs is that rape is violence, not sex. That may be so for women, whose sexuality develops differently from that of men. For men, it is both. Only with a mass cultural resolution of the oedipal complex can adult males divest themselves of the fantasy or reality of violence and domination. This is because the oedipal complex is a personal psychological and a social/political phenomenon at the same time and must be resolved on both levels.

It is a powerful male fantasy that the mother, not the father, wishes to punish her son for being a man. The mother can be contained. Replacing a dangerous male adversary with a less physically powerful one creates a modicum of safety. Men would and do kill one another. Yet it is women who can and must be contained and are often seen as deserving such treatment for, were they not contained, the fantasy goes, they would use power indiscriminately against men much as men currently use it against women and against one another. Men continue their violence toward one another, their competitiveness, even their wars, while defining women as the castrating danger.

Women learn to carry guiltily this surplus of meaning while becoming convinced that they can indeed castrate men through any show of self-assertion or strength. This acceptance of masculine meaning leads girls and women to believe that it is they who are dangerous and must either submit to a man or castrate him. In this way, girls and women contain men's fear of retaliation both by women and by other men. They absorb men's "natural" hatred of women as women's "natural" self-hatred. Sharon G. Nathan (1981) found, in a cross-cultural study, that the less that anatomical differences were hidden in a given society, the more males, not females, demonstrated penis envy themes. Both castration and penis envy are issues in male psychology that have been misplaced along the way.

Thus, I listen to a woman with a creative and satisfying business career explain to me that the men at work like her because, unlike some of the other women, she does not try to "act tough" like a man. I listen to innumerable students explain to me that, although they believe in equality for women, they are certainly not feminists. I hear their wish to please, not to threaten, to contain themselves, not to be the center of their own universe.

In terms of the model presented here, a sense of entitlement and of overly extensive boundaries is characteristic of the psychology of the father, learned as a son. A son is expected to follow in his father's footsteps or to go beyond him, to accomplish what the father could not. Fathers often try to relive their lives through their sons. "For, sons and fathers crown each other's glory with each other's fame" (Roche 1958, p. 188). A daughter should be able to take care of her father and other men, and to look good to him and eventually to other men should he decide to relinquish her, as Freud and Oedipus did not. Both sons and daughters are viewed as extensions of the father's needs, albeit of differing needs. A male learns that he is an extension of his father as his children are of him, and this, I submit, is part and parcel of oedipal psychology. The son learns that women are the spoils and, by extension, that all women are his to possess and to evaluate according to his desires and needs. The oedipal father cannot tell, in a deep psychological sense, where his psychological/physical self ends and that of his daughter begins. He may assume that she wants or enjoys sexual intimacy with him, or that she needs to be sexually initiated, or simply that she is his to do with as he wishes.

Most perpetrators of incest, in fact, report that they were unaware of the harm they were causing and even that they thought the girl enjoyed it: "She liked it"; "She wanted to please me and she did"; "I wanted her to learn about sex from someone who loves her and not from a stranger." A patient who was sexually abused by her therapist reports: "His standard line was, until I learned how to relate to him in the office, I would never be able to relate to men outside" (Pelka 1989, p. 8).

Several decades ago, Karen Horney noted that "the prerogative of gender [is] the socially sanctioned right of all males to sexualize all females, regardless of age or status" (in Westkott 1986, pp. 94–95)—to observe, evaluate, and use the female body for their own purposes. This remains the core meaning of male and female, masculine and feminine, in our society. Although not all men may choose to exercise this right actively, no woman can choose to opt out of this system. All women will be sexualized publicly and privately throughout life; even if they are discarded or judged negatively, it is still against the standard of men's sexual gaze.

Fathers, being male, partake of the masculine prerogative to sexualize all women, and this includes their own daughters. Such behavior is so typical that it fades into the realm of the invisible. It is common for fathers and other adults to comment freely on young girls, particularly as they approach puberty, and on how adolescent girls are developing and filling out. The sense of exposure, shame, and embarrassment, even when mixed with pleasure, are hers for having this body, not his for noticing. Likewise, the sexuality is hers, not his. Suddenly she is glaringly visible, as a body or as body parts.

The male child's body is not scrutinized and commented on in this sexualized manner by adults, and certainly not by adult females. He is commented on with much less frequency and much less negativity. Adults may note changes in the young boy's voice and height, but comments about his hairstyle, clothing, posture, and general demeanor are less common, as are public and private comments about his developing sexual organs by either parent. His testicles or "wet dreams" are not of public note, as are her developing breasts and menstrual periods. If the young boy's mother made his appearance and developing sexuality her business to the degree that fathers normally do with their daughters, the mother would undoubtedly be considered pathologically preoccupied with her son's sexuality and enmeshed with him.

The girl's body is both more visible and more humiliating to her just because the choice to make it visible or sexual is not her own. She is exposed and naked when a boy or man decides to make her so. A father's relationship to his daughter is sexual in a way that a mother's to her son is not. A father, for example, can flirt with his daughter (Goodenough 1957). In a study of families where women had deliberately sought male partners who would share in parenting, the men did not turn out to be male mothers, but more like their daughters' romantic lovers. Certain of these fathers spoke very explicitly and proudly of being in love with their daughters (Ehrensaft

1985). The girl child learns a mixture of shame, pleasure, exposure, visibility, and invisibility, none of which are in her control.

Thus, it comes as no surprise when Mary Catherine Bateson reports in her memoir that her father, Gregory Bateson, "looked at me rather meditatively one day and said he supposed . . . that really the only reason we shouldn't go to bed together . . . was the danger of genetic damage if I should get pregnant. . . . I said, equally low-keyed, that I thought there were other reasons too." "When we traveled off together, Gregory fantasized a romance between himself and me" (1984, pp. 107, 226). Interestingly, she entitled this book *With a Daughter's Eye,* claiming her own sight and movement from the unresolved antigonal phase.

One of the many functions served by culturally sanctioned male voyeurism is to keep boys and men from being scrutinized themselves. Their vulnerable external organ will be neither threatened nor judged (except by other men). In the sexual gaze, they channel their sexuality and relocate their fear of castration, of exposure, of humiliation, into women's bodies.

When Jane was around twelve years old, her mother began to tell her to cover her body in front of her father. Jane was perplexed and resentful, as she was wearing the same nightgowns she had always worn. Why was she suddenly being restricted in this way? Why must she block her father's view, take responsibility for making his sexual fantasies invisible? It is part of the task of the daughter to render the father's sexuality toward her both invisible and gratified, which she accomplishes by absorbing it. She may be able to prevent or contain its genital expression. If not, she must keep it a secret or the shame is hers; it is about her body, not his.

Jane was being taught to embody the dynamics between men and women, men and girls, fathers and daughters, that I have been discussing. Any sexuality is attributed to the daughter, who is mandated to control it by limiting her exposure, her freedom, by rules often invoked by the mother to protect the daughter or to protect the mother's relationship with the father, now threatened by the presence of this more desirable-to-him feminine body in their home.

In much the same way, patriarchal religions, such as Orthodox Judaism and Islam, mandate that women be separated from men and that their bodies be covered to prevent men from being sexually tempted. A male acquaintance recently expressed to me the wish that these customs were more pervasive so that he would not be so often tempted to break his marital vows. He put into words the desire of many men for women to be hidden from view when it suits men's needs and exposed when it meets their needs.

One of the first female professors in the law faculty of a Western university, Novella d'Andrea, lectured at the University of Bologna in the early fourteenth century (de Pizan 1982; Labalme 1984). She was required to lecture from behind a screen so that her beauty would not distract the male students from their learning. She had to be restricted to contain their lust. This was her problem, not theirs.

In his best-selling collection of therapy cases, *Love's Executioner,* the psychiatrist Irvin Yalom (1989) demonstrates how alive and well this tradition is in psychotherapeutic practice. His descriptions of cases involving female patients almost uniformly contain physical descriptions of the women in terms of how attractive or unattractive they were to him. For example, he offers the following observation of the case of a female patient in the title piece:

> Though I had difficulty imagining this shabby old woman having an affair with her therapist, I had said nothing about not believing her. In fact, I had said nothing at all. I had tried to maintain complete objectivity but she must have noticed some evidence of disbelief, some small cue, perhaps a minuscule widening of my eyes. I decided not to protest her accusation that I did not believe her. This was no time for gallantry and there *was* something incongruous in the idea of a disheveled seventy-year-old infatuated, lovesick woman. She knew that, I knew it, and she knew I knew it. [P. 16]

This description reflects a combination of misogyny and self-referential entitlement which, in a just world, would disqualify a therapist from working with female patients at all.

Improvement is also measured in terms of appearance:

> When I went into the waiting room to greet Thelma, I was dismayed at her physical deterioration. She was back in her green jogging suit and had obviously not combed her hair or made any other attempts to groom herself. [P. 59]

This use of the attractiveness test of mental health differentially applied to female patients or clients is far from unusual for male therapists, but surprising for one who purports to be aware of his own dynamics and motives. Yalom does not venture as far into the territory of self-awareness as even Freud did. Sexist attitudes can too easily remain invisible and impenetrable in masculinist society, even among those who are mandated to examine their own motives as part of competent and ethical professional practice.

He begins another case with a female patient in this way:

I have always been repelled by fat women. I find them disgusting: their absurd sidewise waddle, their absence of body contour—breasts, laps, buttocks, shoulders, jawlines, cheekbones, *everything,* everything I like to see in a woman, obscured in an avalanche of flesh. And I hate their clothes—the shapeless, baggy dresses or, worse, the stiff elephantine blue jeans with the barrel thighs. How dare they impose that body on the rest of us?

The origins of these sorry feelings? I had never thought to inquire. So deep do they run that I never considered them prejudice. But were an explanation demanded of me, I suppose I could point to the family of fat, controlling women, including—featuring—my mother, who peopled my early life. Obesity, endemic in my family, was a part of what I had to leave behind when I, a driven, ambitious, first-generation American-born, decided to shake forever from my feet the dust of the Russian shtetl.

I can take other guesses. I have always admired, perhaps more than many men, the woman's body. No, not just admired: I have elevated, idealized, ecstasized it to a level and a goal that exceeds all reason. Do I resent the fat woman for her desecration of my desire, for bloating and profaning each lovely feature that I cherish? For stripping away my sweet illusion and revealing its base of flesh—flesh on the rampage? [Pp. 87–88].

This piece of pseudo-insight incorporates all we have noted about the unresolved oedipal complex. Its sense of entitlement in defense of misogyny with yet more misogyny is offered without shame or apology. As he is clear that he safely belongs to "the rest of us" (read men), he is equally clear that he loves neither the female body nor females themselves, but his own pleasure, desire, and, indeed, illusion.

The cultural ideal for the female body reflects the masculine preference for the young girl, the daughter. Fathers are no exception here and may become distracted from the familiar and aging bodies of their wives by the young and desirable bodies of their daughters. This spanning of the generations, among other things, serves as a form of denial of death, a psychological arresting of time. Oedipus was a contemporary of his parents as well as of his own children, who were also his sisters and brothers. He maintained his grandiosity by overpowering not only smaller creatures but time itself. It has sometimes been suggested by psychologists that the male preference for prepubescent female bodies reflects a thinly disguised homoerotic impulse. I disagree in part. While this may well be a secondary motive, the primary one is the oedipal mixture of sex and power, which can be actualized through fantasied or real relationships with weaker, smaller, younger females. This is both an affirmation, artificially constructed and illusory, of masculine power and a serious effort at denial of mortality and death, also illusory.

Magazines and the popular media bombard us with these images. Middle-aged professors who have affairs with, or even marry, their students, barely out of adolescence, speak of the same desire. Therapists become sexually involved with their clients. Older men marry women the same age as their children. Many fathers have sex with their daughters. How many more fantasize about it? I know of no systematic analysis of the adult oedipal dreams of fathers about their daughters. Yet the oedipal complex is characterized by the projection of adult male sexuality onto women and children and not of the child's onto the parent.

In this dance of entitlement, the father's sexuality is often literally, always psychologically, deposited in the daughter, who must control it. Antigone is so much an extension of Oedipus that generations of readers have hardly noticed her in her own right.

The following list summarizes the phases of oedipal development within masculine psychology:

1. The Early Oedipal Phase (early childhood)

Incomplete gratification of infantile needs by mother and other adults combined with a sense of entitlement to gratification from all other females.

Example of father and other men as central in importance both within and outside the home.

The media, teachers, other adults encourage the boy to explore, compete with other males, and engage in conquest as the essence of masculinity.

Females are the spoils and exist to gratify him.

2. The Oedipal Phase (mid-childhood through adulthood)

The infantile grandiosity is transferred from mother to all other females and often to smaller males. Includes his women and children.

Experiences self as extensive, engulfing, subsuming others, especially females, who are extensions of himself.

Experiences self as superior to females.

Voyeuristic. Fear of blindness (castration).

Sense of entitlement.

Considers himself the parent of his children. Their mother is only a caretaker. She is his caretaker also.

Preference for younger and smaller women.

Experiences sex as power, which can manifest itself as sadism, violence, or domination.

Importance of male bonding, teams, locker rooms, business turf.

Usually does not pass beyond this phase in a patriarchal society, which is also culturally arrested at this stage. He mirrors society, which mirrors him. He is an eternal adolescent in an adolescent culture.

Functions as a denial of aging and ultimately death, as Oedipus decided that he had been too harsh in believing that he himself should die for his sins. Emphasis on staying young manifests as considering himself an appropriate partner for younger women.

Defines both individuals and patriarchal society.

3. The Resolution of the Oedipal Phase (adulthood, but typically is never resolved in patriarchal [oedipal] society)

Relinquishes grandiosity, extensiveness, and engulfment.

Can experience boundaries—where he ends and others begin.

Fragmented vision becomes holistic. Can look at women as full persons rather than as fetishized parts.

Must face his own existential separation and aloneness.

Discovers that he is not a king, just a human being in a world of other humans and other living creatures, all of equal importance with him.

No longer driven by power needs, sexually or in other ways.

Very few men are able to resolve the oedipal complex, since we live in a culture that does not demand or require its resolution but, on the contrary, rewards and maintains it. If men are called upon to resolve it, it is by women, who have taken the lead in this phase of psychological-cultural development. For a man in the oedipal phase of development to allow a woman, or women collectively, the prerogative of taking this initiative is not a psychologically simple task. Even if he is able intellectually to understand that women are treated unfairly, he must cut off access to his own unresolved oedipal conflicts, access to which would thrust him into the experience of his own relative powerlessness, his own mortality, in sum, his own humanity. He is no more and no less than a woman (taken as an insult in the oedipal phase and in an oedipal culture). He would be compelled to see for himself, to discontinue placing women between himself and his own experience of himself.

Needless to say, this is an existential and psychological encounter with oneself from which most men retreat, in several different ways. The most obvious way, considered at length in this work and in many other feminist works, involves continuing the traditional pattern of subsuming and diminishing women and anything associated with them. This might be accomplished, in true oedipal fashion, by either ignoring and excluding women ("No girls allowed in the clubhouse") or by ridiculing women and their ideas ("These women's libbers are frigid, dykes, man haters"). A more intellectual retreat would claim, for example, that feminism is interesting but too narrow, excluding too many important variables, or would acknowledge women's rights in the abstract and in the public arena, while continuing to support women's traditional role in the home and in matters sexual. This separation of roles and isolation of abstract belief from personal experience is the hallmark of post-Cartesian thought and of the distinction made in liberal politics between the public and the private domain.

Our culture provides many easy ways for men to stay in the unresolved oedipal phase. There is little support from other men for relinquishing oedipal grandiosity and sense of entitlement and much support for remaining at the more immature level. As a result, most men never move beyond it. If they do, it is probably because of a meaningful and intimate relationship with a woman who has moved beyond the unresolved Antigone phase, has begun to reclaim her own sight, and can allow this man to see the world as she sees it. Women have always seen from men's perspective; men must now be able to see from women's rather than diminishing and ridiculing women or denying them their own sight. In a reversal of the unresolved oedipal and antigonal phases, their resolution involves self-definition and leadership on the part of Antigone.

ANTIGONAL PSYCHOLOGY OF THE DAUGHTER/MOTHER: A FEMINIST MODEL

Oedipal psychology does not end with the son, but continues as he grows into Oedipus the father. His fate is the fate of his wife and daughters, his sins also borne by them. They are little more than extensions of him, particularly Antigone, the most devoted and dutiful of his daughters. She must also pay for his sins: "You fell a plummet fall / To pay a father's sin" (Roche 1958, p. 193).

Although the Antigone complex rather than the oedipal or Electra did not occur to Freud as an archetype for female development and female sexuality, Otto Rank alluded to "the second great complex, which has for its contents the erotic relations between father and daughter" (1909, p. 77). Rank's formulation in part anticipates one I will present, but emphasizes a dynamic sense of reciprocity between father and daughter more closely aligned with the thought of Freud than with that of modern feminism. For today we are cognizant of the incidence of sexual molestation by fathers or father substitutes of their female children and the devastating effect on their psychological well-being. Incest is neither a romantic notion nor an unfulfilled fantasy when viewed from the female perspective.

What is the plight of Antigone? Her mother is an extension of the men who possess her sexually—first Laius and then Oedipus—and her fate is theirs. She is destroyed by the curse on them and dies by her own hand. Her body is Oedipus' when he requires it, and is disposed of when she is no longer needed. Oedipus need not slay her, as her hand is his and with it she ends her own life. As a blind man, he never looks back to lament her loss or to regret his role in her destruction. Her use to him has passed. One aspect of Oedipus' blindness is his inability to see the value of anyone except to himself. His blindness can be viewed as both a punishment for the way he used his sight and a comment that he has always been blind.

Jocasta is known to us only by her relationship to her men. There is absolutely no indication of her relationship to her children other than to the one who became her husband. She seems to function only in relation to

75

male power and sexuality, as do her daughters. What is their relationship to each other in a male-centered, patriarchal family in which father/son is king? A daughter, in what can be considered the early Antigone phase, learns that men are central and that her function is to please them. She learns her own limits. Along with a deep sense of loyalty to her mother and a desire to please her by becoming the same kind of woman she is, the daughter's Antigone complex is laced with rage at her mother for this betrayal of their relationship and of herself. As she is also a female and her mother's daughter, she learns to diminish and disdain herself. She turns away from and forgets her mother, dutiful to her father and brothers. She becomes her mother, but cannot mother herself.

For a daughter in oedipal society, attachment to her mother is not at all pre-oedipal, but can more accurately be viewed as the early Antigone phase. Attachment to the mother is laced with preparation for the father. A mother typically trains her daughter in softness and attachment, appearance and desirability, sexuality and feminine limits and boundaries, even while some-times encouraging subversive rebellion or hidden strength—that is, she may be strong as long as she doesn't look strong. She may be assertive at work, as long as she doesn't carry it too far or let it spill over into her personal relationships. She may value other females, but not too much. She may not be too independent, as it will lead to danger or loneliness.

Recall that in the anecdote about Jane, it was not her father but her mother who told her to cover her body. As it is her vulnerable female body that leads her to a secondary role in life, she also learns disdain for it. She turns to her father and to men as much from duty as from disappointment in herself and her mother. Her relationship to her mother must be denied, diminished—in essence, made invisible—while that with her father and other men will shape her adult identity. Whether he is largely absent from her daily life or present in a kind and loving or an abusive way, whether he is a source of anger, fear, admiration, or longing in his daughter, she is shaped by his needs. In oedipal society, the daughter becomes the wife and mother, as Antigone essentially becomes wife and mother to Oedipus.

Freud observed early on that "the girl's Oedipus complex is much sim-pler than that of the small bearer of the penis; in my experience, it seldom goes beyond the taking of her mother's place and the adopting of a feminine attitude toward her father" (Freud 1924b/1961, p. 178). While he later amended this analysis, perhaps there is a grain of truth to it. How can the Antigone complex be resolved in a patriarchy, in a man's world? Where can she go? To whom can she turn? As Oedipus extends himself with a sense of entitlement and grandiosity, Antigone appends herself in invisibility and specificity of function. Only the parts of her body that are of use to him matter—in this case her eyes, not her genitals. As his sexuality falls squarely at the center of this tale, hers is virtually invisible. Were he to require it, as he did of Jocasta, then it would have to be available to him, not because the daughter would want it so but because the king would be entitled to it.

Note that Antigone does not escape from her father to marry her own spouse, as does the boy in the oedipal phase. Nor did Anna Freud escape a psychologically incestuous relationship with her father, her mentor, her analyst. It is she who ministered to him through his illness and who continued his work when he was gone, not only her eyes but her very life an extension of his. The girl is the extension of the father, providing him with whatever he cannot provide himself. A son can and does escape from the early world of the mother to a world of men, as the mother is reduced to a person from whom separation is to be accomplished (Spieler 1986). If she conveniently commits suicide, she need not even be killed off.

A daughter in a patriarchal society, however, cannot live outside the world of the fathers. She cannot resolve the Antigone complex as long as the world of adulthood is a man's world, as long as she is the extension of her father or some other man, as long as she is constantly subject to definition by even strange men in public. As Emma Jung commented in a letter to Freud in 1911, "One certainly cannot be the child of a great man with impunity, considering the trouble one has in getting away from ordinary fathers" (Rudnytsky 1987, p. 53). As Oedipus reminds Creon, his sons are men and are masters of their own destiny, but his daughters, who "shared everything I had" (Roche 1958, p. 80), must be cared for. It is the daughters who are most completely extensions of himself, who can forge no life for themselves but the one he gives them. In a patriarchal world, they are reborn of and sustained by him. Yet this "rebirth" is based upon loss of the bond with the mother and, for girls, loss of the self. Therein lie the seeds of the Antigone complex: while a son can become his own man, a daughter experiences complex internal pullings toward her mother, herself, her father, and her children. All are imbued with loss as well as gain.

As Oedipus' sons struggle for power and fully lived lives of their own, Antigone remains faithful and lives only to serve and protect him, never questioning her fate. She dutifully sacrifices her life to her father and subsequently to her dead brother, losing her life to honor and protect him even in death. In the unresolved Antigone phase, women are connected to men or to one another only as helpers of their men. Oedipus notes of Antigone and her sister: "these two girls here, born to care for me, / *they* preserve me; *they* look after me" (Roche 1958, p. 143). Antigone is courageous and defiant, but not in her own name or for her own needs, as is Oedipus.

Antigone, here,
ever since she left the nursery and became a woman,
has been with me as guide and old man's nurse—
unhappy child—
steering me through dreary wanderings;
often roaming through the tangled woods
barefoot and hungry;
often soaked by rain and scorched by sun,
never regretting all she missed at home,
so long as her father was provided for. [P. 100]

In an important sense, Oedipus can afford to put out his own eyes, for he has another pair: "my daughter here whose eyes are mine as they are hers" (p. 88).

Had Jocasta lived instead of Oedipus, Antigone could not have protected her, nor she Antigone. Oedipus, even in blindness and infirmity, retains the ability to provide the boundaries of safety. How far would mother and daughter have gotten roaming the countryside before being raped or otherwise accosted? Would Jocasta have fallen into poverty? For Oedipus' unspoken protection from the external dangers of the masculine world, Antigone exchanges her protection from the internal, from his own vulnerabilities. He needs her in order to deny his own sins and his own death. In this exchange, she is denied her own life. Antigone psychology is characterized by a woman's self-denial and denial of a fully lived life. The needs of those whom she loves and serves take priority over her own and become her own.

Antigone retains her sensory apparatus, but it is to be used for Oedipus' daily needs. Hers is the heroism of the ordinary, not of battle or epic danger but of the small perils of daily life. This is the domain in which women reside, the reflected glory of femininity. Even death has different meanings for those who live the dailiness of life than for those who are shielded from it. The latter often face death as if they had never lived, as a monumental and abstract event, the basis for philosophical tomes. For the former, this meaning, as others, is not less painful but more ordinary.

A woman in the Antigone phase of development is an extension of the oedipal male's eyes and, as such, sees herself as he does, sometimes solely and sometimes in nagging conflict with her own suppressed sight. Those who can bear to see only in the former manner will be traditionally devoted wives and mothers; the latter may glimpse an alternative and struggle to move beyond the unresolved Antigone phase. The former will look to themselves as good as they look to men, will know their own sexuality, if at all, only through men: they will know whether they are young and attractive enough to arouse a man's desire. There are, for example, no clitoral symbols in masculine psychology, literature, or popular culture, all of which are replete with phallic symbols. The clitoris even remains invisible to many women, who know only about breasts, vaginas, openings for the penis, in this unresolved Antigone phase.

Herman Roiphe and Eleanor Galenson point out in a 1981 study that parents typically give little boys pet words for their genitals from a very early age, but rarely do so with girls. They interpret this omission as a cultural manifestation of the castration complex rather than of phallocentric blindness. A recent survey of sex education materials (Lerner 1988) indicates that they, along with parents, typically let the girl child know only that she has a vagina, with no reference to the clitoris. This may lead to confusion and anxiety rather than pride and exploration of her sexuality.

In a violently explicit denial of female sexuality, infibulation and clitoridectomy are still commonly practiced in many parts of Africa and the Middle East, to ensure the lack of sexual desire and satisfaction among women. The enforced belief among many traditional Mexicans and Mexican-Americans is that a woman who enjoys sex with her husband will enjoy it with any man and is, thus, a whore. In a kind of psychosexual clitoridectomy, only a lack of sexual interest is thought to keep a woman faithful to her husband.

I was once approached for a consultation by two Anglo-American therapists in a small California town, who had taken it upon themselves to organize a preorgasmic therapy group for several Mexican-American married women in the area. One of the aspects of the training requested the women to develop assertiveness skills to guide their husbands in approaching them sexually in ways that satisfied them. Several of the women returned to the group having been severely berated or beaten by their husbands. The point is not simply the cultural naïveté of the therapists or of their clients concerning misogyny but the meaning to these men of their wives' sexuality: it was forbidden. They were beaten up for wanting to enjoy sex. Since female sexuality was defined by men, a redefinition in which they were not central could not be allowed. Is this a far cry from the attitudes toward women and sex in the dominant white culture? Or is it a paradigm of women's experience as an extension of masculine sexuality and defined by the simple fact of having a female body?

Only within the last twenty years has the single female orgasm been rediscovered by science and psychology in our society (Koedt 1976). Why did it have to be discovered and taught to so many women in therapy treatment programs? Why would so many women not even know that they could have orgasms, or how many kinds there are? (Do men's orgasms get classified?) They saw their own sexuality through Freud's eyes, demonstrating the power of perspective to render invisible that which does not matter. If the masculinist culture and individual men did not know about women's orgasms or believed that there were two varieties, clitoral and vaginal, then so did many women, who judged themselves lacking by the male standard. Mead (1949) has shown that women have orgasms in societies where women's orgasms matter. Cultures that don't recognize female orgasm can simply make it invisible. There are many ways of making female sexuality and physicality an extension of men's needs.

Now that women's (even multiple) orgasms are expected in many spheres of our society, women may be more prone to fake them. Since a woman's sexuality is still not respected in itself, her orgasm is often seen merely as a response to her partner's ability to perform. She is expected to be both responsive to someone else's desire and readily arousable on demand. If she tries to meet these requirements, her sexuality may become associated with periods of nonarousal rather than of arousal.

Women who do not achieve orgasm have been known as "frigid"; men are "impotent." Nothing reflects more clearly the meanings we impart to the sexual act for men as opposed to women (Kaschak 1976). His is powerful, hers affectionate. His is focused and goal-directed; hers requires warmth and a sense of safety. Both of their bodies have been trained and prepared for this moment of incompatibility. He finds the very power that she loses. While the more progressive language now calls such a woman "preorgasmic," the terminology for the male has not been altered or considered problematic. He is never "prepotent" or "preorgasmic," but just is or isn't potent. Women are by definition impotent.

The recent movie *When Harry Met Sally* contains a memorable scene in which the female lead demonstrates most convincingly, in the middle of a crowded restaurant, how a woman can fake an orgasm. The women in the audience tend to roar in recognition. It would seem that almost every woman has, at one time or another, faked orgasm—at least in the post-1960s, post–Masters and Johnson generation. The male character in the movie is horrified and absolutely positive that no sexual partner of *his* has ever "faked it." His concern is that it would reflect unfavorably on his prowess. Writing in a newspaper column, Richard Cohen (1989) railed against this depiction, upset and humiliated by the notion of this deception. Is a woman's orgasm an extension of her male partner's, a reflection of his, not of her, prowess and potency? Is it something about her or about him?

The primacy of masculine vision often leads women to a blatant form of identification with the indeterminate observer. In a sexual relationship, this woman will tend to be removed even as she participates and will observe herself and her appearance. Through his eyes she sees the eroticized female body. She may be playing a part in which it is more important to be desirable than to desire. Antigone's physicality or sexuality is really only an epiphenomenon of relations between men, and she has no identity apart from them. In an oedipal society, female sexuality cannot exist separately from men. Even conscious efforts to live outside the masculine definition of female sexuality, such as celibacy or lesbianism, cannot succeed without a radical, long-term redefinition of the female body, in which masculine definitions are thoroughly embedded. There is no complete or separate female body, both unfragmented and neither invisible nor hypervisible, possible within an oedipal society.

The life cycle of sexuality is also defined by the masculine perspective and not by a woman's own physical and psychosexual development. That is, she is viewed as a sexual being in the years in which she is attractive to the masculine gaze—typically from early puberty to young adulthood. The incidence of molestation is highest with girls between nine and seventeen years old. Somewhere around the age of seventeen, date rape and, to a lesser extent, stranger rape take over. The oedipal male expresses his sense of entitlement. He often believes that she wants to be raped as much as he wants to do it. " 'A lot of us are unwitting accomplices,' admits sociologist Edward Gondolf. . . . 'It takes prompting and confrontation from women to make us understand.' He knows. As a college football player, he watched a gang rape and laughed. Gondolf awakened to women's suffering and men's responsibility when his wife told him she had been raped before they met" (Toufexis 1990, p. 77).

On a well-known daytime soap opera, the relationship and subsequent marriage of two particularly popular characters, Luke and Laura, began with a rape. There ensued a discussion in the media of whether she could wear white on their wedding day. A recent court decision on corrupting the morals of a minor centered on the principle that, according to the presiding judge, one can't be permitted to dump toxic wastes in a river even if it is already polluted. Popular movies from Spike Lee's *She's Gotta Have It* to the beloved classic *Gone with the Wind* contain explicit or implicit rape scenes in which the woman is pleased, satisfied, and possessed. She becomes his. She must have desired it because he did. The Catholic Church has taught for centuries that a married woman who refuses her husband his sexual right to her body is committing a sin that must be confessed (Finkelhor and Yllo 1985). Women can be forced to have sex or be denied it, as Antigone is.

If girls escape molestation as children, they are not likely to escape sexualized comments, which accelerate as they approach puberty. The adolescent girl is available for comment and evaluation by the determinate and indeterminate observer. The drill continues: she is her body. Women's sexuality, as defined by the indeterminate masculine observer, is often invisible in early childhood, then highly visible, and invisible again toward middle age as women adapt to this unresolved Antigone phase. An elderly woman can sit comfortably on a park bench with her legs apart and her nylons rolled down. No longer the repository of male sexuality, she is not considered sexual or provocative. Yet, if raped, even she may be thought of as "asking for it."

Female sexuality and identity tend to be fragmented, based on body parts. Feelings of loss of oneself and of the early Antigone connection with mother are always embedded in developing heterosexuality in women. Luise Eichenbaum and Susie Orbach (1983) note that sexual connection for women is, in part, an attempt to separate from mother. At the same time, it contains the loss of mother and of the unpossessed (virginal) female self. This is an important aspect of the unresolved Antigone complex. As power is embedded in heterosexuality for men, so is loss and grief for women. For women who want children, this desire is partially based upon the need to heal this wound, to redress the loss, to reestablish the longed-for mother-child bond. Yet they are destined to partial success as they repeat the cycle, Antigone becoming Jocasta, relinquishing both her daughters and sons to masculine society. For men too have their reasons for wanting children. In the *Symposium,* Socrates introduces Diotima of Mantineia, a wise and respected woman, with whom he discusses immortality and love. She eventually persuades him to "marvel not then at the love which all men have of their offspring; for that universal love and interest is for the sake of immortality" (Plato trans. 1951). Women are motivated to recapture the early loss, men the future one.

The oedipal myth can also be read as the fate of those who deny their origins. One thing both Antigone and Oedipus have in common is the denial of their relationship with their mother. They share the same mother, yet neither acknowledges nor appears to remember that fact or the shadowy Jocasta herself. This is not just the denial of death, but of birth as well. The source of the notion that it is men who truly create life can also be seen in the Judeo-Christian belief in a male God who creates all life, as well as in Aristotle's teaching that since semen contains the principle of motion, it alone contains the soul (Aristotle, in Smith and Ross ed. 1912). This masculine cooptation of the cycle of life leads the children to wander alone. As long as the mother is someone to be denied and from whom to separate, then men will be lost and women subsumed.

82

Antigone cannot marry, even though a husband-to-be is found for her. She has given all to her father, leaving nothing for a husband. Says Oedipus:

> *Who will want to marry you?*
> *O there's none—my little ones, not one!*
> *And life for you is all decline: a doom*
> *to empty spinsterhood.* [P. 81]

Her betrothed appears to be devoted enough to Antigone to die for her, so much so that his father calls him "lady-help" and "a woman's lackey" (Roche 1958, pp. 190, 189). An oedipal man should not be an extension of an Antigone woman, but the reverse is appropriate. Perhaps this relationship should be explored further as an alternative model for heterosexual relations.

A summary of the phases of development in Antigone psychology includes the following:

1. The Early Antigone Phase (early childhood)

Attachment to the mother. A real relationship with the mother. Incomplete gratification of infantile needs with a sense that she must learn to limit her needs accordingly.

Example of the oedipal father and all men as central in importance and women as secondary.

The media, teachers, other adults encourage her to limit exploration for the sake of safety and to concentrate instead on nurturing others and on having a pleasing appearance and demeanor.

Often sexually molested as an initiation ritual.

2. The Antigone Phase (mid-childhood through adulthood)

Denial of birth and of origins.

Danger embedded in pleasure.

Denial of own physicality through invisibility or hypervisibility. Eating disorders contain a failed attempt to nurture oneself instead of others, along with its denial.

Clear limits and permeable boundaries.

Experience must not show, especially physically.

Experiences needs of men and children as her own, or as her obligation to fulfill. Exemplified by the pro-life or anti-choice political position.

Physically based self-hatred and shame. Concern with appearance as central to her own value.

Experiences self as extension of father or husband or partner.

Self-esteem based on self-denial, as in eating disorders.

Compulsively relationally oriented. Own identity is secondary.

Sexuality (heterosexuality, and lesbian sexuality to a lesser degree) embedded with loss and grief.

Identification with the indeterminate observer. Uses her eyes to see from men's perspectives.

Strives for safety and protection, to stay small and contained.

Fragmented physical and psychological experience.

Embodies men's and oedipal society's conflicts and meanings.

3. *The Resolution of the Antigone Phase (adulthood)*

Separates from father and the fathers to return to herself and women. Rediscovers pre-Antigone connection with other women.

Faces own vulnerability.

Develops interdependence and flexible boundaries.

Develops own identity as a woman and a human being and only then can deal with men. Experiences self in context.

Redefines meaning of physicality. Moves beyond fragmentation of body parts and psychological aspects of the self to integration.

Uses eyes to see for herself. Develops her own sense of nonexploitive entitlement. Doesn't demand that others also see her way.

Mothers stop making males central and helping to domesticate other females.

As a result, sexuality does not have to contain loss. Development of female eroticism.

The female body is defined by men's meanings in an oedipal society. While a group of men is considered a generic group, a group of women is defined by its differentness from men and by the women's bodies. Women's bodies, in general, and female sexuality, in particular, are viewed as part of everything they do, especially in ways that make them seem vulnerable or otherwise unsuitable for a given task. While a man, for example, may be a doctor or a lawyer, a woman is all too often still a woman doctor or a woman lawyer. Race and ethnicity are treated in this way as well. A black woman lawyer requires adjectives that a white male doctor does not, unless perhaps he is also Jewish. This does not just mean that a woman is a particular subspecies of a gender-neutral professional, although it does mean this, but also that she has a particular kind of body and sexuality, which must be considered in assessing the potential quality of her performance in these roles or her ability to perform them at all. A man's body is considered gender-neutral in nonsexual situations and, as such, not requiring thought or examination for its contribution to his capacity to perform a particular job or task unless it requires force or strength. But it is not defined by his sexuality. Many men speak of their own bodies and sexuality as if they were the normal condition, women's the variation.

Both Presidents Kennedy and Reagan have been reported as engaging in sexual intercourse several times a day (although presumably Reagan's activity was in his younger, prepresidential days). No one has questioned its interference with either man's ability to perform the duties of the presidency. But what if the president were a woman who took sex breaks in an upstairs bedroom several times a day? The reigning rhetoric jokes about a woman president initiating nuclear war in a fit of premenstrual tension, but has it ever been seriously asked whether men's hormones make them more aggressive and violent than women and therefore unsuited for leadership positions?

When Emma Goldman spoke against conscription, the crowds would yell "strip her naked" (Chernin 1985, p. 32). Would a man be threatened this way by a crowd of women? How does this come to be a way both to humiliate and to silence a strong and visible woman? It reminds her of her place—in a woman's body. And that is equivalent to vulnerability and shame, that in itself puts her in danger and diminishes her. Someone in a naked woman's body would lose all power, all pretension to be able to speak. The hostile listeners would have overpowered her.

Although the psychoanalyst Natalie Shainess (1982, 1986) has cited

Antigone as a model of audacity, caretaking, and independent ethics which may well be emulated by today's women, I must take exception for the following reason. The behavior of Antigone and women who are in the unresolved antigonal stage is always in the service of men and only of men in the immediate family. In an oedipal society, this can appear to be independent audacity, but it is never in her own service or even in that of the women in or outside her family. Especially in an oedipal society, the latter would be true audacity and civil disobedience.

As much as any professional woman can lecture on this material and be given a respectful hearing, the moment she steps out of her office or classroom she is equally vulnerable. Her status protects her only where and with whom the status matters. In public, she is defined by her female body and not by status or anything that she does or knows. This is the great equalizer for women of different ethnic, class, or professional memberships.

After the recent earthquake in Northern California, a female therapist of my acquaintance stepped outside of her quaking office building with the client with whom she had been in session. The office faced a busy intersection which was even more congested than usual with frightened people eager to get home and check on the condition of their loved ones and their property. People were driving courteously, however, alternating their movement through the intersection, since the traffic lights were out. The scene was one of mutual respect and constraint, except toward the females standing on the street as the building suffered the aftershocks of the quake. Every vehicle containing more than one male stopped, its occupants hooting or making some threatening or obscene comment. A group of women in the street was fair game for them. In the emotionally charged atmosphere of the postdisaster streets, the sex/aggression equation was perhaps even multiplied, yet the basic rules held: the women were, no doubt, asking for it, simply by being women on a public street. The therapist, a modern-day Jocasta, was unable to protect herself or her female client in the occupied territory of the streets. The client would have been safer with any male therapist, even a blind one, as she would have been treated as an extension of him.

TOWARD RESOLUTION

The purpose of rethinking the Oedipus and Antigone myths is not simply to indulge in an exercise in allegory but to develop a paradigm to aid our understanding of current sexual and gender arrangements. Neither the antigonal nor the oedipal complex is a purely personal or familial drama, but each includes an interplay of those aspects of experience with the sociocultural. The antigonal is not narrowly sexual, but is physically based, as is the masculine definition of women. Both are enforced and reinforced at the interstices of these different, but interrelated, realms of human experience.

In an oedipal culture, a woman cannot define and contain her own sexuality or physically based identity, cannot alone prevent psychological engulfment by masculine meanings or alone resolve the Antigone complex. Her body may be used sexually or denied sexuality; may be dressed up or undressed; may be used for housework, caretaking, or manual labor. She may be protected, attacked, or violated. As long as she is not in control of its uses and the meanings attributed to it, she is oedipally engulfed in an unresolved Antigone stage. Nor is an oedipal complex resolved or even noteworthy, as it is an expression of normal masculinity. While personal change is necessary, alone it is no more sufficient than swimming upstream alone in a rough and treacherous current. One must find or develop more hospitable waters in which to swim.

Resolution of the Antigone phase is a complex personal, interpersonal, and cultural phenomenon. It involves leaving the stage of possession by the father. This is the conflict with the need to be a person in one's own right that must be resolved for the girl to pass to healthy maturity. She must leave behind the safety of invisibility and the danger of hypervisibility, the self-negation of devotion to others. She must make visible herself and her connection to other women and purge the entitlement of men. She must begin to discover her self-defined sexuality. This is the erotic force of which Audre Lorde has said, "When I speak of the erotic, then, I speak of it as an assertion of the lifeforce of women; of that creative energy empowered, the knowledge and use of which we are now reclaiming in our language, our history, our dancing, our loving, our work, our lives" (1984, p. 55).

Many women have reported that physical workouts enhance their sense of confidence and esteem, including their capacity to be sexually aroused (DeVillers 1989). Exercise encompasses mastery of the physical and reintegration of a fragmented body. Yet it is not enough. Sexuality is "unconfined to any single part of the body or solely to the body itself" (Rich 1979, p. 650). A woman must define the boundaries of herself and learn to incorporate men's definitions, sexuality, and needs not as part of herself but as part of the context. She does not belong to them: "the power concealing itself and lurking in the background" (Hegel 1807, p. 740) must devote itself to itself, to its own aims, to its own manifestation. This involves recapturing the early ties with mother/women/self and transforming them into a return to herself as a woman.

Developmentally, children leave the world of their mothers for the larger world of their fathers. In the unresolved Antigone stage, the development of women is arrested at this point. As fathers take children from their early world, so must mothers free their children from fathers. As Antigone's sister, Ismene, states, "I'm just too weak to war against the state" (Roche 1958, p. 167). Can Antigone help her? Can they do something together that they have never done before? Can they re-member Jocasta?

Women must not be isolated, as was Antigone, in an individual family drama, but must be able to tell and to continue to tell one another about their lives. As Carolyn Heilbrun has noted, "There will be narratives of female lives only when women no longer live their lives isolated in the houses (and offices and factories) and the stories of men" (1988, p. 47). This does not mean that women should not be in houses or offices or stories, or in the streets, for that matter. It means that they should not settle for a place in a man's world, that men must no longer be able to subsume women as an extension of their own lives and their own needs. Antigone's may have been the first act of civil disobedience, but it was on behalf of the men in her family. Women must take courage in behalf of themselves and other women, the courage to make their own meanings. As Adrienne Rich has noted, "It is no longer such a lonely thing to open one's eyes" (1979, p. 48).

Presently the masculine impinges upon, limits, and engulfs the feminine in a myriad of verbal and nonverbal, physical, psychological, and existential ways, for this is the essence of the arrangement for which the relationship between Oedipus and Antigone is paradigmatic. In the following chapters, I will trace the complexities of this arrangement in the everyday experience of girls and women, men and boys, and consider, in particular, how these lead directly to the dilemmas of modern Western women, including the development of the sense of self, sexuality, and the so-called psychological disorders to which they are prone.

4

Identity Embodied

In the room of mirrors, girls stand in front of each mirror and practice smiling, practice widening their eyes, practice cocking an eyebrow, practice walking, practice moving. They must practice until their movements achieve spontaneity. . . . They are invisible to each other, invisible to themselves.

—Gabrielle Burton
Heartbreak Hotel

Oedipus was blinded for the sin of looking with arrogance and entitlement. This is a look that seeks its own pleasure and affirmation, seeks to confirm its own central importance. It is the eye of the beholder, in which women's appearance is reflected, evaluated, and given meaning.

For females, the realm of the physical is organized not just around being but, more precisely, around appearing—that is, around the stimulus value of their appearance, their manner of reacting and reflecting. Becoming a woman involves learning a part, complete with costumes, makeup, and lines. Learning to behave like a woman involves learning to sit, stand, and talk in the appropriate ways and to make them appear natural, to have them become natural or, more aptly, second nature (Kaschak 1976). Certainly men also have embodied parts to learn within the gender hierarchy, but for them the physical is characteristically organized around the ability to act upon the environment in much less physically restricted ways. They can sit and move openly, make noises, and, in general, allow their presence to be felt directly by others and by themselves.

LEARNING TO LOOK THE PART

In our culture girls, especially white middle-class girls, are generally protected and expected to look pretty and soft, while their male counterparts are encouraged to be aggressive and to explore their surroundings. Aggressive play is considered masculine, while dressing up and looking in the mirror are considered appropriate play for females (Fagot 1973). Little girls dress up in their mothers' clothes and use makeup to play at being grown up. Little boys can play at being little boys. If they do play at being grown up, it will typically involve an activity or an occupation—soldier, cowboy, astronaut—rather than appearances. Costumes or uniforms are in the service of signaling the legitimacy of the activity, not an end in themselves. Girls are more frequently admired for their appearance than are boys, especially when they are wearing dresses (Joffe 1971). Facial beauty is considered to characterize females and young people (Cross and Cross 1971). When adults, in or out of therapy, recall the childhood and adolescent trauma of not being chosen, for boys it generally involves not being good enough at a sport or an activity to be chosen for a team; for girls, not being chosen for a date or a dance because of their perceived lack of physical attractiveness.

I suggest that the crucial period for the development of women's appearance-based identity extends from the moment of birth, when it is physically based and preverbal, through adolescence, when it is taught and enforced by complex social forces including adults, peers, and society at large through books, magazines, the media, and even the responses of strangers in public. This development continues throughout life, but not with the same fluidity. As empirical research (for example, Ganong and Coleman 1987) catches up with clinical information and nonclinical observation, it also is beginning to indicate that in adulthood, children often reciprocally serve this function for adults, just as adults do for children. In particular, daughters often begin to comment on and evaluate their mothers' appearance, as they do with their peers.

Developmentally, adolescence is the crucial stage for full emergence and crystallization of this constellation of gendered and embodied meaning. That is, while the foundation for identifying women with and by their physical appearance and attractiveness is laid from the first moments of life by parents and other significant adults, it is in adolescence that this truly becomes a difference that makes a difference. It is then that parents and peers exert the greatest pressure for gender role adherence (Unger 1979). For females, the judgments of peers are clearly organized around physical appearance (Allen and Eicher 1973). Not only have adolescent girls been found to be more concerned with their appearance than have adolescent males with theirs but they also consider themselves, in general, less attractive than their male peers consider themselves (Simmons and Rosenberg 1975). Study after study of adolescents and of females of all ages have highlighted their concern, and that of others, with female physical appearance (Henley 1977; Rowbotham 1973; Schulman and Hoskins 1986).

Movements based on rebellion against social values emerge during the years of adolescence. These movements always include a particular code of dress for members—such as that of the hippies in the 1960s or the punk look of the 1980s—which defies the mainstream code, with its strict gender divisions. From early childhood through adolescence, hair and clothes are the most powerful cues used to discriminate gender (Kessler and McKenna 1978; Thompson and Bentler 1971). The very defiance of the strict gender distinction in our culture is always a comment on the importance of appearance in maintaining or defying it. By defying it with yet another strict code of appearance, adolescents signal that the importance of appearance does not change, only the particular code of dress changes.

It is also in adolescence that the physically based self-concept coalesces for both males and females. As Clara Thomson (1942) noted long ago, and Jean Baker Miller more recently, for boys, adolescence is a period of opening up, for girls one of closing down. This is a physical-psychological problem: "Freud believed that girls now had to learn for good that they were not to use actively all of themselves and all of their life forces from a base centered in their own bodies and in their own psychological constructions" (Miller 1984, p. 8).

This is an important distinction from Freudian and object-relations theory, which locate significant development in the earliest years and in the relationship with the mother primarily and the father secondarily. I suggest instead that the development of both males and females is not narrowly sexually based, but is fully physically based as a function of the meaning that society in general and significant adults and peers in particular give to femaleness and maleness. It is not their appearance per se but the meanings that it holds for others and to each person in childhood, adolescence, and throughout life that shapes women and men.

APPEARANCES CAN BE DECEIVING

While the importance of a child's mother in early development should not be underestimated, that of her father usually is. For females, the impact of the father, as a representative of men and the male perspective, in important ways exceeds that of the mother as an enforcer of patriarchal codes. For example, in a fashion typical of many fathers, albeit much more forthright, Harold Searles, a well-respected psychoanalyst, discusses the development of his daughter:

> Towards my daughter, now eight years of age, I have experienced innumerable fantasies and feelings of a romantic-love kind, thoroughly complementary to the romantically adoring, seductive behaviour which she has shown towards her father oftentimes ever since she was about two or three years of age. I used at times to feel somewhat worried when she would play the supremely confident coquette with me and I would feel enthralled by her charms; but then I came to the conviction, some time ago, that such moments of relatedness could only be nourishing for her developing personality as well as delightful to me. If a little girl cannot feel herself able to win the heart of her father, her own father who has known her so well and for so long, and who is tied to her by mutual blood-ties, I reasoned, then how can the young woman who comes later have any deep confidence in the power of her womanliness?

Of his wife and son he opines:

> And I have had every impression, similarly, that the oedipal desires of my son, now eleven years of age, have found a similarly lively and whole-hearted feeling-response in my wife; and I am equally convinced that their deeply fond, openly evidenced mutual attraction is good for my son as well as enriching to my wife. To me it makes sense that the more a woman loves her husband, the more she will love, similarly, the lad who is, to at least a considerable degree, the younger edition of the man she loved enough to marry. [1965, p. 296]

This example is instructive because it is not idiosyncratic but representative of the beliefs of many fathers and mothers, whether they are private citizens or acknowledged experts in human development. It is also important because it is offered unquestioningly by a contemporary psychoanalytic pioneer whose work it is to question just such "natural" assumptions about the family drama. Note the asymmetry of the description, the father-daughter romance filled with "adoring, seductive" enthrallment, the mother-son a "deeply fond . . . enriching" attraction, based upon his wife's love for *him,* her husband. There is nothing in the second description equivalent to the sexualized, romanticized flirtatiousness in the first, which reflects the father's unresolved oedipal complex, as outlined in the previous chapter. Searles, the father, is the central character and primary love object in both scenarios.

In another example, the May 22, 1990, episode of "Nightline" covered the case of the president of American University, who was arrested for making obscene phone calls. Described as a very disturbed man, he was noted in the program as having had some successes in his life, prominent among them having raised "two attractive daughters." How successful would he have been considered had he raised "two attractive sons"? Did his wife, their mother, have any role at all in their raising? There is probably a more modern or enlightened version of this in which a parent is proud of a daughter who is both competent and pretty, intelligent and coquettish. That is, it may be possible for a girl to be competent as long as she looks good to her father or brothers and then to other males while she is doing so, thereby acknowledging their centrality, and as long as her mother and other girls help her do so. Girls' and women's magazines and advice columns aid in this socialization process. This is not so for boys, even in adolescence. If boys become concerned with their looks, which they do less frequently and to a lesser degree than do females, the primary reference group is likely to be their peers and certainly not their mothers. For a boy to be concerned about being attractive to his mother would be to demean or diminish himself. It might even feminize him.

Furthermore, I want to suggest that the same sense of entitlement is at work in both the accusation and the attribution of this former university president. That is, raising daughters to be attractive to oneself and using strange women for one's sexual needs are both within the realm of masculine entitlement to women's minds and bodies. They are based upon the lack of ability or interest in distinguishing women's needs from a man's own, in ascertaining where he ends and his daughters or victims begin. It is rooted in a masculine problem with boundary definition and a grandiosely defined self, which I am naming oedipal. (The issue of boundaries will be developed in detail in chapter 6.)

While mothers also train their daughters to be pleasing to fathers and men through manipulation of their appearance and demeanor, it has been found that girls' preference for feminine behaviors is less related to the femininity of their mothers than to the masculinity of their fathers and to the extent to which those same fathers encouraged sex-typed behaviors (Mussen and Rutherford 1963; Fling and Manosevitz 1972). Karen Hildebrandt (1980) found that fathers interacted more frequently and positively with attractive infants, mothers more with less attractive ones.

Soon enough female peers, trained by their own fathers and mothers, join the chorus, focusing on clothing, dress, hairstyles, and makeup, all designed to make the developing girl attractive to boys and men. Females are the keepers of the details of the body, which early on they are trained and encouraged in a myriad of ways to tend, feed, clean, and clothe. While it is men who make the final judgment concerning whether a woman's general appearance is pleasing, desirable, or arousing to them, it is girls and women who monitor the details, much as Antigone used her eyes in Oedipus' service. In fact, men are not expected to show interest in the details of appearance and how the illusion is created. A man or boy would, indeed, be considered suspiciously feminine if he concerned himself with, for example, the color of eye shadow, the length of earrings, the fabric of which a dress is made. Such attention to detail would destroy the erotic impact.

Females, then, help one another create these effects and evaluate one another's effectiveness. Unless men are paying the bills and consider the money spent to be their money, it is also women rather than men who evaluate the success of the feminine hunt, shopping. It is they who will admire a bargain or a fine purchase. Ironically, for females the multiple meanings in this appearance management include not only helping one another succeed in attracting men for relationships—which mean success, survival, and affirmation of identity—but competing in this quest and giving affirmation when men don't (which is generally when they are not or no longer erotically aroused). This is a form of female bonding, though an ambivalent one. It supersedes male-female relationships, which are less stable and more dependent on erotic visual desirability. Yet embedded in these activities is a well-learned judgment from an external perspective that women also learn to apply to themselves.

A study of children aged eight or nine noted gestures of intimacy among young girls rarely seen among young boys: stroking and combing each other's hair, noticing and commenting upon each other's appearance, including hairstyles and clothing. By the fourth or fifth grade, young girls have been observed discussing who is prettiest and confessing to feelings of being ugly (Thorne and Luria 1986). Schofield (1982) has reported that for a group of children in middle school, boys' status with other boys did not depend on their relationships with girls, while girls' status with other girls depended on their popularity with boys.

Roberta's mother often took her shopping for clothes, and the two of them would carefully match outfits and accessories to develop a particular "look." Once they had returned home, she would tell Roberta to show her father what they had chosen for her, and he would then express approval or disapproval. Roberta felt pretty when her father approved, and he felt proud of her when she looked pretty. This was a loving transaction among three family members, but what was Roberta learning about how to receive love and approval from men and about the role of other women in that process?

Carol's eleven-year-old daughter often criticizes her appearance and asks her to dress in a way that is more "with it" and "cool." This attitude tends to undermine Carol's physical self-concept and to make her feel less successful as a woman. Both she and her daughter agree that the daughter is prettier, if for no other reason than that she is younger and thinner. This is a readily recognizable form of assessment and competition among females, and an accurate reflection in an oedipal society, where younger and smaller women are preferred. It is also a denial by the daughter of her connection with her mother and of the thought that a similar fate awaits her.

Girls cannot identify unambivalently with mothers who are already derogated and diminished. This ambivalence often plays itself out through a daughter's or mother's criticisms of the mother's appearance, clothing, or age that is, all the qualities that make her vulnerable as a woman. This is the daughter's attempt to overcome these restrictions and evaluations by meeting them "more correctly" than did her mother. In this way, daughters are pressed to disidentify with their mothers in order to develop their own self-esteem. Each loses the other as the path toward men and heterosexuality is taken. Thus, women's connectedness to other women is often not direct, but one person or persons removed, and maintained symbolically.

SURPLUS OF MEANING IN THE DEVELOPMENT OF WOMEN'S SELF-CONCEPT

Women are identified with their bodies in a more material and inseparable sense than are men, but not because women, as many male philosophers have argued, are more tied to nature.* After all, men have bodies and hormones, too. Their relationship to mood or behavior has been seriously underplayed by the scientific and lay communities, as the surplus of meaning about bodies, hormones, and sexuality is attributed to women.

Every aspect of the female body is considered to say something about a woman's value as a person and as a woman. She is her body and her face. But it is her appearance that is judged, not her strength, health, or ability to act effectively, not her body's speed or agility but its size and shape, its pleasingness and conformity to masculine standards of the feminine. If her appearance is deemed desirable, then so is she and she is treated accordingly. If not, then she is worth less. She may then be ridiculed or attacked; after all, by her very appearance she is asking for it. It is assumed that she has chosen to be unattractive and deserves to be treated badly for it. Her appearance is not just something about her, as it is for men: she *is* her appearance. Virtually every aspect of it is interpreted to have meaning about her—who she is, how she is to be viewed and treated. This association has been shown to begin as early as among preschoolers, who show no differential treatment of boys related to attractiveness (Smith 1985), but a clear difference in the treatment of girls. This relationship continues throughout life for women and for men.

For example, the comedienne Roseanne Barr is ridiculed, the equally obese actor playing her husband in the weekly sitcom is not. Jackie Mason is romantically paired with the beautiful (courtesy of perpetual dieting, of course) Lynn Redgrave. Could Roseanne Barr be paired in a romantic intrigue with Paul Newman or Robert Redford? A popular model reported that, more than once, when she had disagreed with a man and he had wanted to insult her, he would tell her that she really was not that beautiful.

On the "Today" show every morning, Willard the weatherman wishes older folks happy birthday and consistently and gallantly comments that hundred-year-old women are still pretty ladies. This behavior is gallant precisely because women this age are not considered to be pretty anymore, yet, as women, they should be. In a newspaper article I read of a new fad called the Granny Fanny, which is showing up instead of the traditional flamingo on front lawns: "The Granny Fanny is a piece of plywood cut and painted to resemble the back end of a plump, old woman. . . . Most Granny Fannies show the lower half of a polka-dot dress, bare pink legs and socks. Sometimes you see a frill of lace. . . . Granny's better half is Grampy Fanny.

---

*This notion has also appeared recently in the writing of feminist scholars, such as Merlin Stone's *When God Was a Woman* (1976) and Riane Eisler's *The Chalice and the Blade* (1988), who have also accepted this dichotomy and, as with the concept of relatedness, simply reversed society's traditional evaluation.

Grampy does not expose his legs in Bermuda shorts. He's decently clad in overalls, with a real red bandanna flapping out his back pocket" (Viets 1989, p. 3D).

We must consider carefully just whose perspective or point of view defines female (and male) physicality, for we are concerned here with how powerful, desirable, acceptable, feminine, or attractive women's bodies are in the oedipal eyes of *men,* both individually and collectively. This, of course, compounds the already apparent difficulty of being defined and evaluated on the basis of appearance. In losing control of the meanings of their own bodies, of the bodies themselves, women lose even more—the opportunity to develop a well-integrated sense of self that is more internally than externally defined, that is relatively stable rather than subject to redefinition based on changes in appearance or evaluations thereof, and that is grounded in an accurate testing of abilities and skills rather than passive evaluation.

A particular aspect of this sense of self is reflected in one's sense of personal control over life events. Indeed, psychological research has demonstrated that women and girls in our society do tend to develop a more external than internal locus of control, probably understanding all too well how much their appearance and identity matter in the eyes of men. White males in our society, as a group, are characterized by an internal locus of control, a sense that they control their own fate (Rotter 1966). Despite certain changes, this difference in outlook between males and females has remained consistent (Cellini and Kantorowski 1982).

The female's body, face, and demeanor are expected to be a certain way, and that way is not as healthy, as challenged, as fully used as possible. That way is not defined by the parameters of her abilities, of her physical apparatus, but by masculine vision, by how pleasing her appearance is judged to be within masculine values of feminine appeal. The more her appearance conforms to these criteria, the more desirable a person she is considered to be. Her sense of self is physically embedded and judged in a way that a man's is not. Asking "How good a body does a woman have?" for example, refers to how pleasing it is to the male eye, to the male touch, rather than to how well it serves her. It becomes a sexual question.

One culturally pervasive example that indisputably marks gender is high heels. In a newspaper article concerning women's shoes (see Konner 1988), it was noted that high heels made a woman look charming and attractive in a *man's* eyes, but off balance and unable to flee from a potential mugger's *(man's)* perspective. A convicted mugger explained, "We would wait under a stairwell in the subway station and, when we heard the click of the wobbly spiked heel, we knew we had one" (p. 14). And in a woman's own eyes? While feeling both attractive and vulnerable at once is problematic enough, she still has her own experience of the shoes to add to the picture. They are probably uncomfortable or painful, but she knows she is not supposed to show this or even feel it, as it would detract from the illusion. Embedded in appearance, then, in this case, are suffering and the denial thereof or at least of its importance.

Typically, in this article the woman's perspective is not even considered, just those of various men. This is instructive in our understanding of how her perspective develops. She incorporates in her own experience both the sense of attractiveness and of vulnerability and—secondarily, as something to be hidden or forgotten, to be kept or made invisible—her own separate experience of physical discomfort, perhaps awkwardness, perhaps pain. Whatever her experience is, it is physically based and must be different from the observers' because it is she who is wearing the shoes. All three perspectives—the appreciative viewer, the malevolent viewer, and her own physically based experience—become her complex physical-emotional-cognitive experience, with her initial internal experience (the feel of the shoes on her feet) generally the most weakly represented of the three, since it is not supposed to be experienced at all. Its invisibility, along with the injunction to make it invisible, must remain hidden from awareness for things to run smoothly. Additionally, the masculine perspectives are subject to change with each new viewer, so that even if she passes muster and is positively evaluated one time, she may be negatively evaluated the next time or, as in this example, experience both kinds of evaluations at the same time by different men or by the same man.

The important components here are central in the development of the self-concept in women: (1) the physicalness of woman's identity; (2) that the physicalness is always evaluated; (3) that this physicalness is evaluated first and primarily by individual men or by the masculinist context as mediated by significant others; (4) that what is deemed pleasurable to men is often not pleasurable to women, but harmful, dangerous, or diminishing; (5) that these evaluations can change situationally with the presence or absence of different men and temporally with the inevitable change in fashion; and (6) that women's own internal experience, hurting feet in this case, is secondary and often kept invisible from others and eventually, as a result, from herself. All these components form the complex pattern of the self-concept in women. Some examples will help to explain.

Lisa was considered very pretty as a girl and a young woman. Now in her forties, she is still often complimented on her looks. When this happens, she

always thinks to herself, and sometimes says out loud, "You are not look-
ing carefully. I am just a dowdy, middle-aged woman." Feminine success
is ephemeral and contains within it the seeds of impending loss. For Lisa,
in her early forties, this career is ended.

Whenever she meets new clients, Diane, an accomplished attorney, still
finds herself fearing that they will be disappointed because they will not find
her pretty enough, if they are men, or will be prettier than she and therefore
act superior or condescending, if they are women. After the initial moment
of contact, the fear passes and she is relieved as she passes through the first
moments of contact and appearance-based evaluation. Diane hopes that she
will then be evaluated on her professional competence alone and not on her
competence as a woman professional, which includes appearance.

Furthermore, even attractiveness has its paradoxical aspect, since attractive women, in addition to being viewed positively, may be seen as vain,
egotistic, and materialistic (Dermer and Thiel 1975). Moderate rather than
extreme attractiveness is associated with living a happy life (Freeman 1985),
and curvaceous figures have been found to be associated in the minds of
both males and females with a lack of intelligence (Silverstein and Perdue
1988). If a successful woman is attractive, it is assumed that she got ahead
because of her looks; if unattractive, it is assumed that all she can hope for
is a career (Morrison 1970). Women are always subject to loss of attractiveness in the male eye—if not situationally, then certainly temporally,
through the aging process. These potentially or actually negative evaluations make it difficult for women to develop a stable, positive sense of self.
A sense of self unevaluated—in all the paradoxical ways that women are
constantly evaluated—is impossible.

Hypervisibility and Invisibility

A woman's inner sense of self is more complex and has more potential
points of conflict than a man's, since it includes several components: the
masculine evaluative perspective, the inner experience of the woman, a
sense of impending loss, a sense of loss of the possible—and a need to make
all these fit together, which results in denying, or making invisible, the
unacceptable or conflicting aspects. All these components constitute a sense

of self physically and evaluatively based, fluid, and imbued with a sense of loss and invisibility.

It is not easy for a woman to see herself or to see for herself with her own eyes. To make visible the aspects of her experience or perspective that do not conform with androcentric meanings is to defy or destroy the oedipal context and what has become her own complex experience. The "normal" woman adjusts to the invisible oedipal context while allowing it to remain invisible. She incorporates the masculine experience of her as primary to her self-concept, her own experience as secondary or unconscious, although both obviously become her own socially and psychologically constructed experience. Conflicts are relegated to the realm of the forgettable or the unconscious.

The hypervisibility for women of physical appearance and desirability results, paradoxically, in a heightened sense of invisibility. As a beautiful former model appearing on Geraldo Rivera's popular television talk show (January 6, 1991) stated, she felt as though she were walking around with a cardboard cutout in front of her, to which people responded. She could not afford to let them see what was inside because "it was ugly and not perfect" like the cardboard exterior. The entire group of models on the show affirmed that, as young girls, they were actively pursued by older men.

In an interview, the supermodel Clotilde is quoted as saying, "I am an optical illusion" (*Time* 1989, p. 111), referring to her magical transformation into the natural-looking beauty in the Ralph Lauren ads. "You create an illusion," says another well-known fashion model, Janice Dickinson: "I have no breasts [note the external and visually based definition] but by holding my body in a certain way I can create a cleavage. You can create cheekbones or take a bump on your nose and make it disappear with makeup" (p. 86). From yet another supermodel, Patti Hansen: "I've learned to play different types of people. It's wonderful, all these little tricks you can learn. It's frustrating when I wake up and look in the mirror, because I'm so used to seeing myself made up by different people in different photographs. I want to call them up and say, 'Come over and make me look like something else' " (pp. 99–100).

I have discovered in therapy that many different kinds of women experience themselves as invisible in the world and in relationships, giving them a sense of both safety and diminishment. Not that they are speaking metaphorically, nor are they psychotic; they are simply women and, as such, both desire affirmation and are terrified of the danger of greater visibility.

Invisibility itself is a core ingredient in the developmental learning of females, and examples are all too evident in daily life—from speaking through a male companion to a waiter or waitress to announcing one's wedding as Mr. and Mrs. John Smith, she the former ————. What must it do to one's identity to have been someone one no longer is? To have no name of one's own? Our naming arrangement also renders invisible the connections between mothers and daughters. How many of us are aware that Anna Freud was the daughter of Sigmund Freud? How many of us know whose daughters Melitta Schniedeberg, Marianne Eckhart, and Judith Herman are? (Melanie Klein, Karen Horney, and Helen Block Lewis, respectively.) Women who marry men of another ethnicity also lose their connection to their ethnicity in giving up their names. Celia Chavez can become Celia Cohen; Amy Lim disappears and reemerges as Amy Jones. Alternately, these women can choose to use one name to signal their ethnicity, the other their marital status. As recently as 1974, the American Civil Liberties Union filed suit on behalf of a woman in Socorro, New Mexico, to compel a hospital administration to make her paycheck out in her own name rather than her husband's.

In sociological research, the invisibility of women's perspective is clear in the traditional idea of the postindustrial home as a haven from the harsh world of work. Since it is the place where traditional women do their work, it is no haven for them.

Within the ancient Jewish sexual and marital strictures, male homosexuality is considered a greater sin than lesbianism—not because lesbianism is not considered to exist (as English law, descended from the very sheltered Queen Victoria, held) but because it is not considered to involve genitals: "There is in lesbianism no genital intercourse and no wasting of seed. Thus it is not considered a perversion of God's intent" (Lamm 1980, p. 67). From this perspective, only penises are true genitals. Vaginas may be conferred this status through contact with a penis.

Robin Morgan has touched on this experience in its extreme form in her poem "The Invisible Woman":

> *The invisible woman in the asylum corridor*
> *sees others quite clearly,*
> *including the doctor who patiently tells her*
> *she isn't invisible—*
> *and pities the doctor, who must be mad*
> *to stand there in the asylum corridor*
> *talking and gesturing to nothing at all.*
>
> *The invisible woman has great compassion.*
> *So, after a while, she pulls on her body*
> *like a rumpled glove, and switches on her voice*

101

to comfort the elated doctor with words.
Better to suffer this prominence
than for the poor young doctor to learn
he himself is insane.
Only the strong can know that. [1972, p. 46]

Women clients often communicate to me their sense of invisibility in some way other than through their own conscious awareness.

Erin often seems extremely angry, and her face and body clearly and powerfully communicate a sense of fury. Her anger never seems moderate. When asked about it, she is surprised, not aware that her anger is noticeable. She has a reputation among her co-workers for being angry much of the time but is at a loss to explain how they would know about it. She didn't know that anyone could see her that clearly.

Accommodating to the tension in her relationship with her husband, Toby tells me that she becomes about an inch tall when she backs away from a confrontation. Making herself invisible, she feels shame and fear and danger less than she would if she were to stand her ground or, as she puts it, remain her full size.

Marion brought into her therapy with me a strong fear of being seen. She controlled it by holding very still psychologically, so I could not see her without her permission. She would answer questions only after she had carefully thought about them, would discuss her dreams only after she felt that she had fully examined them for hidden meaning, and would often keep talking when I spoke to her in order not to give me room to comment on anything she had said or done. She was terrified of being seen and terrified of what I would do to her if she were visible to me. Her fears of visibility were complex, but involved being damaged by the meanings I would create about her if I could see her, the meanings that would not be in her control and undoubtedly, in her view, would diminish and blame her for her own fears. This had been her experience, and the strategy of invisibility had been offered to her as a defense against violation: she could behave as a quiet, good woman and not be noticed. At the time I began to see her and at periods throughout our work together, she would become extremely depressed and self-destructive, but generally nobody in her life would notice.

Seeing Oneself from the Outside In

As I sit and write this in a downtown office, I can see through the window women workers, all "dressed for success" (an apt description of how success comes for women), walking by hurriedly in sneakers rather than in high heels. How does this relate to the example discussed earlier? Certainly the use of walking shoes is a comment on the discomfort and impracticality of fashionable shoes. How did the widespread acceptance of this deviation from attractiveness for comfort occur, from the eye of the perceiver to the foot of the experiencer? Apparently during a New York subway strike several years ago, women were forced to walk to work, and this accommodation became a necessity. Economic necessity became the mother (father?) of change, but only of the absolutely necessary change. The sexist value did not change. Since they could not get to the office without this accommodation in footgear, women were permitted to be uncomfortable only in the workplace. At the same time, the walking shoes that women used to get to and from the office became a fashion statement in themselves. And so women were and are still constrained by appearances, the sexist context merely accommodating the economic necessity.

The current economic necessity for women to enter the workplace has also led to some interesting adjustments in the evaluative context. For one, the blossoming of the dress-for-success concept has permitted women to work in previously male-identified occupations while remaining obsessively concerned with, and viewed in terms of, their appearance. Odd that we never had a dress-for-success movement before women in large numbers entered the workplace. The phrase aptly describes just how one can succeed and still be feminine. There are now even dress-for-success maternity clothes. The economic system is also well served, as a new market is created.

Apparently it is also possible for a woman to dress for poverty and failure. The recent film *Working Girl* illustrates just how this system works. The heroine of the film learns how to dress for success and, upon changing her clothing, hairstyle, and makeup, actually gets the job and the man who goes with it and without whom the ending would not be a happy one for a woman. Meanwhile her working-class friends back home continue to dress for failure, poverty, unhappy marriages, unwanted pregnancies, and perhaps alcoholism and abuse. If only they had realized what some new clothes, makeup, and a more sophisticated hairstyle could do for a woman!

These external conflicts become embedded in the self-concept in the following ways: (1) women must always be concerned first and foremost with their appearances prior to, or at least in conjunction with, the quality of their work; (2) women's appearances are never an accomplished deed, but only as good as they are at the moment; (3) if contextual systems, economic necessity, and appearances conflict, women should still be able to satisfy the demands of all of them. The inability to do so reflects on the woman herself rather than on the conflict in external systems and so comes to be an internal conflict of hers.

Men do not have to incorporate women's perspectives into their own in the same way. To use again the example of shoes—one of many possible examples, including clothes, jewelry, and makeup—men's shoes are not central to their attractiveness or erotic desirability in women's eyes, nor do they make them vulnerable, awkward, or cause them pain when they fit correctly. This is not a coincidence or an isolated, nonrepresentative example. It is design from the inside out, based on the physical experience or comfort of the wearer, not on the pleasure of the observer. More important from the psychological perspective, shoe wearing for males does not result in an experience that must be made invisible. It does not create a self-concept that is negative or ambivalent or based substantially on someone else's perspective. Since men's shoes are both more comfortable and more durable, their wearers are not open to accusations of being either frivolous or masochistic. The self-concept in men is less physically based and less evaluative, less complex and less conflicted. There is no internal component that must necessarily be made invisible. It is based on mastery, not on containment or on mastery combined with how one looks mastering a task. Most important, the physical does not signal others about their basic identity, or about how they deserve to be treated, or about whether they are "asking for it." Men's identity develops from the inside out, women's from the outside in.

The emphasis on appearance for women also intersects with race and ethnicity. For example, to fit the dominant norms of beauty, African-American and Jewish women typically spend more time and money on cosmetics, hair straightening, and nose jobs than do African-American and Jewish men. Asian-American women are also beginning to make disproportionate use of cosmetic surgery to have their eyes and noses appear more like those of Caucasians.

A woman once told me that she would not leave the house at night looking too attractive because if she were attacked or raped, she didn't want the police to think that she was asking for it. While a woman can, at any time, be "asking for it," I have not yet heard a description of how a woman can clearly and unambiguously *not* ask for it. A man may choose not to carry too much money with him in a dangerous area, but I have never heard a man choose not to take along money when he went shopping or not to wear an attractive garment so that the police, if he were to be mugged, would not think that he was asking for it. Does a man ever "ask for it," ask to be violated because of how he looks? Perhaps this occurs only if he looks too much like a woman. Perhaps this is also why a woman can't *not* ask for it, as her very existence as a woman can be defined as asking for it. It is one of the meanings that women's bodies carry.

Additionally, it is assumed, from an oedipal perspective, that a woman's appearance actually signals something about her *desire* to be hurt or violated. That is, if a man felt like doing something to her, she must have wanted it too. Since the woman is detached from, yet defined by, her physical appearance or performance, her inner experience is obscured and often foreign to her. She herself must wonder whether she was "asking for it"; until she can learn to sort out the aspect of her complex experience that is context internalized, it becomes her own self concept. Consistently, women in therapy who have been raped or molested as children feel deeply that it was their own fault and are burdened with an excruciating sense of shame. While girls and women may, in fact, not often get what they really ask for, such as respect or equality, it is assumed that what they do get is what they asked for. For example, a woman might suppose that she is asking for the freedom to go out at night unescorted, but she is undoubtedly really asking to be attacked, if that happens. Oedipus' needs are Antigone's.

As another example, I cannot remember how many times I have seen a woman crying and worrying about what it will do to her makeup, crying carefully and dabbing at her eyes at the same time. The word *mascara* itself is derived from the Spanish *máscara,* which means "mask." It provides both an acceptable appearance and a safe invisibility. Her perspective must be, at the same time, outside in and inside out, her experience and behavior incorporating seemingly unreconcilable principles: (1) look good; (2) crying is a feminine way to show pain; (3) #2 is permissible only when it does not interfere with #1—always look good even when you are in pain and crying; never forget about your eyes (appearance) in the eyes of others. Perhaps this is why women have been shown to remember more about people's clothing, hairstyles, and expressions (Kanter 1977), and often concern themselves obsessively with appearance.

In a recent issue of the *Family Therapy Networker,* a therapist wrote about helping women with their shopping and makeup skills in order to make them feel more competent: "during one therapy hour, I take her into my office bathroom, remove all my makeup and put it on again, and then put it on her as well, showing her how, step by step" (Berman 1989, p. 37). In another case: "I did send Joan, the lawyer, to a clothing consultant. It was a way to get her to claim her right to be both competent and feminine [notice the dichotomy], to look the way she wanted to. Joan said the consultation saved her a couple of months of therapy" (p. 37). This is how women achieve self-confidence, by looking the part. Yet the part can be lost with the look and is therefore not easily incorporated into one's identity or sense of self.

The Prism of Self-Image

Women are denied and come to deny themselves actual confrontation with and full experience of the physical. To be a woman means to live one's life in a mirror world, but not the kind of mirrors of which we ordinarily speak. Perhaps a prism would serve as a more apt metaphor, dividing women, like so many frequencies of light, into their component parts. Refracted back are only those parts and qualities that masculine society and individual men deem important, those by which they evaluate attractiveness and femininity. Women's images are refracted back to them evaluated or contextualized, that is, distorted. Some parts of the various and complex aspects of themselves are fragmented, others are completely invisible. In the mirror, a woman sees how she deviates from the ideal in her size, shape, race, or age.

For example, a beginning step in training therapists is to have them view themselves on video. Invariably the women in the group comment on some aspect of their appearance, most typically their weight. The men almost never do this, but instead comment on their own possession or lack of therapeutic abilities. Both may feel challenged or discouraged, but for entirely different reasons. Most frequently, the men see themselves in relation to the task at hand, the women as they appear performing that task. Women are looking into different mirrors. Reflection can be experienced by women either in a mirror or through that human mirror, the indeterminate male observer. This mirrored perspective comes to be their own, as they seek first and within every attribute their own appearance and its value.

Much has been made by object-relations theorists, such as D. W. Winnicott (1960, 1964, 1965, 1969), Margaret Mahler (1968), Alice Miller (1981), and others, of the notion of accurate mirroring as an essential aspect of healthy development of the self. This is, of course, considered to be a function of the mother, who "allows herself to be cathected narcissistically, who is at the child's disposal . . . then a healthy self-feeling can gradually develop in the growing child. Ideally, this mother should also provide the necessary emotional climate and understanding for the child's needs"

(Miller 1981, p. 32). This approach isolates and decontextualizes mothers. Both their separate influence and their separateness from society are seriously overestimated. Perhaps it would read something like this if the invisible were made visible: the mother should be fully at the disposal of the child's physical and emotional needs, as well as those of any other of her children and of her husband. While she must daily deal with denigration and danger, she should convey none of this to the child and, if the child is also female, protect her from similar experiences. She should be able to do all of this with little or no help from the father or any other adults, without getting depressed, anxious, or angry, and, if necessary, while holding down a full-time job.

As noted earlier, the father will typically mirror even more extremely the traditional stereotypes of femininity. The daughter is (read should be) soft and sweet, dependent, clinging, and pretty. Traditional feminine qualities are mirrored. If she has any traditionally masculine characteristics or interests, they are in danger of being defined not as her own qualities or interests as a female person, but as not really belonging to her, as being something that she must outgrow. For example, an adolescent boy who eats a lot has a healthy appetite. Can his female cohort have a healthy appetite? The tomboy (a girl who is temporarily a kind of boy) is not behaving like an active, curious girl (tomgirl?) but like a boy and must lose these aspects of herself in order to develop properly into a woman. In this way, the dichotomy of gender is maintained. If it were ever seen and allowed that females and males might both have any combination of these qualities, our entire gender system would collapse. Indeed, several female psychoanalysts, such as Janine Chassegeut-Smirgel and Muriel Dimen, have stated unequivocally that they believe that a blurring of the distinctions between women and men, mothers and fathers, would lead to psychosis in a whole generation of children (see Baruch and Serrano 1988).

The most common mirror of all in modern society is the television set. It is also, in fact, the most frequently used baby-sitter. Even in families in which the mother does not work outside the home, children spend the greatest proportion of their time not with her but with the TV set. And television, especially commercial advertising, is a primary source of gender stereotyping and of the emphasis on physical attractiveness for females. Billions of dollars are spent every year on advertising cosmetics, physical fitness, and weight reduction (Berscheid and Walster 1984). A. Chris Downs and Sheila K. Harrison (1985) found that the highest proportion of beauty and weight messages were found in food and drink commercials, followed by personal care and household product messages, and then by clothing advertisements. They estimate that children and adult television viewers are confronted with over 5,200 attractiveness messages per year, 1,850 of which deal directly with (female) beauty—virtually all implicitly. The greatest proportion of attractiveness messages consist of female performers with male announcers, the epitome of the indeterminate observer.

A study of the ten most popular children's TV shows revealed that four had no female characters at all. The other six were predominantly male, with females as witches or magical creatures or in deferential roles. Even on "Sesame Street," the most popular educational show for children, not one of the primary monster characters is female. Similarly, popular children's stories show girls and women primarily in observer roles and almost always wearing aprons—even the female animals (Romer 1981).

In Western society, toys also play a major part in socializing and mirroring for children how and in what qualities they should be investing themselves. They are as important as television in physically based gender learning. For one thing, they induce separateness and separate play. They serve most often as a substitute for interpersonal relatedness and, as such, are socially constructed transitional objects. It has recently been reported, in this regard, that girls' toys, more than ever, involve play with hair and makeup. It has been noted that girls' toys, even today, focus on appearance, makeup, dating fantasies, and dressing up dolls, especially Barbie dolls. In addition, there are new games that encourage girls not yet in their teens to compete for the date of their dreams. " 'Girls' play involves dressing and grooming and acting out their future—going on a date, getting married—and boys' play involves competition and conflict, good guys and bad guys,' said Glenn Bozarth, director of public relations for Mattel, which makes the Barbie doll" (Lawson 1989). Many parents say that it is impossible to buck the tide of toys for girls that involve passive play and looks, and for boys that involve active and aggressive learning. One parent is quoted as saying: "I wanted my kids to be raised with a higher degree of consciousness, but you can't force it. . . . I tried to get my daughter to play with GI Joe and my son with dolls. It didn't work. My daughter's favorite toy is Barbie. I am aghast" (p. 5L).

He would also be aghast to discover that there are even more appearance-related toys for girls these days. Toy manufacturers such as Mattel make stick-on painted fingernails for little girls, along with eye shadow, blusher, and lipstick. Maybelline has introduced a bubble gum–flavored lip gloss. A popular doll by Mattel is Li'l Miss Make-up, who resembles a little girl. When brushed with cold water, she develops eyebrows, colored eyelids and fingernails, and tinted lips (Wells 1989). Many of the girls who play with this kind of doll will grow up to read women's magazines and watch soap operas—that is, to be properly socialized as women.

An informal survey of magazines for adolescent girls turned up an emphasis on clothing, makeup, appearance, and how to "get guys." The emphasis was on appearance, appearance, appearance. Several contained articles by males giving advice to females or even ridiculing them, like one from *Seventeen* that explained: "in high school girls . . . appear to be getting a better sense of what they actually want to do with their lives. And, to put it bluntly, it has a dulling effect on their personalities" (Schaefers 1989, p. 68). The more mature woman can read in *Mademoiselle* (August 1989) of the power of the orgasm to increase the beauty of her physical appearance or else can take more mundane paths such as fashion and makeup. The New Woman who reads the magazine of the same name considers career and finances along with beauty, appearance, and how to win and keep her man.

Turning to men's magazines, we start in adolescence with cars and women's bodies (*Playboy*) and move on to *Esquire* and its ilk, which, for example, in August 1989 contained an article called "Women We Love and Women We Don't," the latter being ridiculed for physical appearance, obesity, and the like, as much as the former were admired/desired for their beauty. No articles or ads appeared on how to lose weight, how to attract women, how to have more satisfying sex, and certainly not on how to improve physical appearance. Nothing was said about the glow of beauty induced by orgasm.

With all of these socially constructed imperatives, what woman can accurately perceive herself in a mirror? Self-esteem becomes self-image, and women's images are always found wanting. Some body part is inevitably too big, too small, or the wrong shape. In a study reported by Russell Belk, "women saw their bodies—particularly external parts such as eyes, hair, legs and skin—as more central to their identities than men did to theirs" (1988, p. 52). Of course they would, since they *are*, in a much more essential way, their bodies. Here again it is precisely those body parts, and only those, that are considered worth looking at with which these women identified themselves. The male perspective is incorporated into the female identity.

In the 1988 Olympics, Florence Griffith-Joyner's race times far surpassed what women were expected to be able to perform for many years. Although training has improved for both women and men, women runners have improved vastly more than men have. Why can women suddenly run so fast? Now that they are permitted to, they do—just one example of how powerfully the social context affects physical ability. At the same time, women athletes are continually referred to as "glamorous," "strikingly pretty," or "vulnerable." F. E. Halpert was led to wonder in print in the

Los Angeles Times: "Why is it that women have to cross the finish line with their hair neatly combed and their makeup fresh? Why can't they gasp and sweat and stagger, just like the guys do?" (in *Ms.* magazine, October 1988, p. 39). Why could the ABC-TV commentator Al Trautwig observe on national television, "At some point these women were all normal little girls. Somewhere along the way they got sidetracked" (p. 36)?

In a profile of Margaret Thatcher, we learn that after taking office, she lost weight, had her teeth capped, her hair dyed, her eyelids lifted, and her varicose veins removed. In 1987, Marianne Abrahams, chief designer for the British firm Aquascutum, was called in to revamp Thatcher's wardrobe. "She's begun to look very handsome in the last few years," we learn from Abrahams. "She always had good legs and a stock American size 14 figure, but she feels more conscious now of being very well dressed" (Sheehy 1989, p. 110). Imagine equivalent evaluations of the legs and figure of George Bush or even of John Major, the current British Prime Minister.

In Romania, the editor of the women's magazine *Femeia* criticizes the Ceausescus, who were responsible for untold death and torture. The most serious criticism that she can level at Elena Ceausescu? "Elena was old and ugly. She did not want Romanian women to look young and beautiful" (Ray 1990, p. 2A). A cartoon in a recent issue of the magazine shows her naked and hairy, with sagging breasts.

In a recently publicized legal case, a highly competent and successful woman executive was denied promotion unless she learned to "walk more femininely, wear makeup, and have my hair styled" (Fierman 1990, p. 42). She eventually prevailed in the courts. The recently elected female mayor of San Jose, California, is praised in a local newspaper in the following terms: "Susan Hammer traded her butch haircut and dowdy wool blazers for a colorful new wardrobe, a new shade of lipstick and a fuller hairdo" (*Metro,* January 1991).

In a final example, Shelly Chaiken and Patricia Pliner (1987) found that women who ate smaller meals were viewed as more feminine, better looking, and more concerned about their appearance. Men were rated the same regardless of how much food they consumed. Perhaps this is why one often sees obese women ordering the diet plate in restaurants. The need for public self-denial and denial of appetite in women can easily lead to a private attempt to satisfy an appetite that cannot *naturally* be satisfied. By this I mean that females learn that what is natural to being a woman includes not having much natural appetite of one's own. Women cannot simply eat their fill when hungry, but must instead manage the appearance of not having an appetite—and never satisfy it, while all the time trying to do so. Even women's eating habits are evaluated and interpreted to mean something about their personal value. Women are their bodies and are as good as their bodies.

Ethel Person (1983) has suggested that one of the reasons women choose female analysts is to avoid having to "fake it" or behave in ingratiating ways in order to please a man. His perspective might take precedence over hers. Stanley Moldawsky, writing in a feminist text to make a case for female patients working with male analysts, discusses a patient who lost 100 pounds in the first year of therapy in order to "please me, *as well as herself*" (1986, p. 295; italics added). It is apparent whose pleasure he, and undoubtedly his patient, considered primary. In his description of another successful (in his opinion) case with a female patient, he comments upon his unorthodox decision to see her with her husband at a point close to termination. He made an association to a similar situation involving the wedding of his daughter, during which he also handed her over to her new husband (p. 299). Unknowingly, he speaks for the primacy of the masculine perspective in the feminine experience and makes something of a case for women clients *not* working with male therapists.

WOMEN'S FRAGMENTED PERSPECTIVE

This aspect of women's experience of the physical and the psychological cuts deeper yet. The experience of one's own body with the masculine view superimposed serves as a template for a similarly divided psychological experience. Women's own developing identity, from the first, incorporates the physical contextualized. If one accepts that the unifying principle in organizing experience is the meaning attributed to that experience, and that the majority of the multiple meanings for women come from the masculine viewpoint, then one begins to see that women's perspective must necessarily be a divided one.

If the apparatus through which one experiences life is consistently being evaluated, and is judged not by how well it works but by how well it pleases the erotic or other desires of the perceiver, such as power, control, or a narcissistic wish for centrality, then the most important question is not "How well does my body work?" but "How do I appear?" The answer to "How are you?" becomes "I don't know. You tell me." A feeling is not simply experienced, but is metamorphosed into "How do I look to you feeling this way?" This perspective leads women to depend upon external evaluations not only of their appearance but, by extension, of their complex psychological experience, which can readily become "How do you evaluate my feelings or thoughts and the very fact that I am having them?" In this way, the experience of the viewed is based upon the evaluation of the viewer. The pain of self-denial is necessarily built into this mixture that becomes woman's experience.

There is the additional problem of whether the evaluation of women is *ever* unconditionally positive, since even the positive is both transient and transitory with the presence of different males and the passage of youth. In a study by April Fallon and Paul Rozin (1985), for example, both men and women were found to distort their own body perceptions, but men did so in a positive direction, women in a negative one, never being quite satisfied with their appearances. Kathleen Musa and Mary Roach (1973) found that more girls than boys gave poorer ratings to their appearance than to that of their peers. Women's bodies and, by extension, women themselves are never quite good enough. As Gabrielle Burton aptly notes in her painfully witty feminist novel, *Heartbreak Hotel,* "In the museum of the revolution there is a tit measurer. It has measured every tit that has ever been. Every one is the wrong size" (1988, p. 219).

This is still not the whole story. Added to a divided and ambivalent sense of self is the injunction not to be aware of the very existence of the context or of the profound psychological conflicts it engenders. Women, as a result, have a strong tendency to a particular sort of disconnection from their own bodies and their own cognitive/affective/physical experience—that is, a tendency to watch themselves through male eyes. There are three sources of this process, which I call identification with the indeterminate observer: (1) the priority and constant impinging of the contextual masculine experience of women's bodies; (2) the evaluative component, which can potentially change at any point and predictably does with advancing age; and (3) the demand that women's own experience, as well as the conflict between it and its masculinist context, be made at least partially invisible or not conscious.

The paradox of physicalness for women lies in its being constructed both to be experienced and not to be experienced, but to present what Harold Garfinkel (1967) refers to as an informative display or a source of information and meaning about the particular woman. The body becomes a product to be manipulated and exhibited to its best advantage rather than a living apparatus to be developed and experienced fully. This leaves women with a basic psychological conflict between the actual body and the symbols or meanings attributed to it. As a result, women's bodies typically become more connected to the symbolic than to the physical reality. To put this another way, the physical reality becomes heavily imbued with the symbolic, defined in androcentric and highly evaluative terms.

In the media, women's bodies represent desire, thirst, hunger, fast cars, perfumes, blue jeans, and a myriad of other consumer products. A woman with large breasts is hypersexual. A woman with a certain shade and style of blonde hair is dumb. Eyeglasses and another kind of hairstyle signal intelligence and lack of sexual interest. Store-window mannequins represent women's bodies, but live women represent mannequins that represent women: both the real women and the mannequins are embedded with symbolism and designed to question what is real and what is the mirror.

As the self-concept in women is based directly upon the physical, it alters women's inner experience until it is something other than what it could or should have been. This is yet another aspect of the split in women's experience of self. Women are at the same time defined by and alienated from the physical self and, as a result, the self in general. This is basic to women's psychology, part of being a woman as socially constructed, just as an alienation from the physical is necessary for workers in mental labor, who, to be efficient and effective, must be able to ignore their bodies' immediate needs and wants—training themselves, for example, to sit at a desk for eight hours a day. But, in a different kind of disconnection, their success involves mastery of the physical rather than substitution of the symbolic.

Finally, women's experience of self is splintered in the same way that women's bodies are divided by the sexist gaze. We recall that Belk (1988) reported that women viewed their bodies—in particular, their eyes, hair, legs, and skin—as more central to their identities than men viewed their own bodies to theirs. Apparently a whole cannot be made easily from the sum of these parts, as anyone can see that there are many essential parts missing to form an integrated, whole person. These are instead fragments. As a woman is embodied, so is she disembodied.

A well-integrated self based upon a whole, stable experience becomes extremely elusive, if not impossible. Instead a woman's viewpoint and experience begin in Oedipus' eyes; as he looks at her, her looks are for him. This splintered experience is embedded in women's sexuality and is central to the so-called psychological disorders to which modern women are prone, including multiple-personality disorder, depression, and eating disorders. The last two categories will be discussed at length in chapters 8 and 9, but first, in chapters 5 to 7, I will consider other important aspects of the development of women's identity.

113

5

Relationships:
His and Hers

Tong Chuang Yi Meng. ("Same bed, different dreams.")   —Chinese saying

Recent feminist psychological literature has viewed women in this
society as more relational, empathic, and interpersonally connected, while men are considered to be more independent and
separate from others. This difference has been attributed to our current
parenting arrangements and their consequences for object relations in female and male children. Represented by the clinical theories of Nancy
Chodorow (1978) and Dorothy Dinnerstein (1976) and by the research of
Carol Gilligan (1982), this viewpoint considers men to be more involved
with abstract principles in decision making than with the interpersonal
concerns expressed by women. Along with an analysis of the crucial role of
mothering by women in producing these gender-related differences, these
theorists propose a solution to this problem of differentially distributed
attributes: more equally shared parenting by mothers and fathers, which
would then presumably result in a more balanced development of these
attributes in children of both genders.

There are several points in this analysis that must be questioned, the first
involving its basic premise or question, since that is where epistemology
begins. What is relatedness? Second, do women and men actually differ in
relatedness in the ways described? Does such a gender difference hold as a
function of women mothering, and wherever women mother, or even just
in our own society when women mother? Finally, we must consider carefully the proposal to introduce fathers into the parenting equation as a

factor equal to the mother. If they were to spend equal time caring for children, would fathers equal mothers so that a boy could come to equal a girl in relational capacity? Or would girls become more like boys? Would these changes occur in predictable and desirable (to whom?) ways?

WOMEN'S AND MEN'S RELATEDNESS

While men and women, as psychosocially created groups, may appear to differ in relational capacities and emphasis, it is imperative to view this and any attribute contextually and not just narrowly. As masculinist psychotherapeutic approaches have used masculine models of human functioning, such as business hierarchies (structural family therapy) or cybernetic systems (family systems therapy), this particular feminist model is based upon a familiar feminine situation, the mother-child relationship. Thus, we seem to be asking whether boys grow up to be relational in the way that mothers are with their children. Epistemologically, the answer is certainly built into the question. The answer to the question "Who behaves like mothers?" is highly likely to be "Mothers." If we define being relational as feeling responsible for, and defining, one's self-worth by the success or failure of one's relationships and by being sensitive to the expressed and unexpressed emotional needs of others, then it would appear that women, in general, are more relational than are men, in general. However, if we consider that men's independence and separateness viewed contextually emerge as emotional and physical dependence upon women—wives, lovers, secretaries, graduate assistants, nurses, and so on—then men are certainly as relational as women, if not more so. If we consider that competition depends on a relationship as much as does nurturance, that even domination is a complex interpersonal act, one facet of which is extreme dependency, then it becomes evident that compared to women, men are not less, but differently, relational in different situations.

The mother-child relationship is taken as the model for being relationally oriented and interpersonally connected, and it is girls who turn into women who turn into mothers. Traditionally, many, but not all, women are taught to be relationally oriented in the way that mothers are, but men are also relational in ways that strongly resemble the manner of the cared-for child, with the obvious exception that they come to exercise power in the relationship with the caretaker, in place of the man or men who did so when they were children. The traditional role of the wife includes being mother to her husband (as was Jocasta) and her children by caring for their emotional and physical needs. That of the husband is often some combination of head of household and special child (Oedipus). Clinically, it has been consistently noted that fathers are jealous of their own children and the attention and care they receive from the mother/wife. In this sense, both girls and boys in oedipal society grow up to repeat the mother-child relationship. Women grow up to mother, and they learn to mother both children and men.

Chodorow's (1978) explanation of how this happens begins by acknowledging various complex socioevaluative influences on parenting and on the developing child, but she fails to integrate them into her developmental model. As a result, it becomes a model of only a thin slice of the experience of female and male children in the postindustrial, white, middle-class, nuclear family, functioning in an optimal or "idealized" manner. In this ideal (from a white, middle-class, masculine perspective), but no longer normative and far from representative, case, girls and boys are raised primarily by one heterosexual female parent, with one heterosexual male parent secondarily involved. Girls in these families, according to Chodorow, develop an uninterrupted sense of connectedness and a greater potential for empathy and relatedness. In fact, it is in the nuclear family arrangement that women are most isolated from other women, but connectedness between women is made invisible from this viewpoint.

Chodorow has clearly attempted to develop a universal argument with all the consequent problems and inconsistencies. The fact that this family structure is of historically recent origin, is even now very much in the minority in this country, is not functioning optimally at all, and has never characterized the family structure of many people of color or non-Western families, however, vastly reduces the model's generalizability. In addition, it is weakened by the absence of an integrated analysis of the particular effects of the patriarchal nature of this kind of family or of its current decline. It further lacks a sociocultural analysis of the nature of mothering and fathering, as well as an analysis of how women and men are differently valued and treated, and all the subtle and not-so-subtle ways in which these differences are communicated to girls and boys inside and outside the family. Could it be that none of this matters, that as long as women mother, how and why they do so is irrelevant? Of course not.

This approach searches for the roots of personality and gender differences not just in the nuclear family but more specifically in the parenting arrangements within nuclear families. The traditional, middle-class, nuclear family, as depicted by Chodorow, accounts for fewer than 10 percent of all American households (Wattenberg and Reinhardt 1981). Many children spend most of their day away from Mother, who is as "absent" as is Father. We must then ask whether these daughters have less potential for empathy and relatedness and whether the sons have less need to define themselves as "not mother."

There are currently several other viable child-rearing arrangements, including joint custody, single motherhood, single fatherhood, and blended, extended, lesbian, and gay households. The majority of children growing up in these settings are developing psychologically, and, in particular, with regard to gender, much as do those who still grow up in traditional nuclear families. Of course, this question must be the subject of longitudinal study as these children mature, but thus far there is no evidence of consistently different relational orientations in the female and male children of these families. They differ not as a function of the parenting arrangements per se, but of how well their needs for caring, acceptance, and respect are met. They do not differ, as a group, in gender-related attributes from those raised in traditional nuclear families. Instead the differences occur within groups as a function of the meanings attributed to them. The crucial variable, the power of meta-messages about females and males, of the invisible context as communicated by adult socializing agents of either gender, along with peers, teachers, and the larger societal context, remains unchanged. That is, children learn how to be females or males in a particular society with its particular attributions, expectations, and meanings about the myriad of human characteristics that become organized according to the dualistic gender system.

In colonial times in the United States, child rearing was mainly the job of the father (Hollon 1974). Only beginning in the early 1800s did women begin to devote themselves on a full-time basis to the role of mother and homemaker (Lingeman 1980). Among the !Kung and a variety of other hunting, gathering, and agricultural societies, older children and men also assume primary roles in the care and socialization of young children (Lee 1979). In situations of poverty both inside and outside the United States, children are typically raised by slightly older children. (United Nations data indicate that, on a global level, the average child is raised by an eight-year-old child.)

Even if the relational difference were true for middle-class white women and men in the United States, which is doubtful, it has not been shown to hold for other groups. For example, poor black men and women seem to converge more in their "vocabulary of rights, morality and the social good" (Stack 1986, p. 323). Perhaps oppressed groups have to develop an interpersonal sensitivity, since they cannot afford the luxury of abstract, decontextualized morality and selves. It is not whether women mother and men don't, but *how* both women and men (and sometimes other children) parent that determines what female and male children initially learn about becoming women and men and about focusing on the well-being of relationships.

Chodorow certainly indicates that she is fully aware of the importance of the patriarchal context in which mothering occurs. But then she proceeds as if this were not so, failing to incorporate this aspect of experience in her model. Instead she presents a rather idealistic, almost platonic image of life in the family. She fails to consider, even for those who have grown up in intact nuclear families, the full implication or meaning thereof. For example, within the patriarchal nuclear family, approximately 38 percent of girls and 10 percent of boys are sexually assaulted (Russell 1983). Battery of women occurs in approximately 50 percent of homes (Finkelhor et al. 1986). And these statistics do not include psychological abuse. In addition, it is here that traditional gender roles are first learned, in particular from the father, when he is present.

Much as Freud did, Chodorow and others who follow her approach fail to look closely at what actually happens to girls and women in the nuclear family, which is, in itself, a reflection of and preparation for what happens to women in a patriarchal society: they are often hurt, violated, derogated, and even terrorized. They are even more often limited and constrained by the dictates of traditional femininity. In proclaiming women's embeddedness in relationship a virtue, one fails to consider fully the source of this relatedness, which is not simply the mothering arrangement. The very experiences of danger, constriction, and limitation that are part and parcel of what girls learn in childhood may lead women to attend to interpersonal cues and to the relative (or illusion of) safety of relationship, particularly when the main value imparted to women still remains in the relational realm, in relationship with men and children, that is. Such a reductionist argument fails to consider the complexity of what girls and boys actually learn from parents. It also fails to consider the influence of parents beyond the first few years of childhood and the many other influences on the development of gender-related characteristics through the adolescent and even the adult years. Any approach that fails to integrate these data and this crucial aspect of women's experience is, at best, myopic.

It is imperative to consider the actual behaviors of real mothers and fathers or other socializing persons toward real children within the context of patriarchal culture. In fact, what is constant for women is not a childhood in the kind of family constellation that Chodorow discusses, but a life within a culture that attributes certain meanings and evaluations to females and males. Inclusion and analysis of society's meta-evaluations is a *sine qua non* for understanding the commonalities of female experience, as are specifics for understanding the diversity. For example, the very relatedness of which Chodorow, Gilligan, and others have spoken, along with the various other aspects of female development, is, as they are certainly aware, far from an evaluatively neutral experience.

Children are raised with thousands of repeated injunctions and examples of who they should become. For example, in a study of preschool children (Chasen 1974), the majority of girls already named "mommy" as a projected adult identity, while not one of the boys chose "daddy" as something they would be when they grew up. Women tend to be defined by others and by themselves in terms of their relationships, men in terms of their occupational roles. These are not parallel or symmetrical categories. Whether the relationship of importance in a particular society is mother or wife or sister or daughter or some combination depends, in part, on how women are exchanged in that society. In the Western, white, middle-class group, the role of wife has been most salient for women. In formal religious ceremonies, fathers give their daughters away to other men to become their wives.

Among African-Americans or Latin Americans, the status of mother is more primary. White, middle-class culture may be changing toward that pattern with the proliferation of single parenting among heterosexual and lesbian women and, to a lesser extent, among heterosexual and homosexual men. One of the many adult manifestations of this relational emphasis for women is the adult male-female difference in "parenting permanence": the number of women who abandon the parenting role is minute in comparison with the number of desertions or failure to pay alimony by fathers (Ehrensaft 1984).

Only a minority of children are socialization failures. If mothering by women were a sufficient condition to produce such personality constellations, how would the failures be accounted for? For certainly not all women are more empathic and relationally oriented than all men. Not all women grow up to mother, or want to. Not all those who do want to. The complex meanings of gender and experiences in different situations exercise an important influence.

For example, girls are taught that their self-esteem is based upon their success in relationships. Boys' sense of self-worth will come primarily from the kind of public work they do. The female child is led to develop a greater sense of herself as embedded in relationships in a society that values individuality—but not for women. Her choice, then, is greater relatedness in a society that values individuality above all, or a striving to overcome her training only to achieve greater individuality (individuation-separation) in a society that values greater relatedness for women. She is caught in a dilemma in which either choice includes damage to the self. This results psychologically in a characteristic anxiety and ambivalence which makes its way into the self-concept.

GENDER TRAINING

In the beginning, the parents or other caretakers/socializers are the child's whole world. This is so in a psychological, as well as a physical and social-valuing, sense. The caretakers are not only responsible for meeting or frustrating all the child's physical needs but are the child's physical/psychological world: as they are, so is the world. The young child's primary goal is to please these people, to love them unquestioningly, and to receive in return unquestioning love and devotion to his or her physical/psychological needs. The child is unformed and open to learning physically, emotionally, cognitively, and socially from them. Embedded within the parents' or other caretakers' responses in these areas is always an evaluative component, a conveyance of multiple meanings about the child's behavior, the relationship between these adults and among the adults, younger caretakers, and the child, the parents' behavior, the nature of the child's world, and, by extension, the rest of the world. Most essentially there are meta-statements about the value of that little person and how she or he ought to behave to be valued and loved and to feel worthwhile. Included prominently are literally thousands of messages about how to behave as a girl or a boy. As these are conveyed, they are embedded within the physical, the cognitive, the emotional, both conscious and unconscious, preverbal and verbal, sense of self.

According to Chodorow (1978), gender is not salient to the child during early development. It is perhaps possible to assume that verbal messages—from the first question, "Is it a boy or a girl?" to all the ensuing comments based upon that answer—are lost on the preverbal child. There are, however, no grounds for assuming that more physically based behaviors, from the immediate choice of color and kinds of clothing, to the way the child is held, touched, and allowed to explore, to the tone of voice used in speaking to and about her or him, all of which vary with female and male babies, are lost to the young child. On the contrary, they become firmly embedded within the physical and unconscious, if not verbal and conscious, experience of every human being. Gender assignment and training become a basic organizing principle of the developing child's identity and, as previously noted, appear to be fully organized by twelve to eighteen months of age (Person and Ovesey 1983).

Even if men were to parent children for precisely equal time intervals and in equivalent situations as do women, two crucial differences remain: (1) men parent differently in many important ways, and (2) a man is a differently valued person than is a woman, even if he behaves identically. Fathers are not male mothers any more than women are a class of men. If equal parenting were magically to occur, what would really happen to girls? Would they be abused more, or less? Would they develop the "normal" hatred for men that boys develop for women? Or would they become more independent and separate, while being empathic and intimately related to important others in their lives? Would everyone live happily (empathically and sensitively, yet interdependently and autonomously) ever after in the bosom of the middle-class, heterosexual, nuclear family?

In previous chapters, differences in male and female parenting have been considered. Let us now consider some additional differences. Both fathers and mothers still prefer sons, fathers to a greater degree (Hoffman 1977). Fathers tend to spend more time playing with their children rather than caring for them, and playing more roughly than do mothers (Belsky 1979; Clarke-Stewart 1978; Kotelchuck 1976; Lamb 1976, 1977). Fathers also tend to interact and spend more time with their baby boys than with their daughters (Lewis and Weintraub 1981; Lamb 1976). They are both more active (Lamb 1977; Weinraub and Frankel 1977) and more affectionate (Belsky 1979) with their sons, more interested in their sons' development, and more punitive (Radin 1981). Fathers issue more commands to their children than do mothers, and more to their sons than to their daughters (Gleason 1987). Fathers' ambitions for their sons center on achievement, for their daughters on submissiveness and pleasing others (Alberle and Naegele 1952). Fathers are more likely to comfort daughters than sons and to try to protect daughters from failure (Osofsky and O'Connell 1972). In general, fathers seem to enforce sex role–stereotyped behavior and conformity more than do mothers (Langlois and Downs 1980; Biller 1981). They often think of their children in terms of their own fantasies about what kind of adults they would become, which for boys translates into careers and for girls into romance and appeal (Burlingham 1973).

The propensity for women to become relationally oriented in a particular way is generally exacerbated, rather than eliminated, by parenting arrangements in which the father is more prominent or central. I have worked with several female clients for whom the father was the only parent, beginning at different ages—nine months, five years, and ten years of age. All of these women were even more interpersonally sensitive and carefully attuned to the needs of their fathers and, as a result, of men and children in general. All of them had been dealt with by their fathers in a highly sexualized (normal, not abusive) manner, as is characteristic of fathers' relationships with their daughters in oedipal society (Chodorow 1978; Westcott 1986). They had been raised as a complement to their fathers and had developed a hypersensitivity to them and to their needs.

Fathers consistently tend to reinforce more traditionally feminine and masculine behavior in their children. In the absence of mothering, these girls developed even more extremely the qualities that Chodorow attributes to the relationship with "the generic mother." Does this mean that it is fathering, not mothering, that is responsible for daughters developing these traits? I do not want to slice up experience in this way, but instead to consider some of the particular details of mothering and of fathering, along with their interaction, as they are performed in, and supported by other agents of, society.

In many of the empirical studies of single fathers and their children, experience is sliced very thinly by the use of esoteric self-report instruments and measures of very narrow aspects of family life. The perspective is almost universally that of the fathers alone. It has not yet been considered relevant by adult researchers to understand these relationships from the perspective of the children. It is difficult to find work that attempts to tease out the physical, intrapsychic, and interpersonal details of what actually occurs between parents and their children in single-parent families, or in the even rarer families where fathers are the primary caretakers.

In one study of intact nuclear families in which fathers were the primary caregivers, the author (Radin 1982) reports with almost palpable relief that the fathers in these families were not more "effeminate" than traditional fathers. She interprets her results as suggesting that individuals whose gender-role identities are stable and secure can most easily deviate from traditional roles, and also notes with relief that the children's sex-role orientations did not differ from the expected. Direct teaching was greater with sons, and children had expectations of greater punitiveness and stereotyped behavior from these fathers. Yet the author concludes that there are only advantages to this arrangement.

This is not the place for an elaborate critique of this study or the literature in this area, in general, except to note that it is replete with methodological problems and buried epistemological biases, so that little is added to our knowledge of what actually occurs in these family constellations. Such arrangements are not common enough nor of sufficient longevity to have permitted careful longitudinal studies. Yet there are multiple suggestions that fathers support traditional gender behaviors that maintain

122

the status quo. If the argument of Chodorow and others follows, then in families where men are the sole or primary caretakers, not only should male children be more relational and empathic but females should have more need to separate and should be more hostile toward men. There is absolutely no indication that this is happening. It seems clear that women's and men's parenting per se is not itself the crucial variable here, but that the context of values and meaning, the symbolic system within which women mother and men father, must be considered. What are children taught about what it means to be a girl or a boy in Western, or any other, society?

A basic aspect of the gender system, whereby it is enforced and reinforced, is through shame or humiliation. It is repugnant for boys to be thought of as being like girls, and common for young boys to ridicule girls and to note that certain activities are beneath them or "for girls." Boys commonly ridicule one another and girls for behaving "like girls." Implicit in this attitude, of course, for both masculinity and feminity, is that being "like a girl" is shameful.

High school football coaches can shame their players into being tougher and playing harder by calling them "girls." No well-socialized boy or man wants to be called a girl or a woman. In a 1990 legal case, Kenneth R. Slate was arrested on Christmas Eve trying to enter a closed store in Indianapolis. He had mistakenly bought a pink radio as a Christmas gift for his boss, a construction worker. He preferred to be arrested, which he was, rather than face the humiliation of giving his boss a gift in a color that was associated with females. Other examples are all too easy to come by.

If children grew up in a world where women were unambivalently admired and respected, but where women still mothered, would these notions still prevail? What if it were said that women must care for men's physical and emotional needs as if they were children because men are more dependent and helpless than women, and that is it women who are strong and can be relied upon? How would these different meanings affect the sense of self-worth of girls? Of boys? Misogynist meanings bolster a young boy's sense of self-worth; the young girl's is weakened or turned to defiance.

Such learning is firmly embedded in all aspects of society and cannot be meaningfully reduced to one source. Much as same-sex peers enforce the emphasis on physical attractiveness for girls, so do boys enforce the derogation of girls among boys. In both cases, nothing less than a basic sense of self-worth is at stake.

One of the repeated injunctions to young boys is not to pay much attention to others' feelings and needs, not to be empathic, not to be concerned with feelings or relationships—those domains are for girls. Instead boys should be active, externally oriented, and exploratory. Boys will (should) be boys. On the other hand, girls are taught in a variety of ways to be physically restrictive and to focus on interpersonal situations, on feelings, on safety, to play with dolls and to play "house." Newly marketed games, such as Date Line, Heart Throb, and Sweet Valley High, for the early adolescent girl, center on choosing a date or a boy with whom to go steady. For her own self-esteem, she must be concerned with and responsible for relationships to men and children.

These parameters widen only when the shaming meta-evaluations are reduced or removed. For example, it is somewhat more possible at this time in this society for men to be interpersonally sensitive and women to be assertive and externally oriented. The evaluating context has changed; women and men may behave in these ways without risking ridicule, at least in certain circles. This has not occurred as a function of any change in patterns of male and female parenting, but through the cultural work of feminists who have made changes at the level of meaning attributed societally and individually to these activities.

In addition to the need to gain positive self-esteem and to avoid shame, the development of a greater propensity for relatedness in the female child is based upon the need for safety. A girl turns to relationships not just as a result of being reared by the same-sex parent, but through direct and indirect, explicit and implicit, injunctions from both parents concerning limitations that apply to her but not to her brothers. The world is, in fact, a much more dangerous place for the female child, so she is taught that to be more relational is also to be safer, to be protected.

Even before she can be taught this lesson in words, parents tend to keep female children physically closer to them and to protect them more, as do teachers as early as in preschool. Dolores Gold, Gail Crombie, and Sally Noble (1987) have shown that teachers tend to evaluate the academic competence of preschool boys based upon their age and IQs, that of girls based upon age and compliance to teachers, less compliant girls being viewed as less competent. Teachers also tend to respond more to boys when they behave aggressively, and to girls when they behave dependently and are more physically proximal (Serbin et al. 1973). Several studies have indicated that teachers display a preference for boys (Clarricoates 1978, 1980; Stanworth 1981) and give them more attention than girls in learning tasks in the classroom (Galton, Simon, and Croll 1980).

It is clear that women are actively directed and guided toward a life of relatedness and caring, and not only as a result of being mothered in a nuclear family. Women in this society are *driven* to relatedness by the messages of the culture, which include the demand to be unconscious of the masculine context and of the danger and derision it affords women. The particulars of any woman's situation are intertwined with her racial and class membership, as well as with individual experiences and meanings, but I would argue that sensing the presence of danger is ubiquitous. As hatred of women is a "natural" part of masculinity, so is fear of men a "natural" part of femininity. How many adult women have never directly experienced male violence, either physically or verbally? How many have never witnessed it in person or via the media? Many adult women are not at all conscious of this fear, nor is it necessarily consciously present at all times in all situations for any woman. Yet even when women remain unaware, it is contained unconsciously in their bodies, movements, use of space, even their dreams, which are frequently filled with violent images of males. Tellingly, violence in men's dreams is also typically perpetrated by other men (Lauter and Rupprecht 1985).

SENSITIVITY TO THE AGGRESSOR

One strategy for remaining unconscious of the destructive and shaming context, that most frequently taught to females, is to remain permeable and to immerse oneself in relatedness. For safety and even survival, women learn to maintain permeable boundaries and to be defined primarily through relatedness to men or through their absence of relatedness to a man or men. The psychological boundaries that women develop subsume their relationships with men and children and are not individual boundaries, but relationship boundaries. For this reason, women often do not feel complete if they are not in a relationship.

As Gerald Zuk (1972) has noted, those in power typically advocate rules and rationality, others, relatedness and caring. In marital conflicts, a wife may invoke caring, a husband logic. Yet the same woman with her children emphasizes rules and leaves the appeal to love to the children. That is, seeming autonomy or relatedness are interactional and not characteristics of people in isolation (Hare-Mustin and Marachek 1986). Each aspect depends upon the other.

Yet even relational solutions are fraught with paradox. In a study by Susan Pollack and Carol Gilligan (1982) of violent images in the Thematic Apperception Test (TAT), a projective technique where subjects are asked to tell stories about pictures that represent certain psychological themes, women feared isolation as a result of success and saw increasing violence as interpersonal distance increased. Men, on the other hand, saw more violence arising from intimate situations. The potential paradox facing women if these results are, indeed, valid and generalizable is shocking: if there is a potential for violence in intimate situations and if that violence, as statistics indicate and as we know, is perpetrated for the most part against females by males, then both intimacy with and distance from males are potentially dangerous for females. The streets and the home are dangerous places for women, as strangers, dates, and spouses are all potential attackers. Recently released statistics of the Justice Department (Lewin, *New York Times,* January 20, 1991) indicate that violent crimes, reported and unreported, against people over twelve years of age declined between the years 1973 and 1987. However, most of that decline has been in crimes against men. Violent crime against women is now six times as likely to be committed by their intimates. The women most frequently victimized are poor black women living in urban areas.

Both the psychological literature and clinical experience support the conclusion that females who are abused as children become more dependent upon and more sensitive to their abusers and, by extension, to other potential abusers. This is the self-defense I call "sensitivity to the aggressor." As Judith Herman has noted, "the victims of incest grow up to become archetypically feminine women: sexy without enjoying sex, repeatedly victimized, yet repeatedly seeking to lose themselves in the love of an over-powering man, contemptuous of themselves and of other women, hard-working, giving and self-sacrificing. . . . *In their own flesh* they bore repeated punishment for the crimes committed against them in childhood" (1981, p. 108; italics added).

Again, both statistically and clinically, male children who are abused tend to identify with the aggressor and to become the aggressor in future settings. In essence, then, the feminine (Antigone) style of dealing with fear, in a world where females cannot generally become the aggressor, is to seek safety by hiding, by becoming invisible, and by becoming compulsively relationally oriented. The masculine (oedipal) style consists of seeking safety by becoming the feared individual, by becoming bigger and more visible, and by becoming insensitive to the feelings and fears of potential victims and, by extension, relatively nonempathic. In treatment programs for abusers, one major focus is to teach them empathy, that is, to teach them that other people have feelings that differ from their own and deserve to be respected. This problem is an extension of normal masculinity, as is sensitivity to the aggressor an aspect of the normal feminine style. The difference from the normal in cases of abuse is only one of degree.

Any clinician can attest to the fact that, in couples or family therapy, it is typically the female partner who feels that the relationship is her responsibility, who feels that she has failed if the couple's relationship fails or if there are family problems. In general, it is women who most frequently initiate the therapeutic contact. Jean Baker Miller has noted: "The girl's sense of self-esteem is based in feeling that she is a part of relationships and is taking care of the relationships" (1984, p. 5). A relationship's failure is hers and it is shameful for her as a woman in a way that is not so for her male counterpart, who certainly experiences the same loss of a relationship, but not of self. In or out of clinical situations, the self-esteem of most women, whether they admit it to themselves or not, is directly related to whether or not they are in a relationship. This direct correlation is not true for men.

While women are concerned with relationship management and with being in a relationship, it is men who seem to require relationships for survival itself and who seem to be happiest and healthiest when married (Bernard 1972). So who is more relationally oriented again depends on what the terms mean. It is perhaps not overly cynical to say that marriage appears to be designed primarily to meet men's emotional and physical needs and women's self-esteem and safety needs, and seems to work better at meeting the former than the latter. I do not mean to suggest that humans do not achieve one of the most primary kinds of satisfaction from relationships, but that it is also greatly overdetermined—particularly in contemporary middle-class society, where relationships are considered to serve a myriad of psychological needs: everything from the basic physiological needs to safety, emotional and financial security, friendship, companionship, romance, and sexuality.

If she restricts her movement and independence in the name of relatedness, particularly to males, a woman is offered a semblance of safety and security. After the early years of childhood, continued relatedness to females will not provide a girl with safety or esteem, and thus does she unconsciously, if not consciously, understand that she must switch her allegiance from Mother and women to Father and men. "To the extent that the mother lacks the power and the esteem of others, she has already betrayed her daughter" (Flax 1981, p. 63). Women who make their primary relationships in adult life with other women face potential or actual ridicule, humiliation, or even physical danger in direct proportion to their visibility in both the public and private arenas. Thus do women come to mother men and children, for while their relational orientation may be continuous, as Chodorow (1978) suggests, its recipient generally is not.

Relatedness that occurs not as a response to danger or humiliation, as a means to safety or esteem, but for the sake of affiliation itself is qualitatively and experientially different, as are being a caretaker and genuine caring.

Thus, relatedness must not simply involve meeting the needs of men and children, but meeting one's own needs for nondriven caring and closeness. The relational orientation of many women in our society is, in a large part, a response to oppression, and romanticizing it does not change this fact.

CONCLUSION

Models proposing that psychological balance can be achieved by introducing the father into primary parenting both derive from and lead back to the post-Cartesian dualistic model of male and female psychology. They predict that a balance between the parents will lead to a balance between the genders in relational orientation. But, as has been shown in this chapter, even shared parenting is not equal parenting, just as mothering and fathering a child cannot be spoken of as if they were equivalent activities. To assume that the introduction of the father in parenting children will create symmetry when there is asymmetry in virtually every aspect of male and female relationships, one must ignore the socioevaluative contextual level, as well as the very real details of the intrapsychic, interpersonal, and physical manifestations thereof. In addition, we cannot ignore the very different ways that male parents relate to their children and, even more important, the very different ways they are socially evaluated and esteemed compared with female parents.

The most crucial aspects of this issue, from the overwhelming impracticalities involved in convincing men that they want to or should "mother" to the crucial differences in parenting styles of mothers and fathers, are not considered in a reductionist approach. Why would men *en masse* want to take on a job that carries little prestige for women and less for them, that carries no salary and even less power? Would women want to relinquish their importance in this one arena? Should men be supervised in their parenting for at least a generation? By whom?

Another important difficulty is that the feminist theorists who are proposing a change in the relative evaluations of relatedness and separateness suggest that the qualities identified with females ought to be more positively valued than are those attributed to males. Should we be surprised that women find women's style superior, just as men have previously done with their own? This position is an attempt at change in comparative valuing based only on intrapsychic and interpersonal analyses. The source of the new values is not made explicit. The usual dichotomies are accepted, followed by the usual expression of a preference for one of the two. Only the preference itself is new.

In the antebellum South, children of plantation owners were often wet-nursed and raised by African-American women slaves. Could we consider this relationship the cause of racism or slavery itself? Did these Southern sons grow up needing to separate themselves from blacks as a result of these relationships? If white women had been exclusively responsible for them, would racism have been quelled? Certainly this translation of the argument sounds absurd. The causes are much more complex and multiple. As this comparison should suggest, the solution to the existence of gender differences and oppression itself cannot be found in introducing fathers into the primary parenting process—as if fathers were equal to mothers in this society, as if women were equal to men except in the amount of time spent parenting, as if both genders were only quantitatively and not qualitatively unequal, or as if any qualitative differences could be erased by this simple first-order quantitative change (Watzlawick, Beavin, and Jackson 1967).

A popular intervention used in family therapy, which has already been mentioned briefly, offers a direct parallel to Chodorow's notion that mothers are too involved in child rearing and fathers too little. Family therapists have, for years, identified this constellation as the source of problems. To counterbalance the so-called enmeshment of the mother and child, the father is asked to take a more active role in parenting. Although he may never have participated in these tasks before, he is introduced into the system as an expert with the concomitant power and self-enhancement that such a definition implies. Whether overtly or covertly stated, it is apparent that the mother has failed. Her status and self-respect in an arena to which she has devoted her life are severely damaged by this intervention. This is all invisible to the traditional family therapist who, having created a new balance and eliminated at least temporarily the symptom in the identified patient, the child, happily exits the scene. What actually happens to the other individuals in the family is not of concern.

What really happens to women as the result of such a narrow definition of the problem and of the appropriate solution? Of Chodorow's solution, we must ask the same question, because it also fails to make visible and integrate the societal and contextual levels with the personal. It fails to consider how men might actually parent and what they might do with this increased power in the one arena where women have traditionally held some power. Enmeshed mothers seem to overprotect their children and not let them grow up and away; enmeshed fathers have sex with their children and do not let them grow up and away either. The latter has not been

considered enmeshment by family therapists, but it is certainly the masculine (oedipal) version of it.

When a solution to a problem does not work, people sometimes have an
almost unshakable tendency to try more of the same. This error eventually
leads them to the therapist's office to learn why this strategy doesn't work.
This feminist revisionist argument is of that nature. As parenting by two
heterosexual adults, one female and one male, in a nuclear family is taken
as a given, more of the same is offered as the solution. If men matter more
than women do, making them matter even more and women even less in
one more arena will not only not solve the problem; it will exacerbate it.

6

Limits and Boundaries

*To survive the Borderland means
you must live* sin fronteras
be a crossroads.

—Gloria Anzaldúa
Borderlands/La Frontera, The New Mestiza

The development of psychological boundaries has been considered
extensively in recent feminist and nonfeminist clinical literature. I
would like to introduce into the discussion the distinction between
limits and *boundaries,* as I consider their influence upon each other of
major consequence in human development in general, and in relational
capacity in particular. Limits define the extent to which one may grow,
expand, or explore. Limits identify the point beyond which one may not
venture due to internally imposed deficits, such as lack of skills or talent,
or externally imposed injunctions, such as those introduced by gender
training. Limits eventually become internalized and embedded in the concept of self and others.

Strong externally imposed limits, along with certain other conditions,
which I will describe, lead to weaker psychological boundaries, while weak
limits lead to more extensive, less well defined, or less well internalized
psychological boundaries. Limits contribute directly to the development of
boundaries, by which I mean a clear and consistent definition of oneself, of
one's identity, of exactly "where I end and you begin." This includes
knowing who one is and who one is not.

THE MALE PERSPECTIVE

Even for men, who are typically considered by psychologists to develop a separate and more autonomous self than do women, such an identity lies within the realm of cultural mythology. It is certainly possible for men to appear separate and independent if one ignores all the female supports that permit this illusion. Even more important, from a psychological perspective, one would have to ignore how the masculine subsumes women, children, and even physical space and objects. Men, in general, do not simply have less permeable boundaries than do women, in general; they also have more extensive and inclusive ones, which subsume and engulf. They are not less, but differently, relational.

From early childhood, when they are encouraged to explore the environment physically, to their presence on public streets, to the world of work, boys and men are permitted and encouraged to go up to and even beyond the physical bounds of their bodies. They tend to use physical and psychological space more expansively and confidently than do women. For example, as children, they wander farther and more comfortably from home. They use larger areas for their play activities and, later on, initiate touch more freely and frequently and interrupt women speakers more than do women. They take up more space in general. From the male perspective, all space, public and private, including the women in it, appears to belong to and be owned by men. This belief/feeling/experience has its roots in our legal and social history, whereby women have been considered nothing more than extensions of their fathers or husbands. The word *family* itself originally referred to all the possessions of a male citizen, including his wife, children, and slaves. In the United States, married women now generally have the right to own and dispose of their own property, but in some states the husband's permission is still required.

In 1977, Oregon became the first state to make marital rape illegal. By 1983, a husband accused of raping his wife could be prosecuted in Oregon under the same laws as any other man accused of rape (Morgan 1984). As of 1985, twenty states had abolished the exemption and permitted the prosecution of husbands who rape their wives (Finkelhor and Yllo 1985). In the majority of states, marital rape is still legally nonexistent, although physically prevalent. Conservative estimates indicate that approximately 14 percent of women ever married have been raped by their husbands. Given the pressures not to report these incidents, this must be considered an underestimate (Russell 1982). While men's sense of ownership of women is less formally accepted these days, as a result of legal and social challenges to American laws by feminists, their sense of entitlement and psychological ownership of public and often private property is far from eradicated. (But many other countries' laws are not even this "progressive." For an extensive review of these issues throughout the world, see Robin Morgan's *Sisterhood Is Global* [1984].)

In public spaces, men frequently approach women, even women in pairs or groups, believing and even stating that women are alone when not accompanied by a man. Females are given, and come to require, a smaller area of personal space than do males (Lott and Sommer 1967). Among a group of middle-class children, for example, boys were observed to spend more time playing outdoors than did girls and to take up about one-and-a-half times more space (Harper and Sanders 1975). Outside the laboratory, women alone or in groups also typically claim less space than do men (Edney and Jordan-Edney 1974). And within all-male groups, dominant or aggressive males use more personal space than do other males (Sommer 1969; Kinzel 1970).

Tradition and habit conspire not only to allow women less physical/psychological space than men but to permit them to make less noise, both vocally and in exercising digestive and other bodily functions. Men can chew and exercise bodily functions overtly and loudly without violating a sense of public propriety or their imputed masculinity.

A therapist and mother writes of her experience in Japan: "When we were toilet training our young son, we taught him to pee on a tree in the backyard. Observing this, a Japanese babysitter taught him to first apologize to the tree" (Bell 1989, p. 52). What does it do to the sense of self and others of the typical young boy in the United States, who is taught that he has the right to pee on whatever he can reach? Indeed, contests between young boys to see who can pee the farthest are common. The masculine vernacular even includes the term "pissing contest" to describe a competitive situation. Apparently, the further such a male can extend his body, including its excrement, the more masculine and successful he is judged by his peers and by himself: more and bigger are better.

If women were to treat physical space as an extension of themselves, for example, by roaming freely in the nighttime streets as men are comparatively free to do, their very lives would be in danger. Men in predatory groups have sometimes justified attacking women, saying they deserved it for being out at night (as in the sensationally publicized attack on the Central Park jogger in New York City). Women enter public (another seemingly neutral term) territory at their own risk. "Public" space is, in fact, not neutral: it does not belong to women. Every woman knows this and has a strategy for dealing with or avoiding the danger of public areas, typically either by limiting the ground she covers or by being accompanied by a male.

Women must pass through a war zone every time they step outside their doors, and often again when they step back inside. These days, there are women who can be professors, lawyers, or physicians, gaining limited access to arenas that masculine privilege had previously closed off to them. They can lecture, litigate, or medicate, but the moment they step out of this role into the harsh sunlight or the still harsher darkness of the streets, they lose the protection of status and are defined only by those visible characteristics of their appearance, including gender, race, and age.

At home, in addition to dealing with men they know, women must deal with intrusion by strangers at the door or on the telephone. Obscene calls remind women that they are subject to sexual violence. With the development of technology, engulfment takes on new forms: most single women I know either have male friends or relatives record the announcements on their answering machines or indicate in the message that they do not live alone. These messages may confuse the malevolent caller as well as friends or acquaintances. But this form of camouflage is a necessary addition to women's arsenal for survival in supposedly neutral and private space. It is the strategy of invisibility, which both protects and damages women.

In symbolic ways, women's invisibility must remain intact in public as well. If women sat, moved, or touched themselves in public the way men do, they might be accused of being lewd or even asking to be violated. (Recall the different effects of hypothetical identical descriptions of male and female clients.) Men do not put themselves in danger by behaving in these ways. Nor do they shame themselves. A cross-cultural survey of standing and sitting positions revealed that spreading one's legs in genital display is consistently more characteristic of men (Hewes 1957). I have already discussed the masculinist tendency to define and locate men's conflicts within women, here demonstrated by the fact that men would see a woman in that position as lewd but would not see themselves or other men as lewd. Since they locate their experience within females, they both neutralize their own behavior and subsume women's. Again, women's behavior is defined by what it arouses in the indeterminate male observer.

A female therapist I was supervising told me in a distraught manner that her male client, a few minutes before the end of a session, had reached over and dropped a check in her lap as a signal that he was finished for the day. Another client had removed a soaking wet check from his pocket and handed it to a different female therapist, whom I was also supervising. He explained that he had been sweating a lot that day. He never thought to remove the check from his pocket to permit it to dry out during the session or to avoid inflicting on her the sweat of his body. Could she have been seductive or obnoxious in some way to elicit or deserve this behavior? Had she asked for it?

Both of these acts were probably consciously or unconsciously hostile, but it is the sense of entitlement embedded in the hostility that I want to underline. Can you imagine these situations with female clients and male therapists? What different meanings might be inferred? Were a female client to call attention to her own and the therapist's body in these ways, it would undoubtedly be considered seductive. She would not have the same physical and spatial entitlement and would be violating a boundary that does not exist for men. Or perhaps the meaning in both situations would be about her, as she carries this surplus of meaning just by being female.

As another example, feminist attempts to involve fathers in all aspects of parenting have given rise to a new expression: "We are pregnant." While such a comment by a man may be intended as a sensitive response to feminist requests for equal participation by fathers, consider the perspective. If "we" are pregnant, if "our" womb is carrying our baby, then why was it not impregnated by "our" penis? Just what is shared and by whom? It is the woman's body that becomes the possession of the couple, while the man's remains his own. Hidden under this modern guise is the traditional sense of a man's possession of his woman or, at least, of her useful body parts. As it was the man's alone in the past, when all the children it produced were his possessions, so has the womb become the possession of the couple.

Ernest Becker, in discussing men's need to triumph over physicalness, gives as an example "the widespread practice of segregating women in special huts during menstruation and all the various taboos surrounding menstruation. It is obvious that man seeks to control the mysterious processes of nature as they manifest themselves within *his* own body" (1973, p. 32; italics added). Becker, along with the men of the various cultures to which he refers, considers even women's menstruation to be part of what happens to a man's body. Its cultural meaning derives from men's beliefs and feelings about menstruation, not from women's experience of it.

Another instructive example is provided by an initiation cult in New Guinea, in which it is assumed that "men become men only by men's ritualizing birth and taking over—as a collective group—the functions that women perform naturally" (Mead 1949, p. 98). In many cultures, the symbolic death of a boy and his rebirth as a man is accomplished by men and often involves circumcision or, in certain tribes in Australia, subincision of the penis. This wound is named "vulva" by the men, and the blood from it is considered the menses of ancestral females, stolen by the men to become the source of male superiority (Kittay 1984). Inducing "male menstruation" is a central aspect of these male rebirth rituals. Men thus appropriate for themselves the most physical aspects of childbearing capacity. As they retain the power to make meaning, this ritual is seen not as ridiculous or hopeless but as truly imbuing them with power and superiority. These men then have no reason to envy women, as they wind up possessing all that is female and male.

The sentiment behind such rituals is not confined to far-off cultures. It is well known that the developers of the atomic bomb considered and spoke of the event as giving birth. A recent book on fathering by Bill Cosby was advertised on New York City buses with large posters proclaiming, "Congratulations, it's a book!" Apparently the birth was accomplished by Cosby, its father, all by himself. The basketball star Rick Barry has been quoted as saying that if his children were horses, their breeding would make them worth a million dollars each. One can only assume that their mother is neither a basketball star nor a horse.

All this points us in an important direction. It would seem that men have just as much difficulty separating and individuating as do women, and that the ideal of separation and individuality is a somewhat unnatural act which must be accomplished largely by illusion. If men define women, children, and even physical aspects of the environment as extensions of themselves, then their own difficulties with separation are made invisible. Men so often report experiencing women's reactions to their behaviors as an extension of their own that we must consider that men lack a good sense of where their boundaries end and women's begin. They often seem sincerely to believe, for example, that a woman who is raped wants to be, that a woman who is looked at or commented on lasciviously enjoys it, that a woman who is whistled at on the street feels complimented. Pornographic publications and movies are replete with images of women being dominated, violated, and beaten, usually as though they enjoyed it.

In couples therapy, many husbands express difficulty in seeing their wives' feelings or needs as different from their own. One husband repeatedly pointed out to his wife that she simply should not want certain friends because her contact with them hurt him. Many men even have difficulty seeing that their partners' sexual needs are different from their own. If he does what he likes, he may be truly perplexed that she doesn't also like it—not that he demands that his female partner have the same needs and feelings as he does, but that he makes an often unconscious assumption that she does. It used to be said that, under the marital law, a husband and wife become one person: the husband. The psychological legacy of that condition remains with us.

The masculine must subsume the feminine. As women's boundaries remain permeable and transitorily defined, so are men's extensive and engulfing. For example, a recent article in the *San Francisco Chronicle* (April 23, 1989) discussed female movie stars, such as Kelly McGillis, Brigitte Nielsen, and Sigourney Weaver, who have been successful *in spite of* being tall. The many male stars (Dustin Hoffman, Paul Newman, Robert Redford, Tom Cruise, Michael J. Fox, Mel Gibson, Sean Penn) who are shorter than the average man are mentioned, but their height has not been discussed and has not been an impediment in their career paths. It is written as a fact of life that tall actresses have trouble playing against shorter leading men, not the reverse. Of course, to solve the "problem" the camera must somehow create the illusion that the man is taller. The issue is not how tall the woman is, but whether her male counterpart is taller, or can be made to look taller. While men often seem to fear engulfment by the mother or other women, it is women who are daily engulfed, defined, and limited by the father and other men, often without even knowing it. The practice is so pervasive that it seems the natural condition.

THE FEMALE PERSPECTIVE

While girls and women learn, through externally imposed limits, who they are not or may not be, they also learn that who they are is, to a significant extent, defined by others, by men in an oedipal society. A woman's limits are clear, her boundaries not only negatively and externally imposed but subject to redefinition with the introduction of different men into her life. This includes transitory contact with strange males in public, who may define her as desirable, insignificant, invisible, or "asking for it" by being either attractive or unattractive *to them.*

A girl child's early training involves numerous prohibitions and limitations that do not apply to the upbringing of male children. Erikson (1950) designates "basic trust" as the initial developmental stage in the formation of the core identity in children. But, as Bart (1985) has aptly noted, the first developmental stage for girls should be mistrust. While it is a cliché that "boys will be boys," meaning that they will explore, disobey, and generally expand their known territory as part of the very essence of maleness, there is no equivalent phrase applied to girls because there is no equivalent permissive injunction appropriate to them.

Part of early female training, through both explicit statements and example, involves learning of the danger and intrusiveness with which they must contend. Mistrust, fear, and restriction thus become integral parts of the developing identity. The female child must learn that some males will hurt, others will protect, some will do both. Only when "escorted" by a man will she be considered by other men to be "out of bounds," or boundaried, or to have an impermeable boundary. Only men can draw the line for her between attractiveness and "asking for it" (Grady 1984), if that line exists at all. Furthermore, only a father or a husband can give her a surname. Nowadays, many married women do not take their husbands' surnames, but even then, it is their fathers' names they are then keeping. Only through relatedness to a man can a woman be safely visible and "bounded" or bound up.

No wonder, then, that women learn to survive in connectedness rather than in the self, with permeable, accommodating, shifting boundaries, and often with a sense of invisibility both outside and within relationships. Women can be safely visible only "in relation to," and since this is culturally approved it tends to add to their self-esteem. Paradoxically, at the same time it weakens self-esteem by virtue of its limits. As their limits are defined by others continually throughout life, women's boundaries must remain relatively reactive, unformed, and situational, vigilantly other-oriented rather than self-defined. Ultimately, it is often only the illusion of safety women gain with these boundaries, since violence toward women in intimate situations is epidemic in our society.

A study by Carol Brooks Gardner (1980) focused on the function of men's street remarks to women, including the risk involved in being an unescorted woman in public. It is safer for women to be accompanied by men than to be alone in public, but what does it do to their sense of self? While a certain visibility in the world of men is necessary for the development of a clear and healthy identity, it also presents a tremendous danger. Another paradox is that authenticity, or genuine presence itself, is often gravely dangerous for women. The artist Judy Chicago (1975) writes of women doing art about street harassment; they felt psychically and physically frightened even to discuss the subject among other women and to represent it artistically. As Vivian Gornick has commented, "My father had to be Jewish; he had no choice. When he went downtown he heard 'kike.' . . . When my father heard the word 'kike,' the life-force within him shriveled. When a man on the street makes animal-like noises at me, or when a man at a dinner table does not hear what I say, the same thing happens to me. This is what makes the heart pound and the head fill with blood" (1989, p. 95).

Fear of physical harm by men is considered a natural part of the background of life for women and, as a result, is embodied by women. How often do you see a woman standing straight, eyes forward, confidently striding down the street? Recall the discussion of muggers listening for a woman's footsteps in the street. Now imagine that you are a woman alone at night in the street or in an isolated area, and you hear a man's footsteps rapidly approaching you from behind. What do you feel or imagine?

In a group session with a therapist whom I supervise, one of the men in the group jumped to his feet in agitation and despair. Both the women and the men in the group cringed, fearful that he was going to be violent. They had all had a lot of experience with male violence, but only one, as a child, with female violence. In training classes for psychotherapists, both female and male interns must learn to deal with their fear of anger and especially anger in men, which can turn to violence. Anger in women can be talked about and worked through, or at least contained. Therapists often collude in defining anger as masculine, thus appropriate and acceptable for men but too powerful for women.

At various points in therapy, I have listened to virtually every female client of mine grapple with her physical fear either of men in general or of her male partner. Many have recurrent nightmares about violent men. Several will not venture out at night alone, fearing the anonymous assailant. Others fear that their partners will force them to have sex or that their partners' apparent generalized hostility toward women will be turned on them. Some have heard their partners speak of women deserving to be raped, beaten, or even murdered. Lesbian women often fear ridicule, if not physical attack, both from men they know and from anonymous men in public. Most of these women are not even among the many who have been beaten or raped as children.

Almost any woman can describe a sense of physical and psychological readiness for assault in the streets: "Taking cabs to the airport, sleeping in one's own bed, using public toilets, riding in elevators, driving home, having casual conversations with neighbors or friends, women often feel eerie sensations, 'stomach butterflies' that somehow alert them to danger" (Stanko 1988). Women who have been molested often feel tension for the rest of their lives in certain areas of the body and mind, and often cannot experience sexual arousal without a mixture of tension and fear. People who have been physically abused as children often adopt a physical and psychological posture of perpetual vigilance or defense.

Women are not always actively aware of this fear, as it is so much a part of daily life that it is embedded in the physical, or contained in and by psychological symptoms such as panic attacks, phobias, dissociative disorders, and depression, to name a few typically female maladies. Certainly, not all men are free of fears when it comes to dealing with women. It is my impression, however, that it is rejection, not violence, they fear from women. They fear not measuring up, not being big enough, strong enough, potent enough, wanted enough. They fear the loss of power and entitlement.

If there were a curfew for males—since men in public areas, such as streets and parks, particularly at night, pose a serious danger to females (and to a much lesser degree to other males, increasing proportionally as they resemble females in size, appearance, or behavior)—would there be an increase in violence in the home? How many Americans, in describing our values and customs to a foreigner, would state that we have a curfew for women? Our informal curfew for women is as taken for granted as is men's violence. Here we must ask why this is simply defined as a problem of women's physical and psychological vulnerability and not of men's irrational violence and lack of self-control. There are no large-scale programs to counteract male violence—for example, to teach boys to contain themselves and their aggression, to respect the needs and feelings of girls, or even to understand that those needs may differ from their own. This would involve not just naming the danger but understanding who has the power to define it. This is the very power to delimit, to bound, to create figure and ground, to make visible and invisible. It is the creator of the ground, the owner of the context, who holds the power. It is also the owner of the context who creates its boundary and defines the problem. Only a change that alters the context, that changes the meaning and evaluation of any intrapsychic or interpersonal event, will be change in the oedipal nature of society itself.

To take some everyday examples of the power of ownership of the context, typewriters, when first invented, were considered to be complex machinery that could be operated only by men. Thus, in the United States, the occupation of typist carried a prestige that it lost as it became redefined as a repetitive and trivial task that could be performed by women. Another example is the medical profession, characterized by enormous prestige and financial reward in the United States, where doctors are mostly male. In the former Soviet Union, where the same profession is identified with women, it is accorded much lower status, the typical salary being less than that of certain manual laborers. We may be on the verge of witnessing the same phenomenon in certain branches of law and medicine in the United States, as more and more women gain jobs in those fields. It is not the task itself, but the meaning attributed to it, the evaluative component, from which it derives its status.

In Victorian times, it was observed by Italian dentists that female patients fainted from pain less often than did male patients. This difference was defined not as women's greater strength or courage but as their inferior powers of sensation. Similarly, girls, quicker than boys at intellectual tasks in school, were considered not brighter but more shallow than their slower male counterparts (Russett 1989). "Not-speed" rather than speed became the virtue. It is obvious to us in retrospect that there is a higher-level abstraction involved: maleness is the virtue, femaleness always inferior by definition.

How much has this perspective changed in one hundred years? Joan Schulman has commented on the manner in which certain legislatures in the United States have extended marital protections to cohabiting couples:

> While men in these unmarried cohabiting relationships are increasingly granted the "marital privilege" of rape, women in these relationships have fared far worse in their attempts to obtain privileges of marriage such as spousal support ("palimony"), division of the couple's property or civil orders of protection. In the few states where unmarried women are accorded these rights, courts have first required an express or implied agreement between the parties. No such requirement is made with respect to the expansion of the marital rape exemption. [Schulman 1980, pp. 538–40]

The meanings of women's sexuality in this society, and the uses to which men put it, provide another clear example that it is the male who has the power to define, invade, and engulf, violently or not, to interpret female sexuality as an extension of his. Perhaps the most apparent aspect of women's sexuality in this society is that, as demonstrated by much feminist work and highlighted in a book by Carole Vance (1984), it lies at the intersection of pleasure and danger. Women are constantly at risk in public and in private for sexual harassment, violence, and abuse. They are in danger from strangers and from the men they know and love and perhaps even trust. Women who are raped by their husbands report more long-lasting effects (Russell 1982) and become more sexually dysfunctional than women raped by dates or strangers (Bart 1985).

Here is a fraction of the shocking statistics:

> In a sample of 3,187 women, 1 in 4 had been subject to a completed or an attempted rape; 84 percent of them knew their attackers; 57 percent of the incidents had occurred on dates; the average age of the victim was eighteen and a half (Warshaw 1988).
>
> At least one-third of all females are introduced to sex by being molested by a "trusted" family member.

At least half of all women are raped at least once in their lives.

At least half of all adult women are battered in their own homes by husbands or lovers (Walker 1979). Eleven to 15 percent of married women report having been raped by their husbands (Finklehor and Yllo 1985).

Attacks on wives by husbands result in more injuries requiring treatment than do rapes, muggings, and automobile accidents combined; one-third of all women murdered are killed by their husbands or boyfriends (*New York Times* 1984).

Approximately 85 percent of working women are sexually harassed at their jobs (*New York Times* 1984).

According to the U.S. Department of Justice (Heise 1989), a woman is beaten in the United States every fifteen seconds; at least four women are killed by their batterers each day; a rape is committed in the United States every six minutes.

Internationally the statistics are not any better:

In Nicaragua, 44 percent of men admit to having beaten their wives.

In Peru, 70 percent of all crimes reported to the police are of women beaten by their partners.

In 1985, 54 percent of all murders in Austria were committed in the family, with women and children constituting 90 percent of the victims.

In Papua, New Guinea, 67 percent of rural women and 56 percent of urban women have been victims of wife abuse.

Of 8,000 abortions performed at a clinic in Bombay, 7,999 of the fetuses were found to be female (*Z Magazine,* July/August 1989, p. 61).

These statistics, as well as the variety of stories I have heard as a therapist, an educator, and a friend, are by no means extraordinary. Any group of women could undoubtedly produce a similar range of experiences. The following examples of women's sexual initiations and experiences are composites, drawn from different women I have treated; nothing is invented.

As a child, Anne had been repeatedly molested by her father, a devout Catholic who insisted, all the while he was molesting both of his daughters, that they be given a religious education in a parochial school. As is typical in such cases, her father warned her not to reveal to anyone what occurred between them. She never told any of the nuns what was happening in her home for fear that they would either punish her or not believe her. After several months in therapy as an adult, Anne decided to confront her father. He beat her up and promised to do it again if she ever spoke to him or anyone else about the incidents.

Shortly thereafter, Anne met a man in her Christian Bible study class who was sympathetic and concerned and seemed, in every way, to be the opposite of her father. They began to spend a great deal of time together, and soon Paul declared his love for her and his desire to marry her. In keeping with their religious beliefs, there had been no physical contact between them. After Paul's proposal, Anne confided in him her father's treatment of her and her own fear of sexuality. He expressed his shock and concern and agreed that, should they marry, he would be willing to wait until she felt able to be sexual, no matter how long it took. This was in keeping with his religious beliefs, as was the fact that he, too, had maintained his virginity for marriage.

They married and spent a stormy two years of celibacy together, during which time Paul grew more and more impatient. On two occasions, he struck Anne, although he later apologized profusely. Finally they decided that they should live apart. After they separated, Anne was attacked and raped in the street by a stranger while she was returning home one afternoon from a class. Paul, upon hearing the news from her on the telephone, became despondent. Several hours later, he appeared at her door. When she let him in, he seemed agitated and began to repeat over and over, "Even if we are separated, you are still my wife and I have my rights." Beginning to understand what he was getting at, Anne grew frightened and asked him to leave. Instead he forced her onto the bed, tore her clothes off, and raped her again. He later apologized and said that he didn't know what had come over him. Anne never saw him again, but she could not easily dismiss a lifetime of learning to whom her body belonged.

When I first saw Diane, she was severely depressed and suicidal. Her life seemed painful and meaningless to her. As I got to know her, I discovered not meaninglessness, but acutely painful experiences, from which she drew meaning about her own life as a woman. She revealed to me that her sexual initiation at the age of twelve had consisted of a "gang bang" party that her father had thrown for all his drunkard friends. When they were finished, he had laughed at her and said, "I hope you know your place now." He had thought her a bit too rebellious before that. For a long time, she became even more rebellious and compulsively sought out sex with anyone at any *time. Sixteen years later, she saw and felt no connection between the gang rape and her repeated cutting of herself and involvement with drugs.*

Although Judy had been molested as a child, she considered sex with her husband to be satisfactory. They had married right after high school and he had been her only partner. Yet he often touched her brusquely, hurting her and making her freeze rather than respond warmly. Foreplay was extremely brief and goal-directed. She felt that something was wrong with her ability to respond. Long after she became aware of the connections between her response to her husband and her childhood experiences, she asked him to touch her in the ways she preferred. He insisted that he felt rejected, and that the problem was hers and not his if she could not respond to exactly what he liked to do. He pointed out that he had never had this problem with any of his girlfriends prior to their marriage.

Melanie left an abusive home at the age of seventeen to live with the family of her aunt and uncle. Until the time she moved out four years later to be married and to live in a home with her husband, she was coerced into having sex with her uncle in exchange for her room and board. Although she was not a willing partner, she did not really understand what was happening to her and feared that, if she refused, she would be sent back to her own abusive parents. She has never thought of herself as having been molested or raped.

Sally repeatedly discussed with her therapist the one time she had been raped. At one point in their discussion, she mentioned that her father and two brothers had forced her to have sex with them. She did not consider this to be rape. Less extremely, perhaps, many married women who have been forced to have sex with their husbands would concur, as would their husbands, that this is not rape, but the exercising of conjugal rights.

Laura, a woman in her fifties, is proud of having cleverly talked her way out of a threatened rape by flattering the rapist. She convinced him that he was so masculine that he did not have to prove it by raping her, and he ultimately agreed.

Maureen's childhood experience included no apparent sexual violations, although her father would consistently trot her out to display her to his adult male friends. They would comment on how pretty she was and often would think of their sons or other boys her age who might like to go out with her. She did not think of herself as pretty and so was pleased with this attention. She grew up aware of her own sexuality only when she was able to arouse a particular man. And she was eager to please the men who found her attractive. Seeing them turned on would then turn her on. She was obsessed with her appearance and spent many hours reading women's magazines, shopping for clothing, and trying out new cosmetics, hairstyles, and hair color. Maureen was the epitome of normal femininity.

Harriet reports first being aware of sexuality when her breasts began to develop while she was in seventh grade. As they were large, they became the subject of constant attention from boys at school. In addition to humiliating comments, the boys made a game of running up to her in the hallways between classes and touching her breasts. They would then, as a group, laugh and ridicule her. The humiliation stayed with her and, in her late twenties, she finally underwent breast reduction surgery. Unfortunately, her humiliation and self-hatred could not be surgically removed.

These are all cases of physical, psychological, and symbolic violations. By the latter, I mean men's usurpation of meanings about women's bodies, feelings, and needs. Once men make their own meanings, they not only believe them to the exclusion of any others but they act on them in intrusive and violent ways. Women's physically and sexually based limits come to be delineated by men's needs and sense of entitlement. All these physical violations are accomplished and justified through the making of meanings by men. In this way, men violate women's most basic sense of self and integrity.

And what of that minority who have experienced male aggression only in public? Can they continue to experience sexuality freely in private if they have not been damaged in private? Is the distinction between public and private even a valid one? Do women need reassurance from a partner who is gentle, affectionate, and patient rather than passionate? Do they need to lose themselves in a romantic experience? Women certainly have a reputation for needing romance and "foreplay"—a term that indicates something not to be taken seriously, something that precedes real sex. But several studies indicate that emotional intimacy and closeness with a partner are more important to women than achieving orgasm (Hite 1976; Jayne 1981; Bell 1972). Although women have the most intense orgasms, both physiologically and subjectively (according to their own reports; Masters and Johnson 1966; Fisher 1973; Kinsey et al. 1953), during masturbation, they do not seem to consider it the most pleasurable sexual activity. Women are, with sexuality and other matters, generally sensitive to context, whereas men are more able and ready to have sex decontextualized.

145

In fact, in the days before women's perspective on it was considered, rape was thought to be uncommon and aberrant. Later, it became clear that it is common enough to be considered, if not normative male behavior, then certainly a normal male fantasy. Through the work of feminists, women's view and the frequency of rape were made visible. Now, although it is too common to be considered deviant, rape is still all too often viewed not through women's but through Oedipus' eyes, blind to any but his own needs.

Several studies have shown that unattractive victims are more often assigned more responsibility than attractive ones for their own rape (Deitz, Littman, and Bentley 1984; Seligman, Brickman, and Koulack 1977; Thornton and Ryckman 1983; Tieger 1981). Seligman, Brickman, and Koulack (1977) have suggested that this phenomenon be understood as attractive women being raped because they are attractive, whereas unattractive women must have encouraged or provoked it. Either way, the meaning is about the victim and not the rapist; one way or another, she asked for it. Many studies have shown that males attribute more responsibility to rape victims than do females (Calhoun et al. 1978). Many men would seem to have a positive interest in committing rape as well. In various studies, 35 percent (Malamuth 1981), 44 percent (Check and Malamuth 1983), and 51 percent (Malamuth, Haber, and Feshbach 1980) of males sampled reported that they would rape if they knew they could get away with it. Not all men are potential rapists, but all women are vulnerable to sexual assault or rape.

Rape, as well as unforced intercourse, defines action and status for men, as reflected in the language. In our society, the expletive "Fuck you!" is perhaps the most serious insult one person can level at another. What does this tell us about the meanings attributed to sex and to women? It is *being* fucked that demeans. Apparently fucking is seen as something that one person, a man, does to another, a woman or womanlike person, to express hatred and dominance. The one not in the dominant position is culturally equated with one of the strongest forms of degradation. In certain other cultures and some ethnic groups in our own culture, the insult is extended to getting another man's mother into that degrading-*for-her* position. Rather than being aggressive and demeaning, why isn't the expression a compliment? Why does the very same fuck enhance the male and degrade the female? For precisely the reason that it is not the very same fuck, but his and hers. It expresses succinctly just how different the meanings of masculine and feminine sexuality are.

If his makes him potent and powerful, then hers makes her powerless and even able to be overpowered. The more power he can exert, the more potent he is judged and feels himself to be. The rapist is a powerful masculine figure. If masculinist culture defines male sexuality in terms of power, then power is built into male sexuality. So is entitlement. Rape is not just violence, then, but directly related to, a predominant form of, oedipal sexuality.

As Susan Sontag has aptly commented, "Without a change in the very norms of sexuality, the liberation of women is a meaningless goal. Sex as such is not liberating for women. Neither is more sex" (1973, p. 188). Oedipal sexuality is at the heart of the physical and psychological construction of women. It is what makes women subject to adulation and humiliation, to protection and violation, to being considered to desire whatever men do to them. Women's development is limited by oedipal entitlement and expansiveness epistemologically, physically, and psychologically.

7

Self and Esteem

Everything not forbidden is compulsory.　　　　　　　—T. H. White
　　　　　　　　　　　　　　　　　　　　　　The Once and Future King

Although they emerge from a particular world view, many concepts acquire validity by consensus in a particular culture and appear to its members to be a matter of common sense. Self-esteem, both what it is and how it manifests itself in women in this society, seemed apparent to me as I began to write about it. I have certainly spent enough clinical and nonclinical hours listening to women discuss their sense of self and personal value or, more frequently, the mixture of worth and worthlessness they feel toward and about themselves. Yet beginning a discussion of self-esteem presupposes a particular notion of how the self is constructed and embodied and just what it means to esteem or value that self. Before moving on to consider esteem, let us pause to examine a term we all use repeatedly and whose meaning most of us take for granted. Just what is "the self"?

THE SELF: A SOCIAL CONSTRUCT
BECOMES PERSONAL

Each person's experience is woven of a combination of the complex meanings of the culture and significant influences within it, filtered through personal experience, a degree of choice and chance, and certain biological and genetic aspects and predispositions, such as health, talents, abilities, and perhaps temperamental disposition (Kagan 1984, 1989). The ideal self is made up of the most desirable qualities of masculinity without acknowledgment of any bias. That is, the mature and well-developed self is considered to be separate from others, consistent within any context, autonomous, and independent. The notion of the self reflects a Western, and particularly North American, emphasis on the separateness of the individual and on individuality itself. Gordon Allport (1960) and others have noted the Western predilection for defining people on the basis of their separation from their life contexts. That is, a sharp boundary between inner and outer is culturally and psychologically constructed and eventually believed to exist naturally.

This sort of self is neither natural nor innate; it is a relatively recent Euro-American social invention. Its origins can be traced to the High Middle Ages (Berman 1988). It is only since that period that, for example, homicide with malice aforethought has been identified as a criminal act for which one can be held personally responsible by the judicial system. And Western artists, prior to the Renaissance, did not consider it necessary to sign their works. Even experiences that we consider internal and personal, such as dreams, were understood differently. "Medieval accounts of dreams . . . are not tied to self-examination, because dreams were regarded as imposed experiences, external to the dreamer. The search for self . . . was not an inward search in a twentieth-century existential sense" (Berman 1988, p. 182).

As interest in introspection increased, so did themes of personal responsibility and guilt, along with the role, in the Catholic Church, of the priest as confessor. Within Christianity, there also developed growing agreement that the marital contract was based upon consent rather than coitus. Even the popularity of individual portraiture returned as the sense of inwardness and personal responsibility increased.

René Descartes's famous dictum, "I think, therefore I am," emphasizes not only rationality but individuality. There is a separate *I* who does the thinking and who can stand alone in verifying its existence. Herein lie the roots of the modern Western self. Later in the seventeenth century, the philosophical viewpoints that were to define the modern self were systematized by Leibnitz, who conceived of individuals as made up of infinitessimally small monads that have no means of communication with each other (May 1989). The development of belief in individualism and rationalism reached its apex in the Enlightenment period of the eighteenth century with the ideas of Voltaire, Locke, Berkeley, and Hume. "It is tremendously interesting that the height of the Enlightenment occurred during the decades of the 1770's and 1780's, at exactly the time when the Declaration of Independence, the American Constitution, and the other documents crucial for the birth of America were written" (May 1989, p. 519). The developing belief in individuality clearly influenced the writers of those documents.

The work of Freud was both a move away from this notion of separateness and individuality to the importance of familial relationships in determining individual development and, at the same time, an affirmation of the "self" with its hidden sexual and aggressive aspects (Lowe 1982). Alfred Adler went much further in attributing neurosis to the isolation of people from one another, and Harry Stack Sullivan especially emphasized the centrality of interpersonal experience.

Our culture's emphasis on individuality and separateness also includes a strong sense of personal identity and responsibility: one's actions, beliefs, and values are considered to reflect directly on the quality of one's self. Western and particularly American cultural values lead us to believe that we possess, at the core, one true self that should be and, when functioning correctly, is consistent over time and across situations. Our educational system is oriented toward rights and freedom, at least for males, rather than toward obligations and duties, as it is in the East (Hsu 1971). That is, the explicit purpose of Western education is to afford the individual more freedom, opportunity, and mobility and not greater connection to the group. Once having developed a stable self-concept, we labor to keep it by organizing experience in that way. We pick out, for example, what is and isn't characteristic of us as individuals. A particular way of behaving may be considered superficial or merely a social identity, not the "real" identity or self.

This construction of a separate and individual self directly reflects the masculinist predilection to make invisible the context and interconnections between people and all living things. This is the same perspective that leads to perceiving concepts as universal rather than as contextually bound. Similarly, psychological models that concern themselves with the core construct of a self typically approach it as something that is universally applicable. That is, not only *the* self but the particular *kind* of self that is valued and taught to Western children is considered the universally desirable self.

And insofar as our culture encourages development of and belief in an autonomous self, most of its members labor to construct such a self. If they fail, they feel a lesser sense of worth. Only in Western cultures is the sense of a separate self so highly revered and so vigorously pursued, from striving to be one's "own man" (never one's "own woman") or a "self-made man" to our legal and ethical notions of personal responsibility. Justice, like Oedipus, is blind.

In contrast to this world view, Eastern cultures, such as those of China, India, and Japan, view people as interrelated, and nature as something to be intimately experienced and lived in rather than to be observed, analyzed, and exploited for man's needs. Eastern societies tend to teach becoming part of the group so that no one's individuality stands out (Kojima 1984). In the West, space is considered to be neutral and mathematical, while in Asia space connects the earth with the divine (Eliade 1959); it is never empty, either physically or psychologically. While much Eastern art is concerned with nature and the physical world, Western art is frequently involved with "the Self and its dilemmas" (Berman 1989, p. 337). Often the task in Eastern art is to stay within a genre rather than having to invent a new one, the hallmark of the Western artistic genius.

"The individual's self-concept is not actively developed in Japan to the extent that it is in the United States. There is no show-and tell in Japanese schools. Children aren't encouraged to have a personal opinion" (Bell 1989, p. 50). Many Eastern cultures view infants as too independent, in need of training in dependence and connectedness. Since selflessness is highly valued, the experience, definition, and expression of the self may be quite different from that in our culture (Yang and Chiu 1988). African researchers have also indicated that "in traditional African life, an individual did not and could not stand alone" (Olowu 1988). The greater independence Western children are typically taught and allowed comes to be seen as natural. The turmoil of the adolescent search for self and identity is a direct outgrowth of this teaching. I am not advocating one or the other of these world views, but simply pointing out that both are socially constructed and historically grounded, and that each varies according to gender.

It is, no doubt, apparent that women in our culture stand somewhere between these two sets of values. They are viewed as having obligations to and responsibility for others that often override, or at least supplement, those to themselves. Female identity is situated in the "in between." The ideal for women is different from that for people in general, and both cannot be achieved at the same time by any one woman. Each woman must fail even as she succeeds.

Although the use of the word *self* conveys a single, definite thing, rather than a set of multiple and complex interacting processes or constellations, various aspects of oneself actually become salient in different situations and at different times, depending upon a multitude of factors. Some theorists describe this as our having different selves, but this too isolates and fragments rather than considering the complex organization of feelings and thoughts. It is these constellations that may emerge at any particular moment.

In a witty novel called *The Mind-Body Problem* (1983), Rebecca Goldstein puts forth the notion that everyone has a "mattering map," on which are located, either centrally or peripherally, those things that have meaning or that matter to the person. Such a map would have to be multidimensional and elastic, and would have to accommodate not only beliefs and values but feelings, behaviors, and thoughts—all manner of experience. Clearly, any person's experience is too complex and multiply determined to be able to be mapped completely by any one method, or even by several overlapping methods; it is both stable and in flux.

For example, a woman could enter a culture that considers the epitome of feminine beauty to be the possession of earlobes hanging to her shoulders. If, for any variety of reasons, she were to value and give meaning to that culture and its standards, she might try to stretch her earlobes or else evaluate herself as not measuring up. In the second case, she might apply to herself the abstract principle that she doesn't fit the prevailing standard of beauty; otherwise she might just be bemused by it. In an unresolved Antigone state, a woman sees the way oedipal society or individual Oedipuses see. His experience and meanings are hers and would fall at the center of her mattering map.

The Self in Psychology

Western culture has been strongly influenced by psychological perspectives such as the Freudian and neo-Freudian (object relations and self-psychology), so that most of us consider the self, if we purposefully consider it at all, to be formed in early childhood through interaction primarily or exclusively with one's mother. Most people, both within and outside the psychological disciplines, believe that by middle childhood a self crystallizes; the person has become who she or he is and essentially will be throughout life. Some of the qualities of this self are considered inborn, others learned, and many a mixture of the two.

The issue of the development and organization of the self has been considered by virtually every major theorist of Western psychology, from Freud and his contemporaries, such as Jung, Horney, and Adler, to contemporary neo-Freudian object-relations psychologists extending the work of Melanie Klein, including D. W. Winnicott (1960, 1964, 1965, 1969), Heinz Kohut (1971, 1977), James Masterson (1985), and Alice Miller (1981). Masterson has written extensively about the "real self," while Winnicott, Miller, and other object-relations theorists speak of the "true self" and the "false self." The former is considered to be authentic and at the hidden core of the self. At an outer, more accessible layer is the false self, developed as a protection and adaptation to a damaging psychological environment early in life. These theorists consider it to arise as a result of failures in early maternal nurturance. All these approaches have in common the assumption that there is a true and independent self which, for optimal healthy functioning, should develop in a way that leads to greater cohesion, stability, separation, and individuation. Object-relations thought, from Klein's good and bad breast—a concrete, embodied, and mother-centered representation of the good/bad dichotomy—to the true and false self, avails itself of the dualistic modes that are characteristic of Western thought, in lieu of considering multiple processes or even gradations of categories. These theories see people, indeed life itself, as black or white, true or false, masculine or feminine.

The notion of the good and bad breast divides the experience of the mother's body, each breast being considered apart from the other. The existence of one hill does not allow for a valley, much less for a complex, varied terrain. It is assumed that the infant lacks peripheral vision and thinks in the separate, binary categories and terms of adult masculinist thought. Each infant is a little Descartes: "I suck, therefore I am."

Psychoanalytic-existential contributions include those of Ernest Becker (1971, 1973), who considered the self an abstraction based upon physical and interpersonal experience. The humanistic branch of existential thought has been represented in American psychology by Abraham Maslow, who offered a model of self-actualization of the "separate and autonomous individual" (Maslow 1970, p. 196), and by Carl Rogers, whose concern with the self was also manifested in a particular model of individual growth and development. Any person lacking a sharp delineation of self is considered to be the product of, depending on perspective, a lower level of hierarchical development (Maslow), dependency problems (psychodynamic), symbiosis (family systems), splitting, or just plain defective boundaries (object relations). Constant striving to become an individualized entity and to develop a separate identity is at the core of selfness in our culture.

The Self-in-Context

In a recent study (de Rivera 1989), Americans reported that their sense of self changes only 5 to 10 percent in different situations, while Japanese subjects reported a 95 to 99 percent change. Since Americans subscribe culturally and personally to a belief in a consistent and unchanging core self, to be changeable is to be psychologically unstable.

Although the self and self-esteem are commonly located within the individual and considered to be personal attributes, the recent theoretical work of Joseph Veroff (1983), Walter Mischel (1984), and Patricia Gurin (1985), among others, has highlighted the impossibility of isolating any stable personality characteristic out of a particular context. For example, it has been demonstrated in a variety of sociological and psychological studies (Latane and Darley 1970) that whether a person will help someone in distress depends on the particulars of the situation, including such determinants as whether others are watching.

Feminist theorists such as Nancy Chodorow, Carol Gilligan, Susie Orbach and Luise Eichenbaum, and the Stone Center theorists, including Jean Baker Miller (1984), Judith Jordan, and Janet Surrey (1986), have spoken of the female relational self or self-in-relation—the concept that women and men appear to differ consistently in certain situations and certain kinds of relatedness. The definition of self I want to propose here extends the model I have developed in the previous chapters to a *self-in-context*. That is, the self is an abstract concept by means of which meaning and consistency are attributed to a person in context. The very sense of self is a metaphor, an organizing concept. Rather than speaking of the individual as having or being a self, it may be more accurate to speak of a *sense* of self, which includes the physical, affective, and cognitive experiences associated with this metaphor. The emerging sense of self is a set of abstract symbols and, at the same time, an embodiment of the abstract. The sense of self weaves together self-concept and self-esteem in a skein of meaning. Only by keeping the context in view can the developing sense of self and of self-esteem be understood.

For example, a woman interacting with her husband, children, lawyer, clients, professor, or students may draw upon different qualities and behaviors when with these different people. Are some qualities and behaviors more real, more consistent, more at the core, than others? Different aspects of the context call up different behaviors and experiences within a certain range of consistency. I don't mean to suggest that they are merely a function of situations and other people, but that the demands of a situation, as interpreted by the people in it, evoke certain ways of behaving/feeling/

thinking. For example, in two studies I conducted with a colleague in the United States (Kaschak and Sharratt, 1989) and in Costa Rica (Kaschak and Sharratt 1989), males and females reported that they behaved in more stereotypically masculine or feminine ways depending upon the gender of the people they were with. Both genders in both countries behaved most stereotypically in the presence of males.

There is not one certain kind of self for all women. Instead there are differences as a function of race and class, differences between women in these groups as a result of unique combinations of experience and unique meanings made of those experiences. And the differences within a woman in different situations depend upon the meanings they evoke for her. Work by Jerome Kagan (1984) in Guatemala and in the New York Longitudinal Study (Thomas et al. 1963; Thomas and Chess 1977), among others, suggests that personality is not set in place indelibly in early childhood, but changes, often according to social position and life experiences. This is not to say that there is not great consistency, but not to exaggerate it into stasis so that it obscures complexity. Each person is both like and unlike any other.

One way to find consistency is by looking for it and drawing a boundary around it. In the United States, in fact, people usually insist upon doing so. For example, in a couples session I conducted, one partner repeatedly and paradoxically told the other that something she did was "uncharacteristic" of her. How many times would she have had to do something before the boundary could shift enough for that behavior to become characteristic of her, or even characteristic of her in certain circumstances? A change that is visible and understood must occur in the meaning of the behavior and not just in the behavior itself. A dogged belief in consistency obscures one's vision.

SELF-ESTEEM

Like the self, self-esteem has also been defined with masculinity as the norm and without a view of context. Stanley Coopersmith has defined self-esteem as "the evaluation which the individual makes and customarily maintains with regard to *himself*: it expresses an attitude of approval or disapproval, and indicates the extent to which the individual believes *himself* to be capable, significant, successful, and worthy. In short, self-esteem is a personal judgment of worthiness" (1967, pp. 4–5; italics added). This defini-tion also reflects and reinforces society's emphasis on individuality.

Although we tend to use *self-concept* to refer to the set of beliefs one has about the self, and *self-esteem* to refer to the feelings about or evaluation of these beliefs, I suggest that they are not separable any more than the cognitive is ever separable from the affective, or either is from the evalua-tive: one cannot be expressed without expressing the other. I propose, then, to use the term *self-esteem* in a less divided way, to include the cognitive, affective, and evaluative aspects of the attributions one makes about one's identity and communicates to oneself and others in a multitude of ways. I consider *self-concept* to be interchangeable with, rather than additive to or different from, *self-esteem*—especially for women, since virtually every-thing about women is evaluated. How women look, talk, eat, study, and behave at work, in the family, and in the role of parent are all evaluated differently than they are for men. In fact, men are not typically evaluated at all on many of these dimensions.

That the self is always gendered is by now a given, and I will soon show how self-esteem is also gendered. Attention to the full context in which the meanings of self-esteem are made and maintained for women lead to the two questions I will address in the following section: (1) For women, what judgments of what qualities in what situations enter into self-esteem? (2) How does self-esteem differ in the abstract and in practice for males and for females?

The Paradox of Women's Self-Esteem

Every so-called personal attribute is filtered through the gender system, and studies suggest that more than half the words commonly used in the English language have evaluative connotations (Osgood, Suci, and Tanenbaum 1957). So one can't really say much of anything about oneself that is not both gendered and evaluated. Try it. "I am . . . tall, short, fat, thin, smart, stupid, kind, timid." Each quality matters differently for a female and a male, as well as for particular females or males in particular situations and interactions. This is one way that the meaningful context is incorporated into the sense of self.

Although some girls and women these days can participate in careers, athletic competition, and other previously exclusively male domains, there abound subtle and not-so-subtle messages about the likelihood of engaging in these activities and remaining feminine. A female gymnast is cute. A six-foot-tall female basketball player is not so cute, and may in fact be the butt of jokes. On a recently televised women's basketball game, the commentator rhetorically asked of the audience, obviously assumed to be generically male, "How would you like to be on a date with her? One false move and she'd be able to deck you."

Women's development and identity are characterized by no one trait more than paradox. Within any positive choice is embedded the negative: no aspect is purely positive, and any positive aspect will often be followed by an equally intense negative with which it is intertwined. Women's self-esteem is located at the interstices of the positive and the negative. A woman who *just* works, *just* parents, or does both is open to both praise and criticism. It is impossible to imagine how she could attain untarnished praise and purely positive self-esteem, no matter what she chose. Not surprising, then, that Linda Carli (1990) finds that women, from homemakers to executives, who speak assertively and confidently are listened to less by male audiences than those who speak hesitantly and deferentially. Among the adolescent girls she studied, Donna Eder (1990) found that those in the popular group were inevitably disliked by the other girls, who branded them as "stuck up."

Perhaps the most basic paradox here is that the gendered self develops based on the need for love and approval and the consequent self-esteem it is hoped they will bring. These motivate the child and the adult to conform to society's gender prescriptions, to the expectations and demands of significant others. To seek approval and safety, to avoid humiliation and danger, most people develop the gendered selves they are expected to develop. But as women elicit approval for developing an appropriately gendered self, so do they lose approval and self-esteem because women and femininity are devalued and denigrated. Only women are, for example, unequivocally praised for eating less or even starving themselves, for taking up less space, for putting others' needs before their own. Would a man proudly tell of having consumed only five hundred calories all day? Only under highly unusual circumstances. Would he serve food to his family and eat only when they have finished, as is the custom in many Third World families as well as in many in the United States?

In our society, displaying appropriately feminine behavior (such as good mothering) is no accomplishment, as the counterpart might be viewed for a man, but simply doing what is expected. Women are encouraged to develop less autonomous and individual selves, but if they do so, they are judged immature or even pathological. If women develop more autonomously, they are then judged as inappropriately masculine. For example, women who put their own needs before those of their children are judged harshly, while men are expected to do so. Fathers who remain actively involved with their children after a divorce or who seek custody are applauded, while mothers are expected to do so and judged harshly if they do not.

Whether a woman develops in the direction of interpersonal sensitivity and connectedness or separateness, assertiveness or passivity, or more likely some combination, how these qualities are valued by her and by others obviously depends on what the larger oedipal culture values for women. Although there are ideal qualities that are valued in the abstract, in the particular gendered situation, the very same qualities, including self-esteem, are judged differently for females and for males. A timid and fearful man is evaluated differently from a timid and fearful woman, as is an assertive or competent man versus an assertive or competent woman. Competence tends to be seen as inappropriate for women (Nieva 1981). Women who behave competently can be discounted, disliked, or excluded (Hagan and Kahn 1975), or at least their behavior itself can be discounted (Deaux and Emswiller 1974; Nieva 1981). An active sense of humor is also considered inappropriate for women only. It has been observed in many settings that it is usually men who tell jokes; women's joke-telling attempts are often ignored. Their sense of humor is expected to be responsive appreciation rather than active participation.

There is an entire literature in social psychology dealing with attribution, a segment of which concerns what attributions are made to people when all known information about them is equivalent or held constant with the exception of gender. In such situations, men and work believed to be done by men are typically evaluated more favorably than are women and their work (Goldberg 1968; Mischel 1974). Even in situations where members of both gender groups have achieved outstanding success, as in the case of award-winning professors, women and men may be finally rated as equally competent but their success is attributed to different and predictably stereotyped qualities: the men's to their power and competence, the women's to their sense of concern and likeableness (Kaschak 1978, 1981).

Women have been observed to smile more than men when talking in same-gender (La France and Carmen 1980; Frances 1979) or mixed-gender pairs (Ickes and Turner 1983; Pilkonis 1977), when photographed (Ragan 1982), when greeting strangers (Henley 1977; Mackey 1976), and even when criticizing children (Bugental, Love, and Gianetto 1971). A study by Francine Deutsch, Dorothy LeBaron, and Maury Fryer (1987), based on these observations, suggested that women are judged more harshly than men when they fail to perform warm and expressive nonverbal behaviors.

Supposedly neutral empirical research has both reflected and perpetuated the bias of the researchers in particular and of the society in which they/we live in general. In the service of maintaining an androcentric perspective on and definition of self-esteem, basic methodological principles have been violated and the gendered self has been built into theories and models of self-esteem. One of the major researchers and writers in the empirical psychology of self-esteem, Stanley Coopersmith (1967), conducted the bulk of his research on male samples, from which he then claimed to extract gender-neutral models and scales of self-esteem. As a result, women must respond as must the males in these samples in order to achieve a good measure of self-esteem. However, part of the reason these samples were comprised only of males is the very fact that females do respond differently. The data on females that do not match those of the male subjects are eliminated or excluded from the start. According to this irrational methodology, girls and women are excluded from the development of the measure of self-esteem to which they will subsequently be held. Predictably, physical attractiveness was not a salient factor in Coopersmith's all-male sample and thus is not considered central to matters of self-esteem. The elimination or exclusion of female data almost fails to startle by now, so common has this blindness become in certain studies ("What kind of man is this anyway?"). The shape of the answer is contained in the question.

William James dealt extensively with the concept of self-esteem, which he considered to be a function of how well our achievements meet our aspirations. For example, if one is a psychologist, one's knowledge in that area may be more important to one's self-esteem than knowledge of, say, Greek. But do women judge themselves against what they can reasonably do or be as women, or as men, or as people—which, in oedipal society, still seems to mean men? The lower aspirations of women in areas to which they have been denied access would, according to this reasoning, not result in lowered self-esteem. But women's self-esteem is obviously severely impaired by the cultural messages that they should not be competent or powerful or exercise mastery in many areas. Women's experience and perspectives are invisible in this definition, as are those of all people who lack the privilege of access to free choice, upon which James's definition is based.

According to James, the self is "the sum total of all that he can call his, not only his body and his psychic process, but his clothes and his house, his wife and his children, his ancestors and his friends, his reputation and his works, his lands and his horses, and yacht and bank account. All these things give him the same emotions" (James 1890). Realizing that he wrote these words a century ago, perhaps we can excuse James his unexamined assumption that esteem is for men, and that women are one of the possessions by means of which men can achieve esteem. How, then, to defend Coopersmith, who, in a revised edition to *The Antecedents of Self-Esteem* a mere decade ago, found no need to question this assumption. Nor did he see any need to include fathers in the study of parental effects on self-esteem of the child, but instead got information on the role of the father from sons and mothers—women being seen only as the mothers of boys and otherwise invisibly subsumed within the (generic) category of males. In this model, self-esteem is about how boys are influenced directly by their mothers and indirectly by their fathers.

According to Coopersmith, how much respectful, accepting, and concerned treatment a person receives is paramount to that individual's development of self-respect, but is mitigated by the individual's ability "to define an event filled with negative implications and consequences in such a way that it does not detract from his sense of worthiness, ability, or power" (p. 37). What definition should a girl apply to her own self-worth when she is not even included in the development of theories and measures of self-worth? Women often do not feel esteemed, or easily esteem themselves, beneath the surface because it is the surface from which their esteem derives. Anything beneath the surface must be hidden unless it can be attractively and femininely packaged. Kathleen Musa and Mary Roach (1973), for example, found no relationship between self-evaluation of appearance and psychological well-being for boys, but a strong one for girls. If it cannot be presented to the world, there must be something wrong with it.

Many women have learned to present a confident adult face to the outside world but, in their own minds and often in the intimacy of the therapy hour, talk of how they deserve to be abused or mistreated or abandoned; how deep inside themselves they feel that it is their own fault; how something is fundamentally wrong with them as people or as females; how afraid they are that no one will ever love or want them, that they will never be asked out on another date or participate in another love relationship. Adolescent males and females seem, in many ways, to be similarly dissatisfied with themselves. The difference is that most males are able to outgrow this low esteem and, as a group, arrive at a significant sense of positive self-esteem (Lyell 1973). Females do not.

On a local radio talk show, I recently heard the ex-wives of several movie stars, beautiful and accomplished women by the predominant standard of our society, talk of feeling, after divorce, that no man would want them and of being extremely grateful when *any* man asked them for a date. Their own feelings toward this hypothetical "anyman" ran a far second to their wishes to be desired by a hypothetical man. Their self-esteem was enhanced by

being in a relationship. These women had followed all the rules of femininity in this society and this was their reward: even by winning, they had lost.
Their task became the struggle, late in life, to develop a more positive and
less relational sense of self. The more traditionally feminine the woman, the
more difficult the task.

Many women have explained to me that one reason they married was to
become wives rather than daughters, or that after divorcing they chose to
retain their married names in order to remain wives (adults) rather than
daughters (children). If adulthood for women is too often based on relationships to men, their choice becomes which man's name to carry and by
which man to be defined. While a *Miss* usually changes to *Mrs.* after
marriage, *Mr.* remains himself. The recent increase in the number of
women who keep their father's name after marriage speaks of an attempt
to achieve adulthood in other, more visible ways. Once again, this is only
partially successful. In a recent survey, at least 50 percent of females were
extremely critical of men's treatment of them, but 90 percent preferred
marriage to the single life (*San Francisco Chronicle*, April 26, 1990, p. 1).
The sort of adulthood they seem to achieve by marrying does not lead to
a sense of self-esteem or to psychological satisfaction in general.

Many of my clients have reported that, upon visiting their parents, they
experience themselves again as children, while retaining their adult perspectives. In the same way, an unmarried woman with a highly successful career
experienced herself as a failure, according to her parents' standards for her,
and as a success in her own contemporary world. Yet each was contained
in the other, such that she never felt like either a complete failure or an
unequivocal success.

Since the esteem of many women is directly embedded in the success of
their relationships, they must often sacrifice their own needs for the sake of
a partner or children. Although they have enormous responsibility for these
relationships, most women have little power to control them. This sense of
responsibility often leads women to attempt to control their partners and
children, resulting in everything from jokes and ridicule to pseudopsycho-
logical judgments of women, particularly mothers, as pathogenic or "co-
dependent" for doing just what is required of them (van Wormer 1989). As
a clear example of women's sense of responsibility and concomitant inability to affect the behavior of others, it has been estimated that nine out of
ten women stay with an alcoholic spouse, while nine out of ten men clearly
do not (Kinney and Leaton 1978).

I have talked with many women who were agonizing over important
decisions in their lives, but who expressed to me in various ways that they
had been taught that it is selfish even to think of their own needs and

certainly to put them before anyone else's. Again, they had learned that their self-esteem was based on self-sacrifice. Paradoxically, however, such sacrifice does not add unambivalently to their esteem, for it is only what women are supposed to do. Men also struggle to make decisions that will be beneficial to those they love, but they have not typically learned to evaluate negatively the very concern with their own needs.

A woman is seated in my office. She is unmarried and pregnant. The relationship with the father of her unborn child is an important and satisfying one for them both, but they are not prepared to marry, nor does he want a child. She wants the baby, but considers it selfish to place her own needs before those of others. She tells me she has decided to have the baby. A week later she returns to let me know that she has had an abortion. She just couldn't be that selfish, she tells me. She could easily consider her male partner justified in putting his own wishes first. Will she be blamed for ignoring the baby's needs? She will never be blamed for ignoring her own. Her sense of self-esteem and of having made the right choice was based on self-denial and concern first with her partner's wishes and needs.

As long as simply being a woman is judged as less or abnormal, women will suffer from damaged self-esteem. There must be a basic change in the masculine definitions of self and of self-esteem in order for the contradictions and paradoxes for women to be resolvable and resolved, as these contradictions arise first in the context and then become part of the female sense of self. An unambivalently positive path or paths must exist before women's self-esteem can ever be simply unambivalent. In oedipal society, both love and justice are considered to be blind. Women can no longer afford blindness of any kind.

Women and Mastery

An ongoing study of the top 1981 graduates from a wide range of schools in Illinois by Karen Arnold (1985) indicates that at the end of high school, 23 percent of the males and 21 percent of the females felt that they were above average in ability. By the end of college, 25 percent of the males and none of the females felt above average, although the women had actually done slightly better overall in college. Boys call out answers in class eight times as often as do girls: "If a girl gets that active in class, she is often regarded as an aggressive bitch instead of assertive and confident. By college, many girls are so used to being spectators in the educational process that they participate infrequently or put themselves down when they do" (Myra Sadker, Professor of Education, American University, in Arnold 1985). It has been repeatedly documented that women who attend all-female schools fare better not only in scholastic achievement but in the development of confidence and self-esteem (Lee and Bryk 1986). The recent refusal of students at Mills College, an all-women's college in Oakland, California, to bring in male students attests to the importance of this experience. It enables women to exist in a setting as full participants, to express positive traits without worrying about being judged negatively for them.

Several studies (Marks 1977; Crosby 1987; Baruch and Barnett 1979) suggest that multiple roles seem to enhance esteem for women by offering the potential to draw upon various sources. Meeting the multiple challenges of a complex job also seems to contribute to self-esteem (Merton 1949). For employed women, not just employment per se but a high-prestige job, rather than a husband, is the best prediction of well-being (Birnbaum 1975; Sears and Barbee 1977). I would suggest that the degree to which society and others who matter respect the task be included in this assessment. This same reversal of the traditional relationship is not, in general, true for men: their esteem is not enhanced, for example, by performing household or parenting tasks. Most women probably include relationships and parenting, along with work, on their mattering maps; most men emphasize work more heavily or exclusively. Certainly even these increased opportunities for esteem exact a price from women, as the stress required to perform these multiple roles is rewarded with little significant social or personal support, and possibilities for failure increase. Something will always have to be sacrificed for something else, as long as any problem with multiple roles is defined narrowly as "women's issues" or even more narrowly as an individual woman's problems.

Ironically, the problem for the coming generation is even more complex, as the changes instigated by the women's movement of the 1970s have failed to alter the Oedipus-Antigone relationship, whereby one subsumes the other. The generation of women currently coming of age is not really being offered qualitatively new roles. Just as androgyny was fatally defined as a combination of traditionally stereotyped masculine and traditional feminine attributes, so are women now faced with having to combine the roles of both traditional women and traditional men, and perform them both perfectly. In this sense, they must meet masculine criteria in two different arenas at the same time. These middle-class* or aspiring middle-class women must make a man's career for themselves while also mothering their children and taking primary responsibility for household chores. Mothers in the United States currently have less assistance with child care and housework than do mothers anywhere else in the world (Minturn and Lambert 1974). Between 74 and 92 percent of major tasks in married-couple households are still performed by wives, even when both partners are employed outside the home (Berheide 1984). Working mothers must dress for career success and, upon coming home, change into the garb of a traditional mother and housewife, and, later, of a seductive lover. As demonstrated in television commercials, this is accomplished by letting one's hair down, removing one's glasses, changing attire and perhaps perfume. These women must succeed as traditional men and traditional women in a society that supports neither role unambivalently for women.

Women who don't do both things may now also be evaluated and evaluate themselves more strictly. Once again, incompatible social/economic systems intersect within women, who wind up internalizing and embodying a conflict that undermines their sense of competence, effectiveness, and contentment. In an individual society, failure to meet all these incompatible role demands is identified as a personal failure. As women again, in a surplus of meaning, embody the conflicts of masculinist society, the true source of the conflicts is kept invisible. Unless drastic changes occur in the Oedipus-Antigone arrangement, I predict an increase among young women in eating disorders, depression, anxieties, and other individually located crossroads of these conflicts, which are impossible for the individual to resolve since they are not individual conflicts at all.

*This is probably the first time in history when we can begin to formulate a class system in which women can be included. The attribution of socioeconomic class has truly been a masculinist enterprise, in which women and children have been ascribed status by virtue of the earnings of the man to whom they belonged. Loss of the man was typically concomitant with loss of the status. Even today the quickest way for women to plummet into poverty is via divorce. Gender must be considered in the economic system as well as the psychological and sociological. Marilyn Waring, in her important work, *If Women Counted,* has broken ground in this area.

8

Order Out of Disorder: Disorderly Conduct

I learned to make my mind large, as the universe is large, so that there is room for paradoxes.
                                                    —Maxine Hong Kingston
                                                    The Woman Warrior

How are the pains and fears of human existence approached in a masculinist psychology/psychiatry? One strategy is to organize, categorize, and delimit them. In this way, they are flattened; they lose texture and variability while sounding clear, objective, and even scientific. Psychiatric diagnosis is accomplished by just such separating and flattening out of multidimensional experience, reducing many complex stories into one. The most popular and frequently used beginning texts for psychiatrists and psychologists (such as MacKinnon and Michels 1971; Basch 1980) not only adopt this perspective but use the generic "he" when referring both to therapists and to most patients—with the exception of discussing the ubiquitously popular (with the generic, male, heterosexual therapist) hysteric or histrionic personality as female (MacKinnon and Michels 1971).

The language of diagnosis is distant and often disapproving. Its perspective is external, its voice one of authority. Instead of addressing the all too frequent fear and pain of human existence, of suffering and longing, of loss and disappointment, instead of listening to the voice of the sufferer or of the psychotherapist, it speaks in the neutral, impersonal voice of professional objectivity, using the formal language of disease or disorder. From this professional perspective, disease or disorder is seen to lie within the individ-

165

ual. A border between the individual and complex sociocultural influences is erected and carefully maintained.

The American Psychiatric Association published the original Diagnostic and Statistical Manual (DSM) in 1952 as an attempt to categorize and enforce the medical perspective on what are considered abnormal psychological symptoms and syndromes. In 1958, it was revised and the DSM-II was published. Both manuals were extensive inventories of mental diseases. It was again revised in 1980 and, with the most recent revision, DSM-IIIR, in 1987, many medical concepts were replaced with behavioral and empirical observations. Its highly fragmented cookbook approach results in a strange mélange of value-laden psychodynamic and behavioral assessments.

The current official psychological and psychiatric language of abnormality has evolved into one of "disorder," more palatable and defensible than "disease":

> In DSM-IIIR each of the mental disorders is conceptualized as a clinically significant behavioral or psychological syndrome or pattern that occurs *in* a person and that is associated with present distress (a painful symptom) or disability/impairment in one or more important areas of functioning or with a significantly increased risk of suffering, death, pain, disability, or an important loss of freedom. [American Psychiatric Association 1987, p. xxiii; italics added]

It further states that this system does not classify people, but rather "disorders that people have" (p. xxiii). But it neither reflects nor impedes the prevalent use of these categories to classify people; almost all therapists refer, for example, to schizophrenics, hysterics, and borderlines as if the person becomes the disorder. Imagine how absurd it would sound to do this with physical diseases or disorders: the "canceric," "tuberculic," or "fluitic." This sense of the individual decontextualized, a faithful echo of the predominant Western concept of the self, is psychological in only the narrowest sense.

The authors of this document, from their position of self-proclaimed theoretical neutrality, go on to discuss uncritically a related system, the ICD-9 classification system, noting that it has only a single category for *"frigidity and impotence* despite the substantial work in the areas of psychosexual dysfunction that has identified several specific types" (p. xix; italics added). By taking no exception to this terminology, they implicitly endorse it. Can anyone doubt that the use of these terms to describe female and male sexual dysfunction is not only antiquated but unequivocally biased? As I asked in an article written some fifteen years ago (Kaschak

1976), can it be that the very same orgasmic difficulty in females is coldness and in males is lack of power? From the masculinist perspective, yes, because in the sexual arena, as everywhere else, women are assigned emotions and men are assigned power.

Psychological and psychiatric language need not be as blatantly sexist as this in order to be oedipal. The first question to ask about the system of disorder is the one I have been asking throughout: Whose perspective does it reflect and whose does it render invisible? The nomenclature of disorder is derived from a particular psychological model suggesting that a properly functioning person is psychologically organized in an orderly and predictable fashion, and that a problem is a malfunction in which things are outside that order. Disorders are aberrations, normal development gone awry. They are contained within the person, who is guilty of "disorderly" conduct. Yet another dualism is invoked: you either have a disorder or you don't. Yet another boundary is delineated by those with the power to do so, and is generally accepted as natural: there are those who have disorders within them and those who are normal, who are in order or, perhaps better said, who follow society's orders well. The makers of these boundaries need not be informed about the daily reality of a woman's life. Their perspective is external and dualistic, overlooking the texture of the ordinary.

As Dorothy Smith has aptly noted in her insightful work:

> Psychiatric agencies develop ways of working which fit situations and people which are not standardized, don't present standardized problems and are not already shaped up into the forms under which they can be recognized in the terms which make them actionable. What actually happens, what people actually do and experience, the real situations they function in, how they get to agencies—none of these things is neatly shaped up. There is a process of practical interchange between an inexhaustibly messy and different and indefinite real world and the bureaucratic and professional system which controls and acts upon it. The professional is trained to produce out of this the order which he believes he discovers in it. [1975, p. 97]

Clearly, daily life is not an orderly process. But the more prospective information is eliminated, the more life can be made to appear orderly. Taxonomies, if they accomplish little else, serve this function of reducing the complex to the orderly. Such emphasis on control and order in the psychiatric establishment translates into the popular vernacular through such expressions as "being out of control," "having a breakdown," "falling apart," and "having one's defenses crumble." These are all euphemisms for expressing feelings, usually painful feelings, often to the point of discomfort of others, including the therapist or diagnostician. They are circumstances of disorder.

Decisions about what is and is not a disorder are vested in the voting membership of the American Psychiatric Association. For example, homosexuality, as a diagnostic category, was removed from the DSM-III by vote of the membership of the American Psychiatric Association. This is certainly a democratic way of determining disorders, but it underlines the fact that these disorders are determined by the opinion of those who have the power to vote on them. Imagine the American Medical Association voting on whether tuberculosis exists. Homosexuality is now considered a problem only if the individual who has it so defines it. Why not say the same of heterosexuality? Of tuberculosis? And what exactly does it mean if an individual in a society that considers homosexuality a problem agrees with the majority? Does someone with a paranoid disorder get a vote also? Apparently only if he or she is a member of the American Psychiatric Association.

All these efforts to reform the diagnostic system highlight its basic problem: it is culture-bound while assuming universality. For example, in many societies homosexual behavior is not identified as a problem and is not even seen as being central to one's identity. It is just something that is done at certain ages or in certain situations, not a reification of some homosexual/heterosexual dichotomy. So-called disorders are matters of opinion and perspective.

Many feminists, including the psychologists Lenore Walker, Laura Brown, and Lynne Rosewater, have actively opposed the nature of recently introduced diagnostic categories, but to little avail. Testifying against the DSM-IIIR's inclusion of Self-Defeating Personality Disorder and Late Luteal Phase Dysphoric Disorder (Rosewater 1987; Caplan 1988), they have shown how these presumed disorders pathologize normal and ordinary reactions that are exclusively or primarily women's. Paula Caplan (1990) has proposed a parallel category—Delusional Dominating Personality Disorder—to pathologize men's ordinary gender-related problems as well, and thus make visible the process of pathologizing the ordinary for women only. The new category would include fourteen qualities, among them: the inability to identify and express a range of feelings in oneself; the inability to respond appropriately and empathically to the feelings and needs of close associates and intimates; the tendency to use power, silence, withdrawal, and/or avoidance in situations of interpersonal conflict; and an excessive need to inflate the importance and achievements of oneself and of males in general. If women have disorders within themselves, then men must have them too. But a larger question looms: Are any of these behaviors worthy of being included in a diagnostic system, or is the profession of psychiatry calling ordinary gender-related behavior abnormal?

For women (and theoretically for men, were both groups to be treated equally), disorders all too frequently flow directly from complex physical/psychological/societal experiences and meanings related to gender. In this sense, they are quite orderly and even ordinary. They derive from and contribute to the aspects of women's experience that I have traced in the prior chapters. They are the perimeters that define women's place, for it is time and place that create the ways in which women become disorderly, the ways in which women turn against themselves or social strictures, the conflicts that women embody.

The act of determining pathology, done from the narrowly psychological perspective that is totally external to the person being considered, is divisive of experience. A woman can appear to be in psychological disorder or disarray, which can *seem* to come from within her, as women take in and embody society's injunctions and conflicts as their own. While a more particular understanding comes from knowing how each woman has woven meaning from events in her life, the commonalities of being female in an oedipal society delineate the path on which each treads.

The incidence of psychological problems, as well as the various forms they take, has been shown to be a function of membership in particular societies, classes, and ethnic groups at particular times. For example, hysteria, a condition characterized by emotional excitability, sexual repression, and physical conversion symptoms, was prevalent in women in a society whose standard for femininity was based upon fragility. Ilza Veith has written of hysteria: "Throughout history the symptoms were modified by the prevailing concept of the feminine ideal. In the nineteenth century, especially young women and girls were expected to be delicate and vulnerable both physically and emotionally" (1965, p. 209). In Victorian society, there was a direct injunction that women's physicality and sexuality were not to be visible, or even to exist. Women's senses were considered weak and easily disturbed. Women were supposed to be fragile. Hysterical reactions incorporated and actualized these masculine definitions of women in a parody or an exaggerated form, such as paralysis, blindness, or other physically expressed psychological symptoms: "Perhaps because of this emotional vulnerability there was a striking rise in the prevalence of hysteria throughout Europe. Concurrent with its proliferation, which reached almost epidemic proportions, the malady exhibited a diminution in severity, and the disabling symptoms gave way to the faintings, whims, and tempers so elegantly designated as vapors" (Veith 1965, p. 210).

Other diagnostic categories, such as schizophrenia, have also been shown to vary as a function of different groups. A large body of literature has repeatedly confirmed the greater incidence of this disorder, or at least its diagnosis, among persons of the so-called lower socioeconomic classes (Hollingshead and Redlich 1958; Holzer et al. 1986; Neugebauer, Dohrenwend, and Dohrenwend 1980). Members of this group are subject to more and certain kinds of stresses. They are also more frequently assigned more severe diagnoses since they differ more from their middle-class diagnosticians and tend not to express their distress in cognitive and insightful ways.

Similarly, the patterns of physical/psychological/social development of women in industrial and postindustrial Western societies more readily dispose them to develop particular psychological problems and concerns, as I will demonstrate in the next two chapters. Several writers have suggested that there is a direct relationship between being a woman in modern society and certain disorders, including depression, hysteria, phobias, and eating disorders (Weissman and Klerman 1977; Wolowitz 1972; Fodor 1974; Frances and Dunn 1975). These problems are rooted, equivalently, in the normal development and training of women in this society, in the ways women are treated, in the meanings attributed to women and to their physical/psychological selves and to the meanings and understandings that women themselves develop, internalize, and live out. These are not internal pathologies or disorders that anyone simply *has*.

In Western society, women's bodies and physicality are still a masculine obsession. As the particular definition of them has changed, so has symptomatology. Hysteria has given way to eating disorders, anxieties, and depression—but all are adjustments to traumatic experience. The woman who experiences any of these disorders is well adjusted or attuned to her psychological and social environment.

A woman's identity is organized around oedipal perceptions and evaluations of her based on equating her with her physicalness and, more precisely, on its meaning according to current masculine standards, needs, and conflicts. In this way, conflicts are located in her and not in conflicting demands or meanings. The core of the Oedipus-Antigone arrangement finds women subsumed by masculine meanings and needs.

The meaning of women's physicality has changed since Victorian times and is currently focused upon appearance rather than on fragility. A woman's concern with appearance and its value, images and mirrors, dieting and food, seem so natural to most of us that we do not notice it. In this and the following chapter, I will show how these disorders are actually orderly developments stemming from the training to be a woman in this society.

DEPRESSION

What is the subjective constellation of experiences that we agree to call depression? It includes as a central component a feeling of sadness, embellished by despair or hopelessness. The feeling may differ in intensity and may be intermittent or constant, but it is always more than simple sadness or even the focused sense of grief that surrounds particular loss. The depressed person often senses that he or she is never going to feel any better, that circumstances are bleak and will undoubtedly stay that way. He or she may feel lonely and unable to love anyone or to receive love. This is accompanied by a sense of personal worthlessness and self-blame. There are often also feelings of anger, of being mistreated or misunderstood, of shame and unworthiness. Depression may seem both well deserved and unfair at the same time.

In a severe case of depression, the person may no longer experience the body or emotions as part of the self (MacKinnon and Michels 1971). Instead there is a sense of emptiness and unreality, which tends to be intermittent and accompanied by feelings of longing and especially of loss. This detachment both leads to and flows from apathy, if not anhedonia (an inability to experience pleasure). Yet there is often a vague sense that the emptiness could be, or could have been, filled by an intimate relationship or circumstance. That is, the something missing typically has to do with other people rather than with a sense of one's own self being missing.

Carolyn is a slightly built and carefully groomed woman in her mid-forties. Despite, or perhaps in keeping with, the care with which she presents herself, she seems timid and self-effacing. Having spent eighteen years of her life at home raising children, she has recently returned to school and is studying journalism. She was devastated to learn the week prior to making an appointment with me that her husband of twenty-two years, a professor at a local university, had been having an affair with a nineteen-year-old student. She lets me know of her sense of loss and self-blame, acknowledging that she is no longer very attractive and is just a boring middle-aged woman. She obsessively ruminates about what she has not done or been. She has settled upon her looks and her lack of interest to an intellectually active man as the reason for her husband's affair. She desperately wants to win him back by showing him how much she has sacrificed for him and the children over the years and how much he owes her. She is also shocked that his new lover is only a year older than their own daughter, but realizes that many men have these sorts of relationships in these post–sexual revolution times. Fearing that she has lost her husband forever, she cries intermittently as she tells me her story.

Sonia arrives for her first appointment looking worried and somber. She speaks in a barely audible voice. As she puts it, "life is a drag" and not worth continuing. She has tried to maintain several serious relationships, but they have all ended. She hates being alone, but feels hopeless about finding someone with whom to have a "committed relationship." She is not actively suicidal, but describes herself instead as waiting to die. She says it would be a relief not to have to feel so sad anymore. She is in a perpetual state of hope and longing, while paradoxically not daring to hope. Her sense of despair has varied in intensity but has haunted her since adolescence, when she first began to worry about "winding up alone." Now, in her late thirties, she feels that her worst fear has come to pass.

Angela left graduate school just before completing her doctoral dissertation in biochemistry to marry a fellow classmate. They both agreed that she should remain at home and raise their children. During that time, she had intermittent, serious bouts with depression. The children are almost old enough now that she can consider returning to school, but she feels that her knowledge is outdated and that it would be too difficult to catch up. Instead she has taken a part-time position as a laboratory technician. But even at this job she feels overwhelmed and lacks the confidence to continue. She has discovered that she has developed a preference for the safety and familiarity of remaining at home. Lately she has been awakening at about 5:00 A.M., but feels too lethargic to get out of bed. Instead she lies awake ruminating about the emptiness of her life. She has already missed several days of work.

Dahlia is in her late fifties. She has two adult children, but is disappointed in them both, as one is divorced and one never married. Neither has given her the grandchildren she had hoped for "to make her old age meaningful and to carry on the family name." She ruminates incessantly about her disappointment, wondering, "Why me? Where did I go wrong? All my friends enjoy their grandchildren. Why have my children turned out so badly?" She thinks obsessively about what she must have done wrong in raising them. When Dahlia is severely depressed, she sits alone for hours in her darkened house and cries.

Barbara just turned seventy and lives alone, although her married children live nearby and look in on her at least once a week. Her social security payments do not allow much of a budget for entertainment, so she does not get out often. She misses her friends who have died or moved away. But lately she has lost interest in seeing her friends who do live in the area.

Catherine has had a satisfying relationship with another woman for five years. They own a house together, which they have recently finished renovating and furnishing. Their close circle of friends, most of whom are former lovers of one or the other of them, all feel like family. She is selectively open about her lifestyle at work and has recently told her parents about it. They reacted angrily and have refused to discuss the matter or recognize the relationship. They continue to maintain a cordial, yet distant, relationship with Catherine. She feels no anger toward them and is instead angry at herself for making the wrong decision in telling them. Although she feels alternately angry and depressed, she blames no one but herself for this situation.

Rhonda just turned twenty and has been intermittently depressed since age thirteen, when she began gaining more weight than she wanted. She is about five pounds above her healthy weight and twenty above her desired weight. Although she pays careful attention to her makeup and wears the latest styles in clothing and hair, she is constantly distressed at her appearance and her lack of popularity with the "in group." Secretly she wonders why anyone would want to be her friend.

These cases are some typical examples of the ways in which women become depressed. They encompass many of the ordinary issues that define women's daily lives, including:

The emphasis on relationships as defining success or failure as a woman.
Loss of possible choices, such as access to careers and mastery-related tasks.
Equating the self with appearance in a surplus of meaning.
Self-denial embedded in self-esteem.
Lack of access to emotional and financial resources.
Invisibility of connection to children and grandchildren.
Waiting and feeling valued more than acting.
Having responsibility for what one cannot control.

Female vulnerability to depression in our population has been well documented both clinically (Baruch and Serrano 1988) and through epidemiological study (Gove and Tudor 1973). The gender difference is found in groups of white, African-American, and Latin American women in the United States (Russo, Amaro, and Winter 1987; Russo and Sobel 1981). Both in clinically diagnosed groups and in larger community samples (Girgus, Nolen-Hoeksema, and Seligman 1989), women consistently report and experience about twice as many depressive symptoms as do men. Gender differences in the incidence of depression have also been reported in Denmark, Scotland, Wales, England, Canada, Australia, New Zealand, Nigeria, Kenya, Iceland, and Israel (Nolen-Hoeksema 1987, 1990; Weissman and Klerman 1977). The female-to-male ratio of reported depression falls within the range of 2–4:1, except for bipolar, or manic-depressive, disorders, for which there is nearly no gender difference. These proportions have been repeatedly confirmed both clinically and in various empirical studies (DSM-IIIR 1987) and are not accounted for by a gender difference in willingness to report symptoms of distress (Nolen-Hoeksema 1987, 1990; Weissman and Klerman 1977, 1985).

Some observers (Golding 1988) have suggested that the effect of gender on depression is largely a function of gender differences in rate of employment, education, income, and the like. From this perspective, the various social inequities that impede women's access to a satisfying career and an adequate standard of living result in an increased incidence of the group of experiences we call depression. Certainly such experiences can lead, for both women and men, to feelings of despair and hopelessness, accompanied by a sense of being unable or minimally able to change one's circumstances. In fact, a study by Ronald Kessler and Harold Neighbors (1986) suggested that the effects of race and social class on symptoms of distress appear to be interactive, racial differences being more pronounced at lower-income levels. Ellen McGrath et al. (1990) reviewed this study and reported that the effects of this interaction are twice as strong for women as for men—that is, at lower income levels, racial minorities experience greater psychological distress. Distress is twice as likely among women in these groups as among men.

In addition, compared to elderly men, elderly women are more likely to have lower incomes, to live alone, and to be unmarried (Foner 1986). Yet there are a variety of other experiences that women tend to have while men do not and that also relate directly to an intermittent or chronic experience of depression. Multiple influences can conspire to lead women to periodic or chronic depression. While I do not mean to rule out biological or neuroendocrine factors in all cases, such variables have never been shown to cause rather than to coexist with psychological factors. Furthermore, I consider that even biological changes are made meaningful and altered by the social context and can only be considered contextually (Hamilton 1984).

In the following pages I will consider some additional aspects of depression and how they come quite "naturally" to modern women. The degree of intensity of these constellations of feelings/thoughts and the proportion of time during which they are emergent differ for any given individual, depending on her unique combination of experiences and learned meanings.

The crucial elements in women's development of a sense of self that lead to the prevalence of depression are a sense of unreality or lack of a full experience combined with a negative self-concept imbued with shame and a chronic sense of loss and imposed limits. Although a precipitating event may be identified involving loss, shame, negative judgment, or a physical or psychological intrusion, it is unnecessary: women's lived experience offers a multitude of these events.

Disconnection and Detachment

I have already outlined the manner in which the identity of girls and women comes to be based on their physicalness in general and their physical appearance in particular. That physicalness is commented upon and/or evaluated by men who are important in their lives—such as fathers, brothers, husbands, lovers, friends, sons, and teachers—and by other men who serve only an evaluative function, such as strangers in the street. Other women also participate in enforcing these standards in their daughters, mothers, friends, lovers, and sisters, as well as in themselves. Women's own internal experiences thus become secondary to the experiences they can induce in the determinate or indeterminate observer.

Some familiar comments:

"Hello. Nice to see you. You look good. Have you lost weight since I saw you last. I like your new hairstyle."

"Mom, do you have to wear that old outfit to the mall? What if my friends see us together? Can't you look more like Sandra's mom? Why can't I buy this short skirt? Sandra's mother let her get one."

"I see that you got new glasses. Don't you think they're a bit owlish-looking? You don't want to look like a bookworm, after all."

"Hey, honey (mama, bitch, dyke). Looking good (bad, sexy, fat)."

The more someone's own experience is kept invisible from others, the more it eventually becomes inaccessible to herself. When asked to look inward, a woman may not easily be able to find out what she feels or thinks, or may not be willing to disclose it. She may find an empty place and a sense of longing, but not even be able to identify for what she is longing. Something is missing, but that something is not outside her, as she may think. *She* is missing. She has lost a certain ability to respond genuinely and spontaneously. Her responses are instead imbued with the needs and desires of others, with how she appears and whom she affects.

In the late years of childhood, up to puberty, more boys than girls are depressed (Girgus 1989). In late adolescence, a striking change takes place and twice as many girls as boys are depressed, a ratio that is maintained or widened throughout adulthood. In a study of 300 boys and girls at ages eleven, thirteen, and fifteen, Joan Girgus (1989) found that the most significant issue related to depression is body image. Another study, by Laurie Mintz and Nancy Betz (1986), yielded similar results. Body attitudes are more related to the social self-esteem of females than of males, yet girls reported a more negative body image at all ages. Girls who spent more time shopping, cooking, sewing, and applying makeup were also more depressed than other girls. The author related the latter finding to the passivity of the activities as opposed to behaviors that involve mastery. Once again there is more to the story: these girls were using feminine ways of treating depression, ways that ironically perpetuate it by bringing into play all the means that are supposed to make women feel better, but just make them look better to the indeterminate male observer.

This is combined with women's learning to take responsibility for others and for relationships, to base their reactions on others' needs and desires. In this way, a woman comes to lose her own needs and experiences. She comes to believe/feel that if everyone who matters to her is OK, then so is she. Yet it has been shown empirically as well as clinically that people who derive their sense of self from relationships have a stronger propensity to become depressed (Scarf 1980; Warren and McEachren 1985).

In the case of the woman who appears to have everything—the perfect husband and children, the perfect home and friends—but is still depressed, she may also feel/believe that if she meets all their needs, then they will eventually meet hers. This is, I believe, a common female fantasy. Women learn that these relationships should make them happy and fulfilled, rewarding them for being good girls. These days, for many women, we can add a career to the picture, so that they may be less depressed but more frantic and exhausted—and sometimes depressed, frantic, and exhausted, with even less time to meet everyone else's needs. The many women who have never had the option not to work outside the home, juggling a never-ending work day and caretaking demands, have never had access to good girldom.

As we have seen, this set of experiences leads to a more detached and symbolic connection to the self. Since appearance and relationships top the list of how to succeed as a woman, doing what a woman is expected to do can set the stage for the sense of emptiness and longing that is a large part of depression. An inability to experience the full range and depth of one's own feelings contributes to the sense of emotional distance and emptiness so common in depression. Physical and psychological experience can appear at a distance and are not taken in, leading to a subjective sense of "something missing" and of sadness or perpetual mourning for the missing core of experience or aliveness (Miller 1981). The currently popular psychological model of a lost "child or girl within," although it reifies, speaks to this sense of a missing core of experience or self in women.

Women's invisibility in a variety of psychological situations certainly contributes directly to this sense. How can one remain appropriately invisible and yet experience one's impact on others and on one's surroundings? How can one be subsumed in the category of "man" and feel real? How can one lose one's very name and maintain one's identity? These and other external limits become internal experience as women learn and play their parts.

A girl or woman may unconsciously hesitate, subordinate her own needs to those of others, not express or even know what she wants or needs in a particular situation. Highly successful and dynamic professional women often report deferring to their husbands at home. Women may also fail to speak up in class or at work. Assertive women in the workplace are often judged negatively or ignored. In the classroom, boys often receive more attention and are rewarded for speaking out, girls for behaving well. In fact, one study found that women in a group were ignored even when they had the correct answer to a problem the group was trying to solve (Altemeyer and Jones 1974). A woman may feel in danger when she speaks up, safe but invisible when she hides. Her experience, as a result, is muted. She has to worry about how she is being perceived, how she looks when expressing something. She may come to wonder if she even has anything to say or anything important enough to command the attention of others.

For example, a woman, in describing to me a meeting she had just attended at work, mentioned in passing that she was glad that no men had been present so that she didn't have to worry about how she had acted, that is, how she would look in their eyes. She was aware of what she was playing out, but many women are not. They simply forget that they have anything worthwhile to say. Or they may keep trying to be heard. Other women may gossip, a form of speech deemed trivial and feminine, creating a somewhat illusory connection among themselves, imbued at the same time with caring and competitiveness, longing and envy, connection and anonymity. It has been noted repeatedly that men and women speak and sit differently in same-gender groups. Yet in mixed ones, the behavior of women changes: they become physically and verbally more constricted (Ariès 1976) and alter their topics of conversation to match those of men.

The relationship between the unresolved oedipal and antigonal complexes are learned and played out in a variety of ways. Adults are more likely to do things for girls, while boys are typically shown how to do things for themselves (Latane and Dabbs 1975; Unger 1976). Even in adult educational settings, teachers are more likely to give male students detailed instructions while doing things for females (Sadker and Sadker 1985). Eleanor Maccoby and Carol Jacklin (1974) found only one consistent difference between child-rearing practices for boys and girls. The actions of boys more frequently have direct consequences, such as mastery of a task or direct response, than do those of girls. Thus girls do not see their direct impact on the environment the way boys see theirs. Numerous studies have shown that, as adults, men speak more than women and frequently interrupt them (Kramarae, Thorne, and Henley 1978; Thorne, Kramarae, and Henley 1983). Listeners remember more of what men say, even when women speakers participate equivalently. In mixed-gender conversation, women tend to participate less, to smile more, and to speak more tentatively and ask more questions rather than making declarative statements.

Girls and women learn that it is not what they do but how they appear that matters. They constantly experience others' reactions to their appearance, behavior, and sexuality. As a result, it can become difficult for a female to locate herself, rather than the indeterminate male observer and all the known observers and emotional dependents, in the center of her own mattering map. This creates a muted experience, if not one of invisibility. She has to search among a sea of faces and responses of others to find her own. She may not even know that she has lost herself. Instead she may just have a vague sense of futility about all she does or a sense of shame about being silent or speaking out, especially if she doesn't think she looks right doing it.

The opportunity to develop a well-integrated sense of self that is internally rather than externally defined—that is, relatively stable rather than subject to redefinition based on changes in appearance or evaluations thereof, and grounded in an accurate testing of abilities and skills rather than a passive evaluation—is very elusive for girls and women. It takes removing oneself from oedipal demands and meanings to begin resolution of the antigonal phase.

Negative Evaluations

As already discussed extensively, women are continuously evaluated. Since even positive evaluations are embedded with potential or actual negative ones, there is a pervasive sense for many women of something being wrong even when everything is all right. Many clients, as they improve in therapy, begin to be frightened of feeling *too* good. Wanting to avoid disappointment and the dangers of increased presence and expansiveness, often, as they begin to feel better, they also feel worse. A sense of something always being wrong not with the outside but with the inside, the individual self, is learned and reinforced through childhood and adolescence and continues into adulthood.

As we have already seen, for males in our society, achievement and competence are positively related and unambivalently rewarded. This is not so for females, who may be ignored (Wolman and Frank 1975) in a group or judged negatively (Carli 1990) when they are just as competent as the male members. Competent females may be rewarded or punished or both, depending on someone else's meanings.

The surplus of meaning about how women look and most of what they do is filtered through oedipal expectations for Antigone. This is not so for gender expectations for men: it does not mean something additional about what one is saying or doing to be saying or doing it in a man's body. Men are not interrupted when speaking just because they are men. They are not judged by how they eat and how much they eat. If they are judged by appearance, it is likely that something about their appearance is being judged, not something about their basic worth as a human being, about whether they can think or whether they have something worthwhile to say. They are not ridiculed, ignored, or attacked simply because of their gender. Women carry around an extra weight that men do not. If bad things happen, she probably deserves it. If she is beaten or raped, she must have somehow colluded. The choice often seems to be between not being able to have an impact on the environment or to have her impact noted, and being told she is having an impact on the environment or on others in ways she neither wants nor can control. It depends not on her behavior itself but on masculine meanings attributed to it. Either way, to the extent that she cannot make her own meaning, she is vulnerable to emptiness and depression.

False Responsibility

Women, through childhood, adolescence, and adulthood, learn that they are responsible for what they cannot control. Again, this is more multiply determined than current empirically based causes cited for depression in women in particular, such as the notion of learned helplessness discussed by Martin E. P. Seligman (1975) and others. Much as experimental animals simply freeze or give up in contrived examples of helplessness, so do women's bodies, as previously noted, tend to freeze in difficult or frightening situations. But women are not simply unable to control certain reinforcement or their own access to the rewarding environment as in the learned helplessness paradigm. They are, at the same time, considered to be responsible for those very things they cannot control, such as how other people behave in relationships or whether or not they are "asking for it." Women often have the responsibility, but not the power to exercise that responsibility effectively.

Freud and his followers considered women to have a less developed superego than men. (The superego is that aspect of the psyche that includes both what is popularly considered the conscience and moral ideals. A sense of responsibility, as well as guilt, are included.) Many clinicians and even more women can attest that the very opposite is the case. Women feel themselves to be responsible for themselves, for children, for relationships, for internalized conflicts of the masculinist context of society, for "asking for it," for a surplus of issues and experiences. Only someone who does not understand the lived experience of women can agree with Freud's statement.

Violence against women is part of our religious, historical, and legal legacies. Under English common law, a husband had the right to beat his wife, subject to the "rule of thumb," which prevented him from using a stick any broader than his thumb (Heise 1989). Male violence against women is no longer codified so concretely, but, considering the shocking incidence of rape and other crimes of violence, how far can we say we have come? Most women experience a chronic vulnerability to and anxiety about physical and psychological boundary violations. In the United States alone, a woman is beaten every fifteen seconds, and each day four women are killed (Z Magazine, July/August 1989). This repeated experience of danger often results in the development of sensitivity to the aggressor, in which one's own needs and freedom of physical and psychological movement are subordinated to one's place in a relationship with someone who, tragically, often is a potential or actual aggressor. A compulsive concern with relationship and a fear of not being in one then often develops without conscious awareness of the reasons. Even less conscious accommodations in the restriction of movement and movements in public, and blaming oneself for failures in relationships, characterize this concern.

In my experience, and probably in that of most clinicians, the majority of depressive experiences in women are centered on or triggered by problems in, lack of, or loss of relationships. This is when and why they come to therapy. It both results from and leads to an overriding emphasis on relational aspects of life and, frequently, mild to severe depression even when in a relationship. Women may wonder why they can't control relationships so that they meet all their needs, so that they turn out well, so that they last. It feels like personal failure when a relationship fails. A woman wonders what more she could have done, how she could have looked better or met someone else's needs better. The currently popular twelve-step programs come close to pathologizing women's traditional relational orientation by labeling them "co-dependent" or "enablers" when they try to exercise the control that they don't have but are supposed to, and when they stay in relationships that men would and do leave.

Shame

Shame is as central a component of women's psychology as it is of depression. Women in this society are not just judged by, but identified with, their appearance in an involuntarily exhibitionistic way. Women as individuals can sometimes choose not to be exhibited in a particular situation, but women in general cannot control their own exposure. Women have not been able to eliminate pornography or advertising that uses women's bodies as one commodity to sell another, nor can they typically choose to avoid or eliminate lewd or intrusive comments or physical attack in public or in private, by strangers or by loved ones. As a result, women either consciously or unconsciously experience the shame of repeated exposure.

It is no accident that women often become involved in compulsive shopping, particularly for clothing and items that will presumably enhance their appearance. This behavior is a way of trying to fill up emptiness, deadness, or depression—a particularly feminine way, because it involves appearance. It also involves both covering and exhibiting oneself and so speaks to both the invisibility and the hypervisibility of women.

A woman who had dealt extensively with the issue of physical attractiveness in a variety of feminist therapy settings told me that she had changed her appearance drastically over the years in a sometimes successful attempt not to call attention to herself. That day she had been leered at in a way that made her feel angry and humiliated. Feeling shame at this overexposure, she vowed that from now on she was going to "walk around with a bag on her head." But why on *her* head? It had not occurred to her to put a bag on any of their heads, nor could she have. The perspective of Antigone made her believe that if she could control herself, she could control these indeterminate observers.

As body parts and appearance are objectified and demeaned or admired, the self becomes fragmented, diminished, or hidden. Whether or not a woman deviates from the prescribed standard, she will experience shame. Visibility, which should lead to a greater sense of authenticity and aliveness, paradoxically leads instead to a more direct experience of humiliation. A confident and assertive woman is not often viewed or treated kindly and may even put herself in grave danger. Although these attributes in men may not always bring the desired result, they rarely bring ridicule or threat.

Shame is experienced as not wanting to continue to exist or be visible, as wanting the self to dis-integrate. With the fragmentation of her physically based identity, a woman has a head start in this direction.

Loss

As a result of the physical and psychological limits and restraints to which women are subjected in childhood and throughout life, an impending or actual sense of loss is contained within their psychological makeup. There is the loss of both self-control and self-definition. There is the potential and actual loss of one's own meaning and definition of what life is or can involve. Finally, there is the loss of the possible, the narrowing of choices and limits, missing the full range available in a particular time and society. The expanded choices now open to certain middle-class women are accompanied by more burdens, such as exposure to harassment in the workplace and the double workday.

For women but not men, there is a strong relationship between marriage and depression (Gove 1972; Merikangas et al. 1985), which seems to be related to an increased denial of a woman's own needs and the demand that she meet the needs of others. Married women who do not work outside the home are even more likely to be depressed (Brown and Harris 1978). Women in traditional marital relationships have poorer physical health and self-esteem than those in more equal ones (Avis 1985).

The relationship between marriage and depression for women may also be related to experiencing disappointment. Marriage is only one aspect of a man's life, and it may give him exactly what he expects of it. This is generally not the case for women. Certainly no one in the family is assigned to nurture women. In fact, husbands more often than wives report being understood and supported by their spouses (Campbell, Converse, and Rodger 1976; Vanfossen 1981), and are much more likely to rely on their wives as sole confidantes (Veroff, Douvan, and Kulka 1981). Marriage is a woman's version of success. If it doesn't help her to live happily ever after, then it must be her own fault, not that of impossible or unmet expectations. While marriage, in general, provides a greater protection against depression for men in general than for women in general, an unhappy marriage confers a greater risk for depression on women (Weissman 1987).

Not surprisingly, women experience more change than do men in the transition to parenthood (Belsky, Lang, and Huston 1986; Cowan et al. 1985). Women with young children experience high levels of stress whether or not they are employed outside the home (Thoits 1986), and those with three or more children under the age of eleven at home also have an increased level of depression (Brown and Brolchain 1975). Employed mothers with sole responsibility for children, predictably enough, have extremely high levels of depression (Ross and Mirowsky 1988) unless their husbands help with child care (Kessler and MacRae 1982) and unless such employment is consistent with the values of both spouses (Ross, Mirowsky, and Huber 1983).

ANXIETY AND PHOBIAS

If the socialization process is successful, boys in our society will be taught to protect, rather than to endanger, girls. Or, more likely, they will be taught that a certain amount of threat to women is an acceptable expression of masculinity. In normal development, young boys begin to express sexual interest in girls by mild forms of teasing, as each era finds appropriate: dunking girls' pigtails in the inkwell, producing bugs, snakes, or other animals of which girls are supposed to be fearful, et cetera. These are well-condensed statements of the traditional heterosexual contract and the template for later adult relationships. She is supposed to be fearful and vulnerable. He frightens as well as protects her. Her vulnerability and his power to frighten and to protect supposedly enhance his masculinity and sexuality, as well as her femininity and sexual interest. Many variations on this early arrangement are acted out through adulthood.

The oedipal eye is blind to the violence and damage done to women. If seen at all, this damage is viewed as discrete experiences of individual women and aberrations of individual men. It is abnormal, a disorder. The description of Post-Traumatic Stress Disorder (PTSD) in the DSM-IIIR is still perfunctory in its inclusion of women's stresses. Mention is made of rape as a trauma that can lead to this disorder. Yet the ensuing discussion of precipitating stressors cites only natural disasters (floods, earthquakes), accidental "manmade" disasters (car accidents, airplane crashes, fires), and deliberate disasters (bombing, torture, death camps). Only war veterans and survivors of death camps are discussed. Where have the problems of violence against women disappeared?

In the home and in the streets, there is, in a very concrete sense, a war being waged against women, and women's bodies and psyches bear the scars of living under this stress. Yet the diagnostic category and treatment for Post-Traumatic Stress Disorder were not developed in response to these ordinary situations in which women find themselves on a daily basis, but instead for soldiers, mostly men, returning from the openly acknowledged and visible war in Vietnam. In fact, even in the case of an openly declared war, women veterans do not gain benefits. They tend not to apply for them because, in true Antigone style, "they feel that only men are veterans," according to retired Rear Admiral Frances Shea-Buckley (1989).

When a war is ended, the traumatic incident is considered to have passed. This is not so for the casualties of peace (a state obviously defined from the perspective of a blind man). While Post-Traumatic Stress Disorder has been extended to include women who are victims of rape and other violent attacks, neither the trauma nor the related stresses pass for women, but are an ordinary and daily part of their lives.

The human organism, for survival, adapts to stressful situations in such a way that the overt terror is transmuted into chronic stress (Selye 1978; Tache and Selye 1985) or anxiety. Thus, most girls and women do not typically move through public or private places in abject terror. Instead the overt fear is replaced by a constant anxiety firmly embedded in the body, as well as in the psychological self. Women know instinctively where and how to walk in public in order to avoid danger as much as possible. As noted, compared to men, women maintain a tenser posture at rest (Mehrabian 1968) and, in response to intrusion, freeze more often (Mahoney 1974). Most women learn how to behave in private situations, learn that relationships give them safety and security—and many keep believing this even when it isn't so.

From a chronic feeling of anxiety to a palpable fear in the pit of the stomach, which is probably already tightly constricted in order to appear flat when evaluated, women live with a shifting degree of tension. If they cannot consciously acknowledge the danger to them and its source, then many accept that their problems are individual in nature and fall back on personal psychological strategies. Containing the fear in their own minds and bodies, these women eventually forget that it is even there.

For example, there has been a high incidence of rape and other kinds of attacks on women on the campus of the university where I teach. In response, the female faculty and staff are encouraged not to use their offices on evenings and weekends, and generally do not. One secretary will work late only when she has her dog with her as protection against any men who may have wandered into the building before it was locked. Female students ask the male students to escort them to the garage after night classes or, if no males are available, walk in groups. Some women go to the rest room in pairs only, as attacks have taken place there as well. Some won't take night classes, and many won't even drive at night in case the car breaks down somewhere, making them vulnerable to attack or rape.

These precautions are not extraordinary. This is just one department of one university in an unremarkable city. These are but a few of the "natural" fears and accommodations women make every day. These women are not particularly angry or overtly terrified; it is just part of life as a woman.

A mother's anxiety as a female in a world that is dangerous to women, and her concern for her daughter's safety, are transmitted often preverbally through touch or example. Later she must deliberately educate her daughter in how to remain safe. All these restrictions, along with tremendous anxiety, if not outright fear, become embedded in the girl's developing physical and psychological self. Women's bodies and minds retain a tension and alertness, a characteristic posture and bearing embedded within which is a readiness for danger—not, in masculine terms, a readiness to fight or flee, but a readiness to freeze, to hide, to try to be invisible, to shrink in shame, to lower one's eyes, to laugh nervously, to pretend to ignore the source of danger. Perhaps these kinds of responses should be considered in court as evidence of struggle in a female crime victim.

People often develop obsessive or magical kinds of ideas or compulsive, repetitive behaviors in an attempt to control fearful situations, while not experiencing the actual fear. Women can occupy themselves endlessly with their physical appearance, clothing, weight, and so on, believing that, in this way, they can control how they are treated and, given the surplus of meaning attributed to women's appearance, even how their lives will go. This is a self-focused response to fear in which the individual woman again comes to contain, physically and psychologically, issues that are socially based.

Women's chronic potential or actual anxiety from a heightened vigilance and sense of vulnerability, as well as the constant (actual or potential) evaluation of their worth depending on appearance, results in a predisposition to various anxiety-related and phobic reactions. *Agoraphobia,* coined by Carl Otto Westphal in 1871, is the most common kind of phobia seen clinically (Marks 1969). Generally defined as an irrational fear of the external world, when the nature of that world is considered from the female perspective it does not seem so irrational. Estimates of the percentage of females who experience agoraphobia range as high as 64 to 95 percent (Friedman 1959; Marks and Herst 1970). Whereas most phobias appear to begin in childhood or early adolescence, agoraphobia typically develops in early adulthood (Matthews, Gelder, and Johnston 1981) and in women who have chosen a traditional lifestyle and have been married for about five years (Fodor 1977). These are women who have been, as clinicians like to call it, "overprotected" by their parents.

A panic attack for an agoraphobic is usually preceded by a developmental crisis, such as leaving home or divorcing. The pain and humiliation of the panic attack then lead to phobic avoidance and enforced dependency (Chambless 1982). Agoraphobia is considered, by most clinicians who work with it, to involve a conflict between dependency and autonomy, the development of panic attacks often precipitated by a crisis in relationships (Chambless and Goldstein 1981). The severe panic allows the individual to remain dependent rather than having to deal with her fear of autonomy. She can continue to be protected while not acknowledging this choice. Instead she often feels trapped by herself.

Lynn Hoffman (1972) has pointed out that mastery of fears is not encouraged in girls. Women don't get the same physical training as men in school or at home. Furthermore, a girl or a woman's fearfulness enhances the masculinity of the man who can protect her and, if expressed phobically, can, at least in fantasy, get a woman the protection and caretaking she seeks by diminishing herself.

Since females are socialized to be more fearful than males, and clearly have more reason to be, the typical qualities of phobic individuals—dependency, unassertiveness, fear of being alone and of functioning autonomously—sound suspiciously like those traditionally taught to women, as Iris Fodor (1974) has shown. Ihsan Al-Issa (1980) has suggested that phobias are better thought of as avoidant-dependent responses to stress.

The DSM-IIIR considers agoraphobia to be "the fear of being in places or situations from which escape might be difficult (or embarrassing) or in which help might not be available in the event of suddenly developing a symptom(s) that could be incapacitating or extremely embarrassing" (American Psychiatric Association 1987, p. 240). It is diagnosed far more frequently in women than in men.

Agoraphobic women fear going out alone, traveling, being trapped in close spaces. Is this really irrational? Or an appropriate expression of fear of real danger? Agoraphobia is a more acute response to the ever-present dangers of violation that many other women experience chronically. It is the reaction of a woman who feels that she cannot protect herself at all. Because danger is made invisible by the context, which requires restriction of women rather than of men, it becomes localized in women as one more "women's issue," and shows up as anxiety, and often as panic or terror, when it cannot be held in abeyance. Within these narrow bounds, the anxiety functions as a substitute for fear and rage. But women who experience and express these feelings may place themselves in even greater danger. Certainly they have moved beyond femininity and its built-in sensitivity to the aggressor.

Hannah Lerman (1989) has suggested that many individuals who have been diagnosed as having Borderline Personality Disorders or even Multiple Personality Disorders should be considered long-term chronic sufferers of Post-Traumatic Stress Disorder. I would suggest that the chronic suffering is only half the story and that the other half be made visible. That is, when are the stressors to which women are subjected in the past? Is there ever a period that is truly "post-traumatic"? Perhaps, if we must diagnose, we need a new category such as Chronic Traumatic Stress Disorder (CTSD) for women, differentiated from Acute Traumatic Stress Disorder (ATSD) for what we now call agoraphobia. Despite the DSM-IIIR's definition of PTSD as "the development of characteristic symptoms following a psychologically distressing event that is outside the range of usual human experience" (American Psychiatric Association 1987, p. 247), most of the events leading to CTSD and ATSD are well within the range of the usual experience for women.

DIS-INTEGRATION

The development among contemporary women of a fragmented sense of identity makes certain disorders peculiarly feminine: amnesia, multiple personality, or a combination of these with motor behavior—fugue state. These disruptions are a sort of fragmentation or dis-integration of the self.

The normal process of disconnection, or dissociation, and self-observation in feminine development differs only in degree from that labeled a multiple-personality disorder. Fragmentation of experience results from the multiple perspectives of Antigone. Combined with an identity built upon the fragmentation of the physical—an identification with specific body parts rather than with the body as a whole—normal femininity once again is fertile ground for the development of the prevailing standard of pathology.

As demonstrated repeatedly in the clinical literature, the physical and sexual abuse to which women are subjected in this society commonly results in the development of a dissociative process, an extreme example of what I have called identification with the indeterminate observer. Victims often report having watched their abuse from above or from somewhere else outside their own bodies. This perspective, in combination with fragmentation, is shared to different degrees by most women in this society. It is a means by which to cope with the severe injury of this sort of trauma and one well suited to female socialization, which is built upon a somewhat milder, but just as pervasive, form of fragmentation or disconnection from oneself.

The most recent literature on multiple personality suggests that there are about nine times as many females as males with this disorder (Kluft 1987). Although this is probably a slight overestimate of the ratio, since most males in this category seem to enter the criminal justice system rather than the mental health system, there is a vast preponderance of this disorder among women, who are, I suggest, predisposed to it as a result of the socialization process. In almost every case, this extreme form of dissociation is preceded by childhood sexual or severe physical abuse (DSM-IIIR).

In multiple-personality disorders, the differences between what are called personalities are physiological as well as psychological (Braun 1986). For example, in one patient 5 milligrams of diazepam, a tranquilizer, sedated one personality, while 100 milligrams had little effect on another. Other physical differences, such as seizures, eating disorders, and different neurological and sensory profiles, also vary from personality to personality within an individual. One personality of the same individual might need glasses to read, another might not (Miller 1989).

188

Such splits permit the isolation of fear and anxiety, but also mask the lack of control that a woman in an abusive situation in particular and in an abusive society in general can and does feel. The individual literally comes *a part,* so there is no *me* but only a collection of me's, who are, at the very same time not-me—a solution that exhibits both lack of control and attempts at control. It is, at the same time, a statement of the pain and a statement that "You can't hurt me because you can't find me." It contains within it an acknowledgment of the highly visible form of invisibility that women experience. It says, "I am right here and nowhere at the same time."

Dis-integration is also a reaction to, and a strategy for dealing with, the extreme feeling of shame so often noted in victims of abuse, particularly sexual abuse. Recall that the core feeling of shame is a desire not to exist, to destroy one's feelings and one's very self. The dissociative process, in its extreme producing multiple personalities, is an answer to this need, a partial, passive suicide.

But these problems become decontextualized and viewed as general psychological problems unrelated to the particular circumstances of women in this society at this time. They are treated as disorders or psychopathology, something to be removed or excised from an individual. A noncontextual form of psychotherapy, or even medication, may be considered appropriate to bring the fragmented personality under control.

The daily fragmentation of women's bodies/minds prepares women for the more extreme and visible one. Having done so, it fades into unawareness, leaving behind what seems to be an individual, self-contained pathology. Instead women's own bodies/minds are a familiar territory for embodying and disembodying an initially external battle, as the context becomes the self.

9

Eating

"She become so thin now you cannot see her," says my mother. "She like a ghost, disappear."

And I remember wondering why it was that eating something good could make me feel so terrible, while vomiting something terrible could make me feel so good.
—Amy Tan
The Joy Luck Club

Historically, both food and eating have had different meanings for women and men. During the Middle Ages, for example, elective starvation was viewed as a means for women to achieve spiritual purity (Brumberg 1988). In societies and historical periods such as our own, which emphasize an individual and physical/psychological, rather than a spiritual, concept of the self, women still seek perfection through manipulation of the physical. This is a different, yet related, sort of perfection, one I will discuss in detail in this chapter. What are the current meanings of food and eating in the lives of modern women in Western industrial society?

Much has been written about so-called eating disorders—anorexia, bulimia, and bulimarexia—in women (Bruch 1973, 1978; Chernin 1982, 1985; Brumberg 1988). I agree with those who consider them to be the extreme end point of normal feminine development (Nylander 1971; Button and Whitehouse 1981; Fries 1977; Rodin, Silberstein and Streigel-Moore 1985; Streigel-Moore, Silberstein, and Rodin 1986), although I do conceptualize them not as points on a linear continuum but as part of a complex nexus of meanings around which these issues are organized. Problems with eating and not eating need not be approached as if they differ in kind from normal feminine predicaments and are in need of separate consideration. As predictable and normal ways to become abnormal for women, they derive directly from complex experience and learning. Problems in this arena can thus best be understood by building upon what has already been developed in prior chapters about women's complex psychological development in oedipal society.

But "[a] historical perspective shows that anorexia nervosa existed before there was a mass cultural preoccupation with dieting and a slim female body" (Brumberg 1988, p. 3). There are different reasons for the obsession with female appetite in different historical eras. What is primary and less subject to change is the very fact that it is symbolism and meaning that must be manipulated for women to seek approval and to avoid humiliation. The general rule dictates that, to become a woman, one must accept one's body and one's appetites as symbolic. That is, a woman's appetite and eating must be made to be responsive to the *meanings* of weight and of eating itself along with, or instead of, the physiological cues for hunger and satiety.

The greatest incidence of anorexia, or elective starvation, has been reported in the industrialized countries (Crisp et al. 1976) and among Caucasians (Galdston 1974) of the upper socioeconomic groups. C. H. Hardin Branch and Linda J. Eurman (1980) found that the friends and relatives of the anorectics they studied (all Caucasian) admired the patients' slenderness and control. Studies of African-Americans have shown that those who are more assimilated into white society have more eating problems. While only 5 to 10 percent of all people with eating disorders are men, up to 50 percent of men who seek treatment for this problem describe themselves as homosexual. In a study of homosexual and heterosexual men, Joel Yager (1989) found that the former, although similar in weight and appearance to the latter, were more dissatisfied with themselves and had attitudes toward their bodies more like those of women. This should not be surprising, since, like women, homosexual men feel the need to please and attract the indeterminate and determinate male observer.

Outside the Western industrialized countries, only Japan has reported a significant number of cases of anorexia (Suematsu et al. 1985). Within developed countries, the disorder is still relatively rare, but increasing among black women (Hsu 1987), as it is in older women and Asian women (Nevo 1985) and across the socioeconomic spectrum (Garfinkel and Garner 1982; Andersen and Hay 1985).

For all people, a sense of self begins as an abstraction of the physical, of competence and mastery, of sentience and sensuality. For women, however, as we have seen, a particular aspect of the physical—that is, appearance—becomes the template for the developing identity and sense of worth or value as a human being (a female human being, that is). Appearance signals to a woman and to others just what her basic identity is and can be and, most important, how she deserves to be treated.

Often what is deemed desirable about women's appearance, what is pleasurable to the masculine observer, is either painful or harmful to the woman herself. Women's physicalness is rooted in the shifting sands of desirability. Their physical pleasure thus contains discomfort and self-denial, as described in the example of high-heeled shoes in a prior chapter. Pain becomes intertwined with pleasure. Concern with body shape and size may have its roots in a healthy attempt to develop oneself and to seek love, approval, and self-esteem—but for women, this means learning control and denial of the physical.

There is a significant relationship between most people's self-esteem and their satisfaction with their physical attractiveness. This relationship is consistently stronger for females than for males (Gray 1977; Lerner and Karabenick 1974; Tobin-Richards, Boxer, and Peterson 1983). Peer evaluations and prestige are related to physical attractiveness for women more so than for men (Lerner 1969; Staffieri 1967). The cultural ideal of physical attractiveness is acquired in the preschool years (Styczynsi and Langlois 1977) and matches that of older adolescents by the time children are seven or eight years old (Cavior and Dokecki 1973; Cavior and Lombardi 1973). In one study, at least, physical attractiveness was found to be the only important quality necessary for a man to like his date (Walster et al. 1966).* This focus may broaden to include other qualities as men mature, but it remains central on the oedipal mattering map, and more central for men than for women.

By the time they are nine years old, four out of five girls are on self-imposed diets, and twelve-year-old girls are commonly serious dieters (Wardle and Beales 1986; Hawkins, Tyrell, and Jackson 1983). By the first year of college, one out of every eight women relies on self-induced vomiting or laxatives (bulimia) to control her weight (Heyn 1989). According to

*Reviewing a recent edition of a local newspaper (*Express,* August 2, 1990), I came upon the section in which people seeking a relationship can, in modern style, advertise their own qualities and those of the people whom they are seeking. Within the section describing potential heterosexual partners, almost every advertisement by a woman led off with a description of her appearance, while virtually none by men did. Instead the men described the physical qualities they sought in a woman, along with their own nonphysically based characteristics.

a variety of studies and clinical and anecdotal data, gender clearly seems a much better predictor of dissatisfaction with weight and appearance than does actual weight. In fact, being overweight has been found to affect negatively the quantity and quality of women's relationships with men, while having little or no effect on men's relationships with women (Stake and Lauer 1987).

Consider the following:

If women are consistently more dissatisfied with their bodies than are men, young women are the most dissatisfied, particularly with their weight, hips, and muscle tone (Cash, Winstead, and Janda 1986);

More women than men have rated parts of their bodies negatively (Second and Jourard 1953);

Females aged eleven to nineteen rate their bodies less satisfactorily than their male counterparts (Clifford 1971);

In one sample, eighty-six Midwestern high school females consistently overestimated the width of their faces, chests, waists, and hips (Halmi, Goldberg, and Cunningham 1977);

One researcher found that 95 percent of the women he studied overestimated their body size (Thompson 1986). The more inaccurate they were, the lower their self-esteem;

In a college sample, 59 percent of females rated themselves as low on "satisfaction with figure" (Douty, Moore, and Hartford 1974). It does not take a psychologist to figure out which parts they were dissatisfied with.

THE BODY AS A PRESENTATION

In Western society women are consistently and obsessively concerned not with the process of becoming more physically adept or expressive of the needs of their own particular bodies, but instead with the body and the self as products and conveyers of information to the observer. Since the body is never a finished product, but only as good as it is at the moment, only a work in progress, women must be eternally vigilant about appearance. More often than not, women become the enemies of their bodies in a struggle to mold them as society wishes, to mediate and embody conflicts between the physical and the demands of society.

But the body obviously cannot be infinitely manipulated and decorated.

It often insists on growing in its own way with a wisdom all its own. It can be fought constantly with cosmetics and clothing, with diets and exercise, and, even more extremely, with help from the burgeoning cosmetic-surgery industry. It can be molded, manipulated, and disguised. The better a woman looks, the better life she will presumably lead, the better she will presumably be treated (unless, of course, she looks *too* good; recall the study I mentioned earlier that found most positive attributions being given to moderately good-looking women)—and the more she will get lost in the embodiment of society's and her own conflicting demands.

At least since the 1920s, women have turned to dieting as a means of molding and shaping the body (Clifford 1971; Huenemann et al. 1966; Jourard and Second 1955; Wooley, Wooley, and Dyrenforth 1979). As large bosoms became fashionable in the 1940s and 1950s, the importance of dieting lessened and that of foundation garments increased (Caldwell 1981; Probert 1981). In the late 1960s, with the advent of the miniskirt, attention shifted to lower body parts, skimpily displayed, which precluded the use of foundation garments and instead reintroduced the need to diet in order to conform to the feminine ideal (Mazur 1986). This ideal, along with the growing influence of the visual media, advertising, and fashion industries, created enormous cultural pressure for women to meet it.

Silverstein et al. (1986) surveyed television characters, women's and men's magazines, and popular film stars and found that the current standard of attractiveness is slimmer for women than it is for men and than it was for women in the past. At the same time, women's actual body size has been increasing. According to a recent Gallup poll, richer women are lighter and thinner than poorer ones, but richer men have the biggest waists and broadest chests (Gallup and Newport 1990). Most women, but few men, are dieting at any given time (Berscheid, Walster, and Bohrnstedt 1973; Lerner, Orlos, and Knapp 1976; Miller, Coffman, and Linke 1980). When asked to comment on their bodies, diverse samples of women usually say that they are overweight and that their hips are too big (Ben-Tovim and Crisp 1984; Birtchnell, Dolan, and Lacey 1987; Thompson 1986).

Clearly, training to be worried about and defined by appearance is embedded in the process of learning what it means to be a female in this society. This training comes from parents or parenting adults, along with other relatives and friends, doctors, nurses, teachers, peers, and the more impersonal but extremely effective extension of the oedipal gaze, the visual media.

For example, size and bulk have been found to be positively rated to teachers' attributions of competence for boys, especially older boys. Yet they are negatively related to the same ratings for girls, especially older girls

(Villimez, Eisenberg, and Caroll 1986). And the power of magazines, television, and the movies as conveyers and enforcers of visual cultural standards of beauty cannot be overestimated. If I could design a program that allowed access to only one agent of change, I would choose to influence the visual media and their images of desirability.

The relentless lesson is that if a woman can control and shape her body, perhaps she can control or overcome the caprice of life, the arbitrariness of gender assignment with all its existential-physical-emotional-behavioral meaning. Paradoxically, by gaining control of her body, she succumbs to her fate as a woman. Once again, as she succeeds, she fails. This is another paradox of women's development. The identity or self contains within it this damaging, yet life-defining aspect.

According to a popular anecdote, a woman who was dissatisfied with her appearance, and as a result with the way her life was going, resolved to have a facelift, tummy tuck, and liposuction performed. She had her hair colored and styled and learned to use cosmetics expertly. Having completed this transformation and brimming with optimism, she stepped out into the street. A large truck struck and killed her instantly. Facing God, she could not help but complain. "Everything in my life was going great. Why did you do this to me now?" she asked. "To tell the truth," God replied, "I didn't recognize you."

THE BODY AS COMBAT ZONE

Various theories and interpretations of the symbolism surrounding eating disorders within this cultural context have been developed by some very astute observers and interpreters of women's lives. Some of the ways that eating disorders have been understood are as internalized expressions of hatred of women and of women's bodies; as fear of sexuality; as fear of becoming an adult woman (Millman 1980; Bruch 1973, 1978); and as reactions to women's relationships with their mothers (Chernin 1981). Certainly the conflicts surrounding women's desires and appetites, about taking up space, and about adult sexuality are expressed elegantly and painfully in eating disorders in women.

I cannot overemphasize that all the various manifestations of difficulties with eating are only an extreme or parody of the normal. As I am sure that these interpretations all have their place, I am equally sure that if the cultural standard for women's appearance were to change overnight so that

195

bulk became desirable, women would begin stuffing themselves and we observers and chroniclers of the human condition would have to search for the symbolism of large size. Perhaps we would then have to talk of the desire of men to regain their mothers, of women always being required to be in a state of motherhood by being larger than the baby, of hiding or denying sexuality. Psychologists already make some of these meanings about women who are considered obese. This search for meaning, even among psychologists, typically focuses on women's size and not on men's. This is again a reflection of the problem and not a solution or even an analysis of it. Are fat men equivalently considered by psychologists to be denying their sexuality? Are thin or anorectic men? Are they considered to be enmeshed or in conflict with their mothers?

And do we have a psychological model of the kind of struggles that women might be having with their fathers and their relationship to eating disorders? Let me offer a model of an "anorexogenic" father. He responds in oedipal fashion to his daughter's appearance and its pleasingness to him. He teaches her, however subtly, to deny her own appetites in favor of his. He probably responds to her in a variety of sexualized ways. He teaches her to define her self-worth as a reflection. He expects perfection in these standards and, if a mother is present, expects her to enforce and reinforce them. Many studies indicate that the families, and particularly the fathers, of anorectics have perfectionistic standards and explicitly require high academic achievement of them (Suleiman 1986). While Peter Dally and Joan Gomez (1979) have found that issues of academic achievement are more often a trigger for anorexia than are sexual issues, they refer only to overtly troublesome and culturally visible sexual issues.

I suggest that what ties these issues together is a more general need to be pleasing to Father in whatever ways he deems appropriate. In fact, at least one study (Gordon, Beresin, and Herzog 1989) did find that fathers of preanorectic children are characterized by a sense of entitlement, which includes everything from ruling the family autocratically to demanding the largest and best portions of food for themselves. The mothers in these families tend to be deferential and solicitous of the needs of others, especially their spouses. The authors also suggest that these fathers have an engulfing sexualized interest in their daughters. These fathers, in all ways, fit our definition of the oedipal man.

Let us take as a starting place, then, not a constellation of behavior-feelings-thoughts extreme enough to be brought to the attention of professionals as an illness or a visible disorder, but the place of food and eating in the lives of normally socialized women in our society. The sources of women's obsessions with food and eating are made invisible by a culture that defines the problem as being individually and personally, rather than contextually, located. Thus, we have a proliferation of commercially based diet programs and articles and books for women that focus on weight reduction as a matter of individual control. Americans spend $10 billion a year on diet aids and programs, and the majority of these consumers are women (Romano 1980). Both men and women laugh at women for their obsession with dieting. It is another "natural" narcissistic quirk of women. If its contextual meaning is made invisible to the society and to the individual herself, then she becomes a prisoner of the unexamined meaning. Only the body remains visible; the complex cultural and personal conflict is, of course, embodied rather than understood. Only when they reach the extreme of "eating disorders" are problems with larger implications noted. Even so, "eating disorders" then become the problems of certain disturbed individuals. Much as food itself tranquilizes and permits a narrow focus on complex conflicts, so do programs that deal with dieting and/or correcting so-called eating disorders.

NORMAL EATING

I submit that the normal eating pattern for women is a dieting pattern. Consider the following women, each of whose example contains a strategy for both denial of appetite and manipulation of appearance.

Susan keeps a list of every calorie she eats, and exercises every day. If she goes over her allotted calories, she is unhappy and berates herself. She immediately worries about how much weight she has gained from the one transgression, but never weighs herself. Susan, in her mid-thirties and a professor at a major university, is in many ways an extremely competent and effective woman.

Jane has a different strategy. She eats nothing before 5:00 P.M. At that time, she allows herself to eat a large meal. She maintains her average weight this way. Jane is a woman in her mid-fifties who has raised a family, worked in a paraprofessional capacity, and has now returned to school for an advanced degree. She is a talented artist.

Andrea has yet another strategy. She allows herself a different food each day, something she is really craving. To maintain control, she eats only that one food for that day. Sometimes she loses control and eats too much. Then she feels guilty. She also feels too fat unless she is about ten pounds below her ideal healthy weight. She feels that the extra weight, which settles in her hip and thigh areas, is like a burden that she carries around and is not really part of her. She hates it and wishes it would go away, but often does not have the willpower to deny herself food.

Diane has recently completed a commercial diet program, in which she lost twenty pounds. Her lover often complained of her excess weight in the stomach and hip areas and let her know that he was attracted to slim, young women. After Diane lost the weight, he left her for one of these women. Diane is in her late forties, as is her former lover. His new partner is nineteen. Diane struggles to maintain her new weight, has bought a new wardrobe of stylish clothes, and is actively dating. She feels much more attractive and desirable than she did with the "extra" twenty pounds. She hopes to be able to compete for men and to find a new man.

Theresa, in her late twenties, has a thin and shapely figure that is often admired by others. She wears form-fitting clothes and bikinis in the summer to show it off. However, she feels that her breasts sag and, although this is not apparent when she is clothed, it bothers her enough that she is consider-ing plastic surgery to "correct" the problem. Her husband supports this plan, although he does not comment on her "defect."

Cheryl has, for some twenty years, followed the same diet: coffee and toast for breakfast, yogurt or salad for lunch, and fish or some other nonmeat meal for dinner. When she gets too hungry, she smokes a cigarette to lessen her appetite. She has been warned by her doctor to give up smoking, but she persists because she knows that without it she will often not be able to curb her appetite. She tells herself that only a few cigarettes a day will not harm her as much as the stress of constant dieting. She is in her early fifties and has been smoking since adolescence.

Elena has recently become involved in body building, but is unable to lose enough body fat to enter successfully into competition. Most women in body building face this problem, since women's bodies are difficult to mold in the form of men's. Elena is considering taking steroids. She has a history of thyroid problems and is aware of the dangers of steroids, but minimizes them in favor of achieving her goal.

When I see Jean, she tells me, "I'm not feeling well, but it's OK because I've lost three pounds already."

Ann, somewhat guiltily but conspiratorially, lets me know that she is premenstrual and, thus, has been eating chocolate again. I am to understand the complexity of feelings that she has about it.

Charlotte lets me know that "I was so anxious that I vomited today." She is the envy of all her friends because she can vomit so easily.

Lane mentions that she is having stomach problems and looks forward to having diarrhea so she can lose some weight.

Can you find yourself among these examples, or add your own strategy to these? Nearly every woman, unless her body is still young and "perfect" enough to exclude her from this sorority, for now, no doubt can. Chances are that men will not find themselves represented here and may even be somewhat perplexed about women's obsession with dieting.

I could continue indefinitely with such examples, as could any woman, for virtually every woman in this society who has access to sufficient food has a dieting strategy. She can tell you about it easily or conspiratorially, for it both connects and identifies women in this and many other societies. By unspoken female agreement, women help one another enforce their rules of dieting. Each knows that any other woman will accept and understand her strategy and also that she has a dieting strategy of her own. Not all the women in the foregoing examples are clients. This does not separate them from one another or from me. Concern with food, dieting, and appearance unites them. It is, however, obvious that they are women; anyone who doubts this can reread the foregoing examples substituting male names and note how jarring they sound.

What if a man, for example, were to confide in another man with a guilty but conspiratorial smile, "Listen, Craig, let's have a salad for lunch because I slipped and ate some chocolate last night when I was home alone," or "I got depressed after Mary called and canceled our date, so I ate an entire cheesecake," or "I got so upset at gaining three pounds that I binged last night"? Certainly there has been a societally fueled move in the last few years for both men and women to become more conscious of their bodies from the perspective of staying healthy and young-looking. Yet the glorification of youth and the accompanying dread of old age and death do not have the same meaning for men as they do for women.

Men's concern with eating and exercise is health- and youth-related. Women's concern is still primarily with how their attractiveness will be affected. Advertisements often present exercise programs for women as something that will put an end to dieting forever, helping women to look slim and trim. An ad for the ski machine NordicTrack says: "Not mascara. Not perfume. Not even a pair of new stonewashed denim jeans. Nothing can truly improve the way you look like being in shape." Of many, many other examples, a recent newspaper article discussed the new ways that people are aging: "Grandma has been given a facelift, symbolically, if not literally. And she may not even be gray"; while "Grandpa may be playing in a softball league" (Ghent, April 2, 1989). Even in the New Age old age, men remain active and women remain youthful-*looking*.

The obsession with dieting is most prevalent among, but not exclusive to, middle-class and upper-middle-class women, who have the luxury of too much available food. It does not appear to be confined to the United States. I have experienced firsthand this female concern with eating and not eating among women in such diverse areas as Western Europe and Central America, where I have both taught psychology classes and conducted research on gender roles. It seems that if they are not starving from a lack of available food, then many women will starve themselves voluntarily. With a transition to economic surplus, physical size becomes more symbolically based. There seems to be an extensive women's culture, within which concerns with appearance are integral and which transcends the national borders created by men. Thus, a group of women can fall into a discussion of various diet strategies, admit their lapses and failures, their exercise and starvation regimes, and instantly understand one another. This is a language that connects even women who are strangers to one another in every other way. They can discuss the highly desired and forbidden fruit. They can comment on each other's appearance. They can share dieting strategies and monitor one another's transgressions with unspoken agreement about just what constitutes a transgression. This connectedness to other women is based upon self-denial and self-control and proceeds from the viewpoint of the indeterminate observer.

In our current social milieu, smaller is considered better for females only. While this is subject to geographical and ethnic variation,* the general principle holds that women should be smaller than the men they are with. Women's bodies, as their worlds, can grow within parameters that can still be subsumed by those of men. Exercise and sports have become a bit more acceptable, as long as women stay feminine about it. This means not becoming too big or muscular, and remaining concerned with presenting a feminine appearance. This has recently been accomplished to feminine

---

*For example, taller seems more common and more approved on the West Coast than the East; and among certain ethnic groups, such as Latins, a slightly fuller figure is preferred.

perfection by the runner Florence Griffith-Joyner, who won the women's 100 meters in the 1988 Olympics by running faster than any woman had run the race in the Olympics. Called the world's fastest woman (Page 1991), she not only credited her husband with training her but retired immediately thereafter to promote hairstyles, clothing, and two-inch-long airbrushed painted fingernails. Apparently, this is a feminine way for a woman to become a sports figure.

While it is important to understand why certain body types are in fashion these days and what these trends mean in the context of the current masculinist social milieu, it is not unlike understanding any other fashion or trend. The principle behind it holds across time and cultures: it is the gender division itself, and not specific attributes, that remains constant. It is the oedipal context, the ability of men as a group to define women as a group that frames this issue at different historical moments. The specifics of appearance may change, but the fact that women's worth is equated with appearance in the eyes of determinate and indeterminate men is constant.

LIFE OR DEATH

One of the most shocking revelations I have ever heard came from a group of women, all participants in a therapy group for postmastectomy patients. Virtually all of them agreed that one positive outcome of their illness was the fact that they had lost weight, and would continue to do so. Even if they were eventually to die of the illness, it seemed, they could at least have the dubious satisfaction of dying thin. What does this say about women's obsessions with their bodies and appearances? It says that appearance is more important than life itself. It says that the meanings of life and of death for women differ from those of men. Appearance *is* life. To how many men would a terminal illness have this welcome side effect?

Reading the local newspaper, I came across an advertisement from a major department store, which "invites you to a special seminar, focusing on the *beauty needs* of women in cancer treatment" (*San Jose Mercury News*, April 2, 1989; italics added). In bold print are the words "BEAUTY AND CANCER." Women do not only focus on beauty in the face of cancer but may even risk developing cancer for the sake of beauty. Statistics indicate that the only group in which the rate of smoking is currently rising is young females, many of whom, as Cheryl does, use cigarettes as a dieting tool. What, in learning to be female, allows or impels millions of women in our own and many other countries to focus on and manipulate their bodies endlessly in search of a societally sanctioned appearance? What does it say of identity and self-concept? It speaks of a disconnection from the body and physical experience for women. It speaks also of a profound denial by society and often by women themselves of the damage that is done to women's bodies and psyches. It speaks of the sort of self and sense of self that women develop. Both women's physical and psychological makeup are disconnected from their potentially truer inner and outer experience. They have learned to substitute the symbolic for the actual physical and psychological, as if arranging flowers or a performance instead of themselves.

As women's bodies are the battleground for the masculinist conflicts and meanings of the zeitgeist, they become women's battleground, the embodiment of these conflicts. Women and men are *both* obsessed with women's bodies, figures and faces, hair color and clothing, primarily with the particular parts deemed important from the masculine perspective. One woman, for example, complained to me that, when she was an adolescent, her mother was constantly commenting on her weight and her hairstyle. "But," she said, "I never really felt noticed. She only saw the parts of me that were important to her."

The scrutiny of women's bodies in all stages of dress and undress leads to a strong sense of shame at such heightened visibility. Women experience shame about their natural appetites and unfeminine appearances. This sense of shame leads to a desire to disappear, to hide the body, to become invisible. One can express such a desire by emphasizing and flaunting appearance or by trying to hide it. This is another version of the reaction that is seen very specifically in victims of child sexual abuse, whose two most characteristic responses are compulsive and hostile sexuality or anxious and fearful nonsexuality—and both these strategies make a woman disappear. They are attempts to achieve safety as well as to avoid humiliation. One can attempt to take control of one's own body, to offer or allow its use before it is taken. Similarly, one can shrink the body until the very self seems to disappear. At the same time, one can keep trying over and over to get one's body just right, and fail forever.

PARTS OF A WHOLE

Women commonly identify themselves with specific body parts. This self-concept derives directly from how women are viewed in this society and illustrates the direct impact of context on the physical and the psychological. What one defines as excess fat comes to be experienced first as *only* a part and second as *not part* of me, a removable part under which is waiting the real me. If one experiences oneself in parts, then it follows that a part may be removed without the whole being changed, that is, "part of me" can become "not part of me." The parts are both embodied and disconnected, or disembodied. It also follows that if a woman does not want this part, this fat, to be part of her body, then it is not. If the excess is "not me," her body can still at least potentially fit the ideal. She can continue to strive forever to reach her potential.

Marcia Millman (1980) has said that fat people disown their bodies and think of themselves only from the neck up, and Kim Chernin (1981) has noted that all people with eating disorders recede from the physical world. Women's disowning of the physical is based on an obsessive concern with it. The body is an incessant, obsessive concern, but only as symbolically construed. Women are engaged in a raging battle between the pleasures of the natural appetite and appearance. To add to this, as the appetite becomes unnatural and instead symbolic, it also becomes compulsive, disconnected from hunger and instead connected and driven by deprivation and a quest for acceptance and approval. What women disown, or attempt to disown, is the shame and humiliation of the physical by making some or all of their bodies "not-me." They are simultaneously making two statements: "I am my figure" and "I am not my figure." In this way, the external and internal battles are embodied. As a result, however, their eating becomes secret and compulsive, furthering shame even as it avoids it. The paradox of women's individual solutions is seen again.

As women's bodies are found wanting, so do women find their own bodies wanting. They can be fed until they are physically full but symbolically starved, or the reverse. To be full as a person is to be empty, a failure as a woman. If one is starved for basic respect and affirmation, for the esteem of others for who one is, but instead is esteemed for who one is not, one remains forever starved. The "not-me" survives and is fed as the me remains undeveloped and invisible.

This sort of partitioned sense of self is also exemplified by the "thin within" approach to weight loss. From this perspective, there is a real me, a platonic ideal self, waiting to emerge from the chrysalis of fat that encases it. An extreme example of this configuration is the weight loss of the talk show host Oprah Winfrey, who, having lost some seventy pounds, conveyed this literally and symbolically by pulling behind her onstage a wagon of animal fat equivalent to the amount of weight she had lost. The obvious message that she was more like an animal when she was heavier and is now infinitely more desirable as a gendered person (woman) aside, the point of this chapter could not be better exemplified: the me and the "not-me" had changed places.

Encouragement to experience oneself in parts also comes from certain popular psychological and psychotherapeutic models, in particular the Gestalt and the object-relations schools. From the jargon of the Gestalt approach, the manner of expressing conflict or ambivalence—"part of me feels this and part of me feels that"—has entered common parlance. Ironically, an approach that emphasized developing a whole, or a gestalt, has been influential in leading people to think of themselves in parts, as if they could not contain an entire conflict within a single psyche. I consider this sort of fragmented thinking harmful to all people but particularly to women, who already have a propensity to build their psychological selves on a physical identity fragmented into evaluated parts.

The object-relations school of therapy posits such inner self-representations and parts-objects as the grandiose self, the idealized parental imago, the nuclear self, the self-object, the cohesive self, and so on (Kohut 1968; Kohut and Wolf 1987; Kohut 1971). These fragments are all brought inside to fill the empty interior space of the self through the psychological mechanism of projection (Cushman 1990). But it is imperative for women to be able to maintain the notion of a complex and varied self *without* having to fragment it.

MOTHERING IN CONTEXT

In addition to these components, Chernin (1985) and others have emphasized the role of the relationship with the mother in eating problems of women. A mother, however, does not exist in isolation, that is, without a father or the all-pervasive cultural father of oedipal society (Leonard 1983). Women's problematic relationship with food begins not just in the separate relationships with Mother or Father but in an attempt to resolve the interaction or relationship between the two individually or culturally. If a daughter is not in a family with a female and male parent present, she is still in a society defined by the values and perspectives of the fathers. Mothering is shaped and defined not just by the individual mother but by the needs and perspective of the father. That is what is meant by *mothering in context*.

What is good mothering in an oedipal context? For that matter, what is good enough fathering? Feeding and nurturing must necessarily include preparation to live in the larger world, which must necessarily include self-denial. The good mother must feed and nurture her daughter, but she must also teach her not to eat just for pleasure or to fulfill her appetite or only for nurturance. For eating affects her body in many complex ways, and the good mother must be prepared for all of these. The daughter must be fed for health, to grow strong and big, but not too strong or too big. A mother must communicate a complex set of injunctions that are at odds with each other. Eat for health, for satisfaction, even for confirmation of the mother's effectiveness. Secondarily comes the injunction to eat only within the context of management of one's size and appearance. A girl's having a healthy appetite is not an unambivalently happy thing for her or for her mother, whose job it is, as a modern-day Jocasta, to prepare her for the world of men. The daughter must struggle to accept food while negating its effect on her body. While denying any appetite, she must try to allow it to be satisfied. She must swallow and digest all these conflicts.

If the good mother doesn't do her job well enough, then the good father must enter in to let his daughter know how important it is that her appearance be pleasing and that her eating be directed toward this end. To succeed as a woman, she must learn to manipulate her appearance, and food is an important tool toward that end. Daughters must learn to please their fathers in the same ways that their mothers do or in ways that their mothers cannot.

Arliss and her daughter, Hannah, often go shopping together. They invariably include in their outings a stop for lunch at a local restaurant. There they share the dieter's special, while talking about Hannah's latest boyfriend. They are a close mother and daughter. Hannah's father beams with pride when she models her purchases for him on her slim, trim body.

Jessica's mother would struggle with her about what to eat and what not to eat. Everything was either forbidden or compulsory in the service of promoting health while controlling the weight of her growing adolescent body. Her father would then pronounce judgment, which was often, "You are too fat." Jessica does not binge, purge, or starve herself, but she diets incessantly. She worries about calories, about losing control, about how her body looks. From time to time, she loses control and devours an entire bag of potato chips or candy. For the most pleasurable experience, she prefers eating alone, as then she doesn't have to maintain control or be seen indulging herself. This secret pleasure is often more enjoyable than sex and always more shameful. Unless she is starving or ten pounds under her healthy weight, she feels too fat. She squeezes into the tightest clothes she can wear and obsessively worries about her body getting too big, too full, too flabby, too ample. Stomach, hips, and thighs are the problem areas.

Jessica suffers from no pathology or "eating disorder." She is just a normal, average female.

For women, eating becomes tied to appearance, self-control and self-indulgence, nurturance, guilt and shame, not just to hunger or its satisfaction. It soon becomes psychologically, rather than physically, motivated. Some women cannot tell when they are hungry. Others are always hungry unless they are stuffed. Forbidden fruit, hidden pleasure, is embedded with shame and the pain of failing to meet the standards of control or appearance. Fat people, especially women, are the frequent butt of jokes. While men are more often overweight, it is women who diet more. Only women are judged by the size of the portions of food they eat, by body parts, by the ideal of staying eternally young and desirable. In the United States alone approximately 300,000 women have had their breasts enlarged, and 15,000 to 20,000 per year have them reduced (Lehman 1979). How many men undergo anything resembling this? For men, lifting weights to make the body larger is not as complexly motivated, nor is it in any way self-negating. An adolescent boy who eats a lot has a healthy appetite. The more he can eat, the more of a man he may be considered, as evidenced by eating contests held by college fraternities.

Can his female cohort have a healthy appetite? What is a healthy appetite for a woman? The less she can eat, the more of a woman she is. She may eat before a date or a party to appear appetiteless. In a TV commercial currently being shown, a woman discusses how she can eat desserts in front of her husband now that she is married to him rather than just dating. She still chooses a sensible (low-calorie) dessert. Less is more; self-esteem for women is based on self-denial.

FOOD OR SEX

Having seen how limits are imposed upon women in this society, having considered the danger, actual or potential, on which those limits are based, the ridicule and humiliation, explicit or implicit, it remains to translate these experiences into the personal realm of eating. Women are often left with internal adventures or battles centering not on the external world but on their own bodies and psyches. These are the safe realms, the hidden, invisible adventures. I wonder, in fact, how the world of food and eating would look if this realm were understood as women's adventure? *Tune in tonight for the adventures of Amanda as she encounters a five-pound chocolate cake. Will she succeed? Can she overcome her own raging appetite and resist or will she succumb to the forces of hunger? Can she prove that she is a real woman?*

Women's relationship with food is highly charged and eroticized. Chernin noted that her own feelings about food are reminiscent "of the way people in the nineteenth century used to feel about sexuality and particularly about masturbation" (1982, p. 6). This is certainly a realm in which most normal women invest the essence of their passion, albeit in secrecy, like a guilty sexual secret. I wonder what would be revealed by asking a few hundred or thousand women whether they would prefer sex without any negative consequences (unwanted pregnancy or disease) or being able to eat any food they wanted without any negative consequences (gaining weight). A novella called *Vanilla Days/Chocolate Nights* published in a women's magazine actually deals with a woman's fantasy lover who knows her tastes so well that, before making love for the first time, he covers his entire body in chocolate: "This dear man. . . . How well he knew me" (Frank 1990, p. 7).

At the meetings of a women's group to which I belong, the proceedings are regularly conducted over chocolate. What men's group would do this? Many of these women, as others, are embarrassed to eat too much in public, to be seen indulging their appetites. One confessed on the second day of meeting that, after resisting all day, she had "succumbed at night in her room" to some chocolate.

In a study of Rorschach responses (Zivney, Nash, and Hulsey 1989), girls who were sexually abused before nine years of age, in addition to having morbid images, gave many responses centered around food and clothing. The authors interpreted this finding as reflective of unsatisfied primitive needs. I would not necessarily disagree with this particular meaning of the girls' perceptions on the Rorschach, but would suggest that they have been given an early and strong dose of what it means to be a woman in a man's world and are, and will likely continue to be, obsessed with issues of feeding, appearance, self-denial, and shame in just the ways I am discussing. Their obsessions, fears, and pain may be more intense and overt than those of a female who has not specifically been abused in this way, but it is a difference in degree, not in kind.

While Hilde Bruch (1978) has suggested that anorectics are demonstrating the triumph of mind over body, I would offer a less dualistic interpretation: that is, women embody the conflicts of society concerning their bodies and appearances. Within this framework, like everyone else, they struggle for approval and self-respect and to avoid shame and humiliation. But eating itself and certainly a "healthy" appetite are shameful for women, so that self-affirmation can be achieved only by self-denial.

I don't know which invention of society, the mirror or the scale, has been more psychologically destructive to women. This may seem like a trivial criticism in a world where men have developed bombs capable of apocalyptic destruction. But these two seemingly innocuous devices, as utilized in a misogynist society, have caused as much of a different kind of harm as drugs or bombs have.

Concerns with eating connect women to other women, to children, and to men in different but powerfully embedded ways that could easily be lost to them with the resolution of the conflicts or abandonment of the obsession concerning eating. They would lose the connection with men through approval/humiliation and with women's sharing of these concerns. They would stand alone, facing a basic existential issue. They would also lose a secret and compelling pleasure.

The physicality/sexuality of women in postindustrial society is inextricably intertwined with food and feeding. Women's highly charged conflicts around food and eating represent a failed attempt to return to Jocasta and the self, to a self-centeredness and self-nurturance only beginning to be possible for a few women in a patriarchal society. The prevalence of problems with eating also demonstrates an increased attempt to reach this goal, and the difficulty of doing so. Here are contained both the problem and the solution, and maybe even a form of safe sex for women.

A recent artistic renaissance has sprung from women's regaining their sight. "The Dinner Party" by Judy Chicago is a prime example of this genre. It is an artistic representation of a dinner table set with dishes that represent a variety of women of historical or current significance to the artist. The table, as well as many of the designs on the plates, is triangular in form. It also symbolizes the omnipresent, yet invisible, connection of women to food and sexuality. As the presentation of food and eating in women's magazines is sensuous, so is it here. The interior/exterior blurring contains the ambivalence in the desired and the forbidden, in satisfaction and denial, in the visible and the invisible. In this work, the triangle, an ancient symbol of the feminine, is made visible. The inner and the outer are united. Such art, along with a blossoming of literature, theater, and music, represents a cultural beginning toward seeing with women's eyes and struggling to take back women's senses and voices.

10

A New Model for Feminist Psychotherapy

And the end of all our exploring
Will be to arrive where we started
And know the place for the first time.

—T. S. Eliot
Little Gidding

Psychotherapy has in common with epistemology the focus on meaning and how it is made and acquired in the experience of everyday life. Feminist psychotherapies and epistemologies share a focus on making visible the hidden effects of gender in ordinary life. They are both oriented toward exposing masculinist meanings and their damaging effects in general and in particular, and toward developing alternative meanings and choices based upon the actual lived experience of girls and women. In this way, women can be helped to see for themselves prior to, or instead of from, the perspective of the indeterminate or determinate masculine observer. The more intimate focus is obviously not sufficient to bring about large-scale cultural change in oedipal society. This does not seem to me to be an argument for not doing feminist psychotherapy, but it is an argument for not *only* doing feminist psychotherapy. Feminist change must, by its very nature, be multifaceted, involving confrontation with meaning in every sphere of experience.

Insofar as feminist psychotherapy concerns itself with the detailed meanings of a particular woman's experience, it contributes to the feminist cultural project of giving a respectful hearing to the diverse, yet similar, experiences of women. In this and many other ways, it can contribute to the

210

individual and cultural resolution of the antigonal and oedipal complexes. The dilemma is not so much whether to work at the micro- or macrofeminist level, but not to separate and dichotomize them in this way, as each feeds and nourishes the other. Psychology and psychotherapy are intimately involved in the integrated understanding of the dis-integrated. Feminist psychotherapy works toward helping women remember forgotten experiences and making invisible meanings visible. It seeks out both the embodied and the disembodied in women's experiences and takes as its goal returning to women control of their own bodies/minds/hearts.

It is frequently said that feminist psychotherapy does not involve a particular model or method of therapy, but instead adds or integrates a feminist perspective on any of the many models of psychotherapy available. I suggest that we not abandon prematurely the development of an integrated feminist model for psychotherapy. The model of the nature of personal development (in context) that I have developed in this book leads directly to a model of change (in context) upon which feminist psychotherapy can be based. The building blocks of such a model are as follows:

1. All experience is interrelated and is organized by meaning. *Meaning* is not a cognitive or an intellectual term, but encompasses thoughts-feelings-behavior or mind-heart-body.
2. Meaning is conveyed in this and in any culture by all agents of socialization, including parents, siblings, other relatives, teachers, peers, the visual and written media, and is also organized and reorganized by each person.
3. The most centrally meaningful principle on our culture's mattering map is gender, which intersects with other culturally and personally meaningful categories such as race, class, ethnicity, and sexual orientation. Within all of these categories, people attribute different meanings to femaleness and maleness.
4. The meanings of maleness and femaleness in our society are represented by the oedipal and antigonal complexes and their interrelationship.
5. Feminist therapy involves identifying and changing the personal/cultural meanings explicit and implicit in the unresolved oedipal and antigonal complexes as they are embedded in each woman's (and man's) most personal experience.

Feminist therapy begins with a woman telling her own story or stories. The feminist therapist, as any therapist, must give the client a respectful audience. This is nothing but effective therapy, but must be underlined here because the feminist therapy setting is often the first place in which a woman has the opportunity to become visible and seen, and eventually to begin to see for herself. Yet a woman's story is only the starting place. To facilitate the process, the feminist therapist must actively continue the process of questioning her own meanings and ferreting out the indeterminate observer who will be hiding in them as well as in those of her client. She must try to see through the client's eyes at the same time that she sees through her own and those of the indeterminate male observer. This is the multiple perspective familiar to so many women in oedipal society, here used for women's own sake.

Feminist therapy has in common with many other approaches a focus on the relationship between therapist and client as microcosmic and as a fulcrum for movement and change. This relationship must also be understood within a context of meanings and values. This involves searching for multiple meanings, each connected to a particular perspective and always understanding from what perspective a particular meaning is made, including that of the therapist. A feminist perspective involves acknowledgment of and search for the invisible, for what lies at the margins of any story, and for ways that women's invisibility translates into invisibility to herself. Where there is visible conflict experienced psychologically or physically, the signposts are already in place.

Psychotherapeutic approaches have often focused on finding the one true meaning of an experience. Whatever their theoretical orientation, therapists also frequently commit this error. For example, a woman I know tells of having been raped one summer when, as a student, she was hitchhiking through Europe. A man picked her up, drove her to an isolated area, and attacked her in his car. For a few minutes, she fought and screamed, soon realizing that there was no one nearby, or at least that no one was going to respond. At that point she froze and just hoped to get it over with as soon as possible. Being in a foreign country and knowing that she would be blamed for hitchhiking, she did not bother to report the rape or even to tell anyone that it had happened. Yet, over the next few days, she could not rid herself of the idea that her father, whose seventieth birthday was that week, had precipitously died. She called home collect and was reassured that he was fine. She did not speak of this incident until several years later, when she decided to tell her therapist about it. "Obviously," he said, "you were enraged at your father for not protecting you." A few years later another therapist, upon hearing this story, told her, "Of course you called home. You wanted your mommy." Which one was correct? Which therapist was a father and which a mother? Her meanings had met up with theirs.

Both of these therapists sought *the* correct meaning of the experience.

Perhaps the woman was also enraged at her father for being a man, as it is men who rape women. Perhaps she was enraged at her mother for not being able to protect her. Perhaps she felt damaged and feared they would not love her anymore or that she, by extension, had damaged her father. Perhaps she felt that she had betrayed them both and that they would want to destroy her. Perhaps she felt damaged, destroyed, dead herself. Perhaps she felt too much shame to tell them directly what had happened. Perhaps she wanted to protect them although they had not protected her. In this way, she could still feel that she had some control and power, although she had just been shown how powerless she really was. Perhaps calling home made the incident in Europe, and Europe itself, seem less real, home more real. Perhaps calling collect helped her to feel taken care of in some way.

I could go on and on about what meanings were embedded in this experience and never touch on them all, for I am also speaking only from my own perspective. I could ask the woman herself, for whom it would be much more painful to engage in this exercise than it is for me. Most readers could also add to the picture, particularly if I were to sketch in more details about this woman, her family, her ethnic and religious background, the man she was engaged to marry. I do know that she felt it was her fault for hitchhiking, or at least that anyone she told would so believe. She was aware that if she told her parents, they would attempt to curtail her freedom and she would feel even further diminished. She bought her freedom at the high price of aloneness and shame—a very female strategy that allowed her to win by losing.

We could also try to imagine a male hitchhiker having the same experience, and this exercise would lead us to more gendered meanings. Try, for example, the comments of the two therapists: "Obviously you were enraged at your father for not protecting you"; "Of course you called home. You wanted your mommy." Would either have been made to a male client? Would they have made him seem smaller, more helpless, and more contained—more feminine? That is, more feminine than the very experience of being raped would have made him? Should this have happened to a man, the oedipal strategy would have entailed enlarging and strengthening himself in some way, perhaps by perpetrating the same damage on another individual.

We are not on a quest for *the* right meaning. Complexities of meaning must be carefully disentangled and disembedded. Part of the feminist therapist's job is to be able to retain this complexity in the service of moving toward greater simplicity by relieving women of the physical/psychological burden that gendered meanings engender. Invisible meanings that are damaging and dis-integrating must be separated from those that are enhancing or that can connect the client to herself and to other women.

The surplus of meaning attributed to women is an ongoing focus of the process of feminist therapy. Hidden meanings from the perspective of the indeterminate masculine observer, when made visible, can then be relinquished or replaced by alternatives. One way to unearth these meanings, in listening to any woman's stories, is to ask, Who is this about? Is the experience just about you? Is it about you at all? Who else is it about? Whose perspective is invisible? How would it be interpreted differently if it were about a person in a man's body? The focus on meanings involves freeing women from the prison of meaning by returning those that belong to the indeterminate observer of oedipal culture, as well as to particular identifiable Oedipuses.

Traditional psychotherapies work toward the goal of making conscious the narrowly personal and leaving the rest unconscious. That is, influences other than the narrowly defined personal remain invisible. Feminist psychotherapy involves awareness and understanding of the way everyday experiences, including so-called psychological disorders, are organized according to gender and other culturally salient variables. As meanings are changed, the invisible is made visible. This is not a simple cognitive experience, but one that is highly affect-laden and embodied and that profoundly makes visible the connections among women. It is consciousness as used by Paulo Freire (1969) and certain European (Italian) feminists, the making visible of women externally and internally, in society and to themselves.

I would distinguish what I mean here from the early model of consciousness raising in the women's movement in the following ways. First, I do not consider it to be a time-limited means to an end, but an ongoing way of making sense of experience. Therapists and the women with whom they work must continue to ask themselves and other women, What are the multiple meanings in this situation and which ones have salience for me at this time? Which are masculine meanings applied to women? Am I using my eyes to see for myself? Feminist therapists must ask questions of their own as well as of their clients' experiences: Which ones are unique and which are shared by other women? Which other women in particular have been in this situation? An African-American woman may share certain meanings with other African-American women, other meanings with white (European-American) women or particular white (European-American) women, and yet others with African-American women and men. A lesbian woman who is Jewish may have certain experiences and meanings in common with heterosexual Jewish women, others with heterosexual or lesbian women of color, and others with only lesbian women, Jewish and non-Jewish. Points of overlap and of difference help to make visible new and different meanings, to continue to question reality.

What I am describing requires holding the tension of the complex perspective, continuing to look for what or who is being kept invisible. Feminist therapy is an exercise in peripheral vision, double vision, inner vision. Children notice details that seem irrelevant to an adult. Part of becoming an adult in this society means learning to make consistent stories and images, overlooking contradictory and paradoxical details as "natural" or as background rather than as what Teresa de Lauretis calls "a horizon of meanings" (1986, p. 5).

Yet dealing with a woman's pain and fears, joys and pleasures, is not simply a sociopolitical exercise. It is an intimate meeting of the most personal kind, filled with meaning, with fear and caring, courage and sadness, anger and grief, loss and gain. It is meaning as it permeates the body-mind-heart. Some of the meanings are those shared by women in this society and can be anticipated. There are particular aspects of women's experience and identity in current society that will be addressed characteristically in feminist therapy and that must be addressed in order to help a woman move through the resolution of the antigonal complexities. I have already explored many of these in the previous chapters, and it remains only to consider them in conjunction with the specific process of psychotherapy.

I do not consider current systems of pathology or pathologizing itself to be useful in understanding the experiences or the problems of women in context. Such taxonomies are not only divisive of experience but narrow and individually based. Locating the interstices of each woman's experience and every woman's experience is a more useful way to begin to understand more fully the source of successes and difficulties. For example, assessment in therapy with a woman, at this historical time and cultural place, might more usefully include understanding the issues in the following list and locating them on her mattering map. Obviously this sort of assessment is a process that is embedded in and not separate from and prior to the therapy, as are more traditional assessment procedures.

1. Quality and centrality of relationships with other women, men, and children. How much and in what ways do these relationships determine the sense of self and of self-esteem? What particular aspects are enhancing and debilitating to others and to the woman herself?
2. History and current personal experience of limitations imposed by parents, peers, teachers, the media, and other significant sources and of more apparent violations, including, but not lim-

ited to, the more obvious ones involving violence, incest, and rape.

3. Own evaluation of appearance and of its centrality on her mattering map.

4. Physical presentation of self, including habitual aspects of posture, carriage, gait, expression, musculature, movement, as well as situational variations when dealing with specific issues and experiences in therapy.

5. Degree of fragmentation experienced physically and psychologically.

6. Sense of invisibility and hypervisibility or exposure in general and in particular circumstances.

7. Eating/diet strategy.

8. Losses and disappointments, especially loss of the possible and of the sense of self.

9. Anger at and loss of the mother (Jocasta) and enmeshment with an individual father or cultural (oedipal) fathers.

10. Degree of identification with the indeterminate observer.

11. Extent of sense of responsibility for events and behaviors of people whom she cannot control.

12. Experiences of shame.

13. Sense of self and of self-esteem.

Assessment locates the unresolved antigonal issues. While, in more traditional approaches, some of these are sometimes assessed with clients for whom they appear to be salient, I am suggesting instead that they are issues for every women in this society at this time and should routinely become the focal points of any assessment procedure.

For example, in their initial interview in a traditional family systems–based clinic setting, the female partner in a heterosexual couple was extremely distressed to learn that the therapy would be observed through a one-way mirror. Her male partner, who had made the appointment, had not informed her of this aspect of the interview. Her distress concerned her appearance; she had come from work and was dressed in jeans. She finally agreed to continue the sessions, but requested a later appointment time in the future to give her a chance to go home and change her clothes. Her partner was to all appearances extremely concerned that she look good, and complained bitterly that she was five pounds overweight and did nothing about it. By not informing her that they would be observed, he seemed to be attempting to get the therapy team to see her from his perspective—not looking right. To complete the picture, he was dressed in a suit and tie. Both agreed that his appearance was perfect, hers defective.

Who is this about? When the therapist had them tell their story, from their perspective it was about the wife and her defects, with the husband's disappointment and hostility perhaps secondary. The therapist, trained in a family systems perspective, understood them to be in a power struggle in which both were equal participants. The fact that the struggle centered on her appearance was not considered meaningful by the therapist. The goal of therapy was to recalibrate the system so that the struggle could be resolved.

From the feminist therapist's viewpoint, what is most immediately noticeable is the unresolved Oedipus-Antigone relationship. The battleground is her body and appearance, which are charged with containing both their conflicts. Both see through his eyes, although she no doubt has her own buried perspective. Both accept his right to comment upon and define her appearance and appropriate size. As a result, her sense of hypervisibility and shame is apparent. His sense of entitlement and weakly defined boundaries is also part of the picture, as are his fear of clearer self-definition and of standing alone. His dependency is hidden behind hers. Her sense of lesser worth, along with his avoidance of his own fears and conflicts, is part of the complex picture. Their relationship could not simply be recalibrated. If these issues are not addressed, they will manifest themselves in another way. Even if they are addressed, they are manifested in a myriad of ways. From this broader perspective, this cannot be a struggle between equals, as the entire weight of the indeterminate male observer is behind him.

As another example, a woman client I saw often worried about how her son was developing. She felt that she had not been a good enough parent to him and had damaged him by working outside the home when he was young. It had never occurred to her even to consider whether her husband had influenced their son's development by also working outside the home. It is more than likely that the employment arrangements of both parents affected the son, with the effect mediated by the meanings he learned to attribute to it. That is, if he understood his mother's working outside the home as his father's failure, the effect would be quite different than if he understood it as his father's success as a man. It would differ again if he understood it to have meaning about his mother and not his father at all and/or about himself.

I needed to understand which of these meanings had become part of this woman's sense of self. In this case, the son was not resentful, but the father/husband was. He didn't overtly blame her, but she did the job for both of them, seeing the situation through his eyes and those of the indeterminate male observer. Family relations were her responsibility and her fault. How her children "turned out" (as if they were products rather than people) reflected on her and was a measure not just of her job performance but of her self-worth. She worried incessantly although, in fact, her son's ailments existed mostly in her imagination and were mainly a comment on her own imperfection in her eyes.

In understanding this situation, we begin with the woman's own story and try to ferret out the perspectives of the determinate and indeterminate (oedipal) male observers. Unlike the prior case, they are not situated in the meaning of her appearance but in the meaning of her responsibility for relationships, for what she cannot control. She experienced these discrepancies, however, much as did the woman in the prior case, through a pervasive sense of shame and impaired self-esteem. She also felt the guilt of someone who is responsible to and for others. She would often become quiet, depressed, and self-critical. The strategy of the first woman client was to dress up and be physically hypervisible. This one became quiet and invisible. Both are easily located among the unresolved issues of Antigone.

Another woman let me know that her boss at work had confided in her that an extremely ugly woman had applied for a management position in the company. She laughed nervously as she told me this story. Predictably, her boss did not add a qualifier that this was so in his eyes, but assumed instead that his eyes were universal, that he was simply describing something about the woman. Implicitly he affirmed his own right to judge her, a classic oedipal move. This particular client experienced recurrent bouts of depression, which she believed she should be able to overcome or control by sheer will. She suggested to me that if she could be freed of this problem, she might even consider trading places with the ugly woman, such was her sense of desperation. With this comment, she pointed out her own perceived attractiveness. She also implicitly affirmed his power to judge. She had joined his perspective as the oedipal observer; their eyes were one. That is, implicit in her comment was his judgment of her as attractive and not worthy of ridicule for her appearance (at this time), but probably for her inability to control her depression, which was interfering with her job performance.

She was both relieved at the current assessment and frightened at a potential future one that might be out of her control. Ashamed of joining with him and letting herself and me see her doing so, she was yet more ashamed of her inability to control her depression. In her own way, she was attempting to connect with the other woman to remove herself from a vulnerable antigonal position. This she accomplished by connecting with the shamefulness of her position. Yet she also both gained and lost something by seeing with her boss. Her own sense of self-esteem was, at this moment, both increased and decreased. She may have won the battle, but it was a pyrrhic victory. The work of her feminist therapy involved helping her to see and deal with several unresolved antigonal issues.

A client complained to me that a male co-worker consistently commented on her appearance, but not in an offensive way; he said something only when she looked nice. She wondered why it always annoyed her. She blamed herself for getting angry inappropriately. Another woman told me that her teenage son is playful and teases her a lot as a way of showing affection. The night before, when she asked him where he was going for the evening, he replied that he and his friends were going to pledge a fraternity and participate in a "gang bang." By this "joke" he was telling her that he was not really like that, but that he has a right to be. She laughed awkwardly (the awkwardness being manifested mostly in her body) as she told me about the comment, worried about his eyes and mine and lowering her own (a characteristically feminine gesture). The awkwardness contained her inexplicable (to her) sense of exposure, violation, and shame combined with the inability to see all this clearly through her own eyes. After all, he was only joking and he was her son (but it was time for him to be bigger than she was).

Another client explained that where she worked, women were not treated fairly and promoted equally with male employees of the same level and ability. She had been angry about it, but explained that the women could never pinpoint any reason for not being promoted, as the reasons were kept invisible. Whispering campaigns indicating that the particular woman was not "a team player" would circulate.

In academia, there is a similar criterion for promotion called "collegiality." Is she one of the boys or not? Most women respond by trying harder and doing more work. They feel responsible for what they cannot control and assume that they are facing an individual problem. All these issues refer back to the unresolved antigonal and oedipal relationship and consistently involve, whatever the combination of other issues, a woman's self-esteem, responsibility for what she cannot control, and sense of shame. These aspects of the unresolved Antigone phase are invariably at the heart of the matter for women and, thus, for feminist therapeutic work.

The artificial separation of mind and body must be approached in a unified fashion in feminist therapy, first and foremost because they are not separate; second, because the physical focus of meanings attributed to women, the ordinariness of violations of women's physicality, and the surplus of meaning attributed to appearance and to doing any particular activity in a woman's body are such central experiences. As this becomes an increasingly visual culture, so do visual meanings become more central.

Meanings are inscribed in the musculature, skin, bones, internal organs, and, most likely, even the endocrine and immune systems. The therapist must notice how women move, sit, stand, and use their bodies characteristically and situationally. In this way, they express general and specific effects of gender. When do they get very still or freeze or appear to be making their bodies either invisible or hypervisible? Meanings are expressed through multiple and redundant channels of communication, the physical being a primary one.

The therapist is also subject to all the attributions to and violations of physicality that come with having a woman's body. The meanings of the physicality of both participants and their interaction are also part of the therapeutic relationship. For example, judgments about their own and each other's appearance may need to be considered, along with the meanings that each and the indeterminate male observer make of them. As they have both experienced the limits and violations involved in learning to be a woman, either or both may manifest tensions and fear in their bodies situationally or characteristically. Obviously it is the job of the therapist not to have these experiences unconsciously whenever possible, but to be aware of and work with her own Antigone issues. My point is that the physical is not to be screened out, but included, in feminist therapy in all the ways that it manifests itself. The entire spectrum of physicality and not just sexuality narrowly defined is meaningful in and out of feminist therapy. How meanings are embodied, as well as how being in a female body defines any experience, is an ongoing aspect of feminist therapy.

A therapist of my acquaintance introduced the topic of her move to a new downtown office to several of her women clients with the comment, "You can window-shop on the way over." The most overt meaning this comment carried was that the move, which was inconvenient for many of her clients, who had been seeing her in a less congested neighborhood, also had its positive aspect. While this comment was certainly multiply meaningful, I want to focus on its surplus of meaning to her as a woman and to these other women. It had not occurred to her to make such a comment to her male clients, since she thought they would not be as interested in window shopping and certainly not interested enough to make the change a positive one for them. She may or may not have been correct, but I want to make a slightly different point with this example from the point I have already made about the equation between women and appearance. The feminist therapist is also a woman and may herself be unaware of the surplus of meaning with which she is operating and may slip into the perspective of the indeterminate observer. Appearance is extremely important to this particular therapist and a way to cover other deficiencies. The role of physical/psychological self-consciousness was as important to the therapist as it was to her client, since both have been trained to see for Oedipus.

I have already suggested that a feminist therapist must continually grapple with the physically/psychologically embedded oedipal perspective in order to be able to help her clients develop a complex vision. Although I would be delighted to be proved wrong, it seems that it would be close to impossible for a male therapist to be able to ferret out the oedipal perspective from within his own, as they are likely to be identical. Perhaps with extensive feminist supervision or consultation, he would be able to do some of this. More important, his very presence in the role of the therapist would come to replicate the oedipal-antigonal relationship. He could not show the client another woman's view nor serve as the lost Jocasta, providing the female nurturance that most women in oedipal society give rather than receive. He could not return her to her origins and, in this way, to herself.

This is not so of the female feminist therapist–male client relationship, in which case she might be able to aid him in passing through the unresolved oedipal phase and developing a sense of clearer boundaries and empathy/respect for women. A male therapist who has done some of this work in resolving the oedipal complex could be very helpful to other males in this regard. Certainly this work must also be done if boys and men are to learn to resolve their grandiosity, to contain themselves, to maintain their own boundaries and resolve their own conflicts, to learn empathy, and to respect girls and women.

Any venture into therapeutic work with women must involve a search for their lost sense of self and esteem. A central aspect of any feminist therapy will be the emergence of paradoxes in women's lives that do not allow their self-esteem to be unambivalent. The example of women's esteem based on self-denial has been considered at length. Ambivalence about improving in therapy is also paramount, as it involves greater visibility, authenticity, and perhaps danger. It is very common for women who begin to feel and function better to become frightened of losing these gains. They are accustomed to paradox, to the negative always being embedded in the positive, to there being a price to pay for any gain. Women, as we have seen, are also judged negatively for being too competent. Thus, improvement and happiness are often accompanied by a profound fear of loss and danger. Getting better has to mean, at the same time, getting worse.

Loss is, indeed, a major theme in women's lives and, therefore, in feminist therapy. Improvement leads to separation from the therapist, giving up perhaps the only relationship since the loss of her early relationship with the disappeared mother, Jocasta, where her needs are central. In oedipal society, women all lose their mothers, as they become them. Feminist therapy returns the experience of centrality in someone's eyes to each woman so that she eventually can become more central in her own eyes. This time neither leaves the other for the father, so that a sense of primary connection can remain. Even if their paths don't cross again, each retains a primary commitment to herself and to women, to seeing from her own and women's, not men's, perspectives. Each can keep the other clearly in sight, having regained her own vision.

All feminist therapy includes the work of mourning the various losses for every woman, central among which is the loss of the possible as a function of gender restrictions. Disappointment is well embedded in female psychology and must be acknowledged before the work of regaining the possible can begin. This mourning contains all the steps described by Elizabeth Kübler-Ross (1969) as stages in the mourning process. That is, a woman who is in the early unresolved stage of the Antigone complex will be engaged in denial of the damage to her and other women based solely on gender. This can take the form of believing that she is completely fulfilled as a woman by being a wife and mother or by believing that she is one of the boys at work: she can be a traditional female or a traditional male and ignore the price that she pays for each. Another strategy is to include with this denial an adaptation of the stage of mourning known as bargaining. This is most clearly encompassed in the belief of many women that they can "have it all" by being superwomen or by having a truly egalitarian marriage and equally shared parenting arrangements despite societal and personal pressures to the contrary. They believe they are somehow different enough to supersede the usual restrictions and difficulties.

If they pass through these stages, female clients inevitably arrive at disappointment and grief, accompanied by tremendous anger at the injustice done to them. These are the steps by which many women arrived at feminism through the early consciousness-raising process. Interlaced with grief comes an intense experience of anger, which is an indispensable stage in this process. The shock is sometimes less intense these days, as many aspects of women's experience, such as abuse, molestation, and rape, have been made culturally visible, and women now often enter therapy aware of having had these experiences. Just as important, they sometimes have the idea that they don't have to accept them as part of everyday life as a woman. This process is not a linear progression. Any of these emotions may be experienced and reexperienced.

Anger is directly related to power and to the ability to change, and is a personal and individual response shared by virtually every woman who has gone through the process of consciousness raising or feminist therapy. The issue of women and anger has been discussed at some length by many feminists and its role in change and therapy by most feminist therapists (Kaschak 1976; Bernardez-Bonesatti 1978; Lerner 1985; Eichenbaum and Orbach 1983). It is a stage in the process that is eventually channeled into activity or activism, understanding, and change. This is not by way of suggesting that women then never get angry again, but that they do not remain in a state of perpetual anger. I address this issue in this way because a woman's anger on her own behalf is highly unacceptable in oedipal society, which does permit her, as it did Antigone, courage and defiance in the service of others. As a result, many women and men associate feminism with anger in women about their own plight and, thus, find it unacceptable and to be avoided, feared, or ridiculed. To them, it is frightening and expansive. It contains a sense of entitlement. It is masculine.

For example, a *New York Times* review of an important feminist work, *If Women Counted* (1988) by Marilyn Waring, described it in the following terms: "this angry yet humorous, well-written and accessible book . . ." (Stevenson 1989, p. 36). Why is being angry considered a criticism that is so *prima facie* irrefutable that it needs no explanation? Is the anger well and appropriately expressed? Does it advance or detract from the argument set forth? Is it genuine passion, and is this permissible to women? Are all these questions irrelevant when a woman is angry?

Respect for a woman's own experience would constitute a cultural revolution in itself. What if women took pride in their own experience rather than turning to physical and psychological cosmetic surgery in the service of hiding it? What if women could let experience show? There is a line in a Leonard Cohen song in which he describes looking for a woman who had lines on her face. He is probably the only man in recorded history ever to do so and, even at that, who knows what he wanted her for?

The Antigone complex cannot be resolved individually or within the drama of the nuclear family, as can the oedipal of Freud's individually (within the nuclear family) focused masculine psychology. This is because we are viewing these complexes as just that—complex—as defining individuals within the cultural context, as well as the culture itself. Resolution of the Antigone complex requires a reconnection with other women and a reaffirmation of the positive quality of this connection, of women and of oneself as a woman. It involves changing the meanings of a masculinist, oedipal culture. Herein lies yet another paradox: one of these oedipal meanings is that women's primary connection should be to men and children, and that the world of women is always smaller than and subsumed by that of men. It is somewhat shameful in an oedipal society for women to be dissatisfied, much less angry about it, and to want to expand their connections to other women and not to be subsumed by men.

Male bonding is considered desirable and masculine. Even male heterosexuality often has more to do with how men look in the eyes of their oedipal peers than with their women partners. Yet female bonding is unfeminine unless it is in the service of improving the care of men and children. Quilting bees, PTAs, and women's auxiliaries are fine. Women's business organizations are less fine, but marginally acceptable as long as they have the narrow goal of assimilating their members into the masculine melting pot of the business world.

In circumstances of necessity, such as poverty and the relative absence of men found in African-American ghetto communities and in the barrios of Latin America, the oedipal gaze may note that women band together and are able, in this way, to develop strength and courage. Yet the oedipal perspective can then solipsistically blame these women for having developed a matriarchy that must, of course, weaken men just as patriarchy does women and is, thus, responsible for the difficulties of the group as a whole. That this is an oedipally defined matriarchy is highlighted by its paradoxical nature. These so-called matriarchs have all the responsibility with very little power. Only the oedipal perspective would develop this notion of a matriarchy and would continue to blame women, no matter what their strategy or success. From a feminist perspective, a beginning step in resolution of the antigonal dilemma is implicate in these arrangements.

One of the tasks of feminism and of feminist therapy is to maintain the tension between women as a category and each individual woman, between micro details and broad strokes, similarities and differences. Neither should be used as a way to avoid dealing with the others if we are to achieve as full a picture as possible of each woman's experience. Many women have a preference for looking at one or the other side of the picture and may have difficulty integrating either the more personal focus or the broader sociopolitical focus, which links them to other women when they are struggling in modern society to be individual people and not just women. There is also, of course, a tension involved in neither exaggerating nor denying the differences between women and men at this time in oedipal society.

Feminism and therapy both involve understanding the meanings of ordinary, everyday life and focusing not just on the figure but on the ground upon which it stands—ground shifting if not ground breaking. What is ground is somewhat arbitrary. Living as I do in earthquake country helps me maintain this perspective: the ground can never be taken for granted and can become figure at any unpredictable moment. Similarly, one can never study gender relations as a category or a monolithic construct involving woman in isolation. One is always a self-in-context. The self is as much a part of the context as the context is of the self. Each feeds and defines the other.

Psychotherapy involves naming not just the unnamed but the unnameable, speaking not just the unspoken but the unspeakable. Feminist therapy begins with the questions, with meaning, as do feminist politics and epistemology. These are not separate activities, but not identical either. Change involves replacing the arrogant oedipal gaze with what Marilyn Frye has called the loving eye, which "does not prohibit a woman's experiencing the world directly, does not force her to experience it by way of the interested interpretations of the seer in whose visual field she moves" (1983, p. 82).

Feminist therapy involves returning her own vision to each woman and, in this way, contributes to the feminist cultural vision. Perhaps my work—just as it owes much to the work of other feminist theorists and practitioners who share my vision—can add to the foundation for those who wish to help women to see for themselves, for once they do, nothing ever looks the same. Seeing is believing and knowing for oneself, often for the first time.

References

ALBERLE, D., AND K. NAEGELE. 1952. Middle class fathers' occupational role and attitudes toward children. *American Journal of Orthopsychiatry* 22(2):366–78.

AL-ISSA, I. 1980. *The Psychopathology of Women.* Englewood Cliffs, NJ: Prentice-Hall.

ALLEN, C. D., AND J. B. EICHER. 1973. Adolescent girls' acceptance and rejection based on appearance. *Adolescence* 8:125–38.

ALLPORT, G. W. 1960. The open system in personality theory. *Journal of Abnormal and Social Psychology* 61:301–10.

ALPERT, J. L. 1986. *Psychoanalysis and Women: Contemporary Appraisals.* New York: Analytic Press.

ALTEMEYER, R. A., AND K. JONES. 1974. Sexual identity, physical attractiveness and seating position as determinants of influence in discussion groups. *Canadian Journal of Behavioral Science* 6:357–75.

AMERICAN PSYCHIATRIC ASSOCIATION. 1952. *Diagnostic and Statistical Manual of Mental Disorders.* Washington, DC: American Psychiatric Association.

———. 1958. *Diagnostic and Statistical Manual of Mental Disorders II.* Washington, DC: American Psychiatric Association.

———. 1980. *Diagnostic and Statistical Manual of Mental Disorders III.* Washington, DC: American Psychiatric Association.

———. 1987. *Diagnostic and Statistical Manual of Mental Disorders.* 3rd ed., rev. Washington, DC: American Psychiatric Association.

ANDERSEN, A. E., AND A. HAY. 1985. Racial and socioeconomic influences in anorexia nervosa and bulimia. *International Journal of Eating Disorders* 4(4):479–87.

ANZALDÚA, G. 1987. *Borderlands/La Frontera, The New Mestiza.* San Francisco: Spinsters/Aunt Lute (p. 195).

ARIÈS, E. 1976. Interactional patterns and themes of male, female and mixed groups. *Small Group Behavior* 7(1):7–18.

ARISTOTLE. 1912. De generatione ánimalium. In *The Works of Aristotle Translated into English.* Edited by J. A. Smith and W. D. Ross. Oxford: Clarendon Press.

ARNOLD, KAREN D., AND TERRY DENNY. 1985. The lives of academic achievers: The career aspirations of male and female high school valedictorians and salutatorians. Paper presented at the annual meeting of the American Educational Research Association, Chicago.

AUERBACH, J., L. BLUM, V. SMITH, AND C. WILLIAMS. 1985. On Gilligan's *In a Different Voice. Feminist Studies* 11, no. 1 (Spring):149–61.

AVIS, J. 1985. The politics of functional family therapy: A feminist critique. *Journal of Marital and Family Therapy* 11(2):127–38.

BALMARY, M. 1979. *Psychoanalyzing Psychoanalysis: Freud and the Hidden Fault of the Father.* Translated by N. Lukacher (1982). Baltimore: Johns Hopkins University Press.

BART, P. 1985. Rape doesn't end with a kiss. *Viva* 2:39–42, 100–101.

BART, P. B., AND P. H. O'BRIEN. 1985. *Stopping Rape: Successful Survival Strategies.* New York: Pergamon Press (p. 89).

BARTKY, S. L. 1988. Foucault, femininity, and the modernization of patriarchal power. In *Feminism and Foucault: Reflections on Resistance.* Edited by I. Diamond and L. Quinby. Boston: Northeastern University Press.

BARUCH, E. H., AND L. J. SERRANO. 1988. *Women Analyze Women in France, England and the United States.* New York: New York University Press.

BARUCH, G. K., AND R. C. BARNETT. 1979. Multiple roles and well-being: A study of mothers of preschool age children. *Working Paper No. 3.* Wellesley, MA: Wellesley College.

BASCH, M. F. 1980. *Doing Psychotherapy.* New York: Basic Books.

BATESON, G. 1979. *Mind and Nature.* New York: Dutton.

BATESON, G., AND M. C. BATESON. 1987. *Angels Fear: Towards an Epistemology of the Sacred.* New York: Macmillan.

BATESON, M. C. 1984. *With a Daughter's Eye.* New York: Washington Square Press.

BECKER, E. 1971. *The Birth and Death of Meaning.* New York: Free Press.

———. 1973. *The Denial of Death.* New York: Free Press.

BELK, R. W. 1988. My possessions myself. *Psychology Today* (July): 51–52.

BELL, L. 1989. Song without words. *Family Networker* (March/April): 48–53.

BELL, R. 1972. Some emerging sexual expectations among women. *Medical Aspects of Human Sexuality* 6:136–44.

BELSKY, J. 1979. Mother-father-infant interaction: A naturalistic observational study. *Developmental Psychology* 15:601–7.

BELSKY, J., M. LANG, AND T. HUSTON. 1986. Sex typing and division of labor as determinants of marital change across the transition to parenthood. *Journal of Personality and Social Psychology* 50:517–22.

References

BEM, S. L. 1981. Gender schema theory: A cognitive account of sex-typing. *Psychological Review* 88:354–64.

BEN-TOVIM, D. T., AND A. H. CRISP. 1984. The reliability of estimates of body width and their relationship to current measured body size among anorexic and normal subjects. *Psychological Medicine* 14(4):843–46.

BERHEIDE, C. W. 1984. Women's work in the home: Seems like old times. *Marriage and Family Review* 7(3):37–50.

BERMAN, E. 1989. Going shopping. *Family Networker* (September/October): 36–37.

BERMAN, M. 1984. *The Reenchantment of the World.* New York: Bantam.

———. 1988. *Coming to Our Senses: Body and Spirit in the Hidden History of the West.* New York: Simon & Schuster (p. 182).

BERNARD, J. 1972. *The Future of Marriage.* New York: Bantam.

BERNARDEZ-BONESATTI, T. 1978. Women and anger: Conflicts with aggression in contemporary women. *Journal of the American Medical Women's Association* 33:215–19.

BERNAY, T., AND D. W. CANTOR. 1986. *The Psychology of Today's Woman: New Psychoanalytic Visions.* New York: Analytic Press.

BERSCHEID, E., AND E. WALSTER. 1974. Physical attractiveness. In *Advances in Experimental Social Psychology.* Edited by L. Berkowitz. New York: Academic Press.

BERSCHEID, E., E. WALSTER, AND G. BOHRNSTEDT. 1973. Body image. *Psychology Today* (November): 119–31.

BILLER, H. 1981. The father and sex role development. In *The Role of the Father in Child Development.* 2nd ed. Edited by M. Lamb. New York: Wiley.

BIRNBAUM, J. A. 1975. Life patterns and self-esteem in gifted family-oriented and career-committed women. In *Women and Achievement: Social and Motivational Analysis.* Edited by M. Mednick, S. Tangri, and L. W. Hoffman. New York: Hemisphere-Halsted.

BIRTCHNELL, S. A., B. M. DOLAN, AND J. H. LACEY. 1987. Body image distortion in non–eating disordered women. *International Journal of Eating Disorders* 6(3):385–91.

BLEIER, R. 1984. *Science and Gender: A Critique of Biology and Its Theories on Women.* New York: Pergamon Press.

BOGRAD, M. 1984. Family systems approaches to wife battering: A feminist critique. *American Journal of Orthopsychiatry* 34(4):558–68.

BOLEN, J. S. 1984. *Goddesses in Everywoman: A New Psychology of Women.* San Francisco: Harper & Row.

BRANCH, C. H. H., AND L. J. EURMAN. 1980. Social attitudes toward patients with anorexia nervosa. *American Journal of Psychiatry* 137(5):631–32.

BRAUN, B. G., ED. 1986. *The Treatment of Multiple Personality Disorder.* Washington, DC: American Psychiatric Press.

BRODSKY, A. M. 1973. The consciousness-raising group as a model for therapy with women. *Psychotherapy: Theory, Research and Practice* 10:24–29.

BROVERMAN, I. K., D. M. BROVERMAN, F. E. CLARKSON, P. S. ROSENKRANTZ, AND

S. R. VOGEL. 1970. Sex-role stereotypes and clinical judgments of mental health. *Journal of Consulting and Clinical Psychology* 34(1):1–7.

BROVERMAN, I. K., S. R. VOGEL, D. M. BROVERMAN, F. E. CLARKSON, AND P. S. ROSENKRANTZ. 1972. Sex-role stereotypes: A current appraisal. *Journal of Social Issues* 28:59–78.

BROWN, G. W., AND M. W. BROLCHAIN. 1975. Social class and psychiatric disturbance among women in an urban population. *Sociology* 9:225–54.

BROWN, G. W., AND T. O. HARRIS. 1978. *Social Origins of Depression: A Study of Psychiatric Disorders in Women*. New York: Free Press.

BRUCH, H. 1973. *Eating Disorders*. New York: Basic Books.

———. 1978. *The Golden Cage: The Enigma of Anorexia Nervosa*. Cambridge: Harvard University Press.

———. 1985. Four decades of eating disorders. In *Handbook of Psychotherapy for Anorexia Nervosa and Bulimia,* pp. 7–18. Edited by D. M. Garner and P. E. Garfinkel. New York: Guilford Press.

BRUMBERG, J. J. 1988. *Fasting Girls*. Cambridge: Harvard University Press.

BRUNSWICK, R. M. 1940. The preoedipal phase of the libido development. In *The Psychoanalytic Reader: An Anthology of Essential Papers with Critical Introductions,* pp. 231–53. Edited by R. Fleiss. New York: International Universities Press.

BUGENTAL, D. E., L. R. LOVE, AND R. M. GIANETTO. 1971. Perfidious feminine faces. *Journal of Personality and Social Psychology* 17:314–18.

BUIE, J. 1989. Course helps fathers know best. *APA Monitor* (August). Washington, DC: American Psychological Association.

BURLINGHAM, D. T. 1973. The pre-oedipal father-infant relationship. *Psychoanalytic Study of the Child* 28:23–47.

BURTON, G. 1988. *Heartbreak Hotel*. New York: Penguin Books.

BUTTON, E. J., AND A. WHITEHOUSE. 1981. Subclinical anorexia nervosa. *Psychological Medicine* 11:509–16.

CALDWELL, D. 1981. *And All Was Revealed: Ladies' Underwear 1907–1980*. New York: St. Martin's Press.

CALHOUN, L. G., J. W. SELBY, A. CANN, AND G. T. KELLER. 1978. The effect of victim physical attractiveness and sex of respondent on social reactions to victims of rape. *British Journal of Social and Clinical Psychology* 17:191–92.

CAMPBELL, A., P. CONVERSE, AND W. RODGER. 1976. *The Quality of American Life: Perceptions, Evaluations and Satisfactions*. New York: Russell Sage.

CAPLAN, P. J. 1988. The name game: Psychiatry, misogyny and taxonomy. In *Women, Power and Therapy,* pp. 187–202. Edited by M. Baraude. New York: Harrington Park Press.

———. 1990. Delusional dominating personality disorder (DDPD). *Psychology of Women: Newsletter of Division 35, American Psychological Association* 17, no. 1 (Winter):5–6.

References

CARLI, L. 1990. Gender, language and influence. *Journal of Personality and Social Psychology* 59(5):941–51.

CASH, T., B. WINSTEAD, AND L. JANDA. 1986. The great American shape-up. *Psychology Today* (April): 30–37.

CAVIOR, N., AND P. DOKECKI. 1973. Physical attractiveness, perceived attitude similarity, and academic achievement as contributors to interpersonal attraction among adolescents. *Developmental Psychology* 9:44–54.

CAVIOR, N., AND D. A. LOMBARDI. 1973. Developmental aspects of judgment of physical attractiveness in children. *Developmental Psychology* 8:67–71.

CELLINI, J. V., AND L. A. KANTOROWSKI. 1982. Internal-external locus of control: New normative data. *Psychological Reports* 51:231–35.

CHAIKEN, S., AND P. PLINER. 1987. Women, but not men, are what they eat: The effect of meal size and gender on perceived femininity and masculinity. *Personality and Social Psychology Bulletin* 13(2):166–76.

CHAMBLESS, D. L. 1982. Characteristics of agoraphobics. In *Agoraphobia: Multiple Perspectives on Theory and Treatment.* Edited by D. L. Chambless and A. J. Goldstein. New York: Wiley.

CHASEN, B. 1974. Sex-role stereotyping and pre-kindergarten teachers. *Elementary School Journal:* 225–35.

CHECK, J. V. P., AND N. M. MALAMUTH. 1983. Sex role stereotyping and reactions to depictions of stranger versus acquaintance rape. *Journal of Personality and Social Psychology* 45(2):344–56.

CHERNIN, K. 1981. *The Obsession: Reflections on the Tyranny of Slenderness.* New York: Harper & Row.

————. 1985. *The Hungry Self: Women, Eating and Identity.* New York: Harper & Row.

CHESLER, P. 1972. *Women and Madness.* New York: Doubleday.

CHICAGO, J. 1975. *Through the Flower.* New York: Doubleday.

CHODOROW, N. 1978. *The Reproduction of Mothering: Psychoanalysis and the Sociology of Gender.* Berkeley: University of California Press.

CIXOUS, H. 1980a. The laugh of the medusa. In *New French Feminisms,* pp. 245–64. Edited by E. Marks and I. de Courtivran. New York: Schocken Books.

————. 1980b. Sorties. In *New French Feminisms,* pp. 90–98. Edited by E. Marks and I. de Courtivron. New York: Schocken Books.

————. 1986. *The Newly Born Woman (La Jeune Née).* Translated by Betsy Wing. Manchester: Manchester University Press (p. 68).

CLARKE-STEWART, K. A. 1978. And daddy makes three: The father's impact on mother and young child. *Child Development* 49:466–78.

CLARRICOATES, K. 1978. Dinosaurs in the classroom: A re-examination of some aspects of the "hidden" curriculum in primary schools. *Women's Studies International Quarterly* 1:353–64.

————. 1980. The importance of being Ernest . . . Emma . . . Tom . . . Jane . . . : The perception and categorization of gender conformity and gender deviation in primary schools. In *Schooling for Women's Work.* Edited by R. Deem. London: Routledge and Kegan Paul.

CLIFFORD, E. 1971. Body satisfaction in adolescence. *Perceptual and Motor Skills* 33:119–25.

COHEN, M. B. 1966. Personal identity and sexual identity. *Psychiatry* 29:1–14.

COHEN, R. 1989. Fakin' it. Critic at Large. *Washington Post,* August 13, p. 9.

COOPERSMITH, S. 1967. *The Antecedents of Self-esteem.* San Francisco: Freeman.

———. 1981. *The Antecedents of Self-esteem.* 2nd ed. Palo Alto: Consulting Psychologists Press.

COWAN, C. P., P. A. COWAN, G. HEMING, E. GARRETT, W. S. COYSH, H. CURTIS-BOLES, AND A. J. BOLES III. 1985. Transitions to parenthood: His, hers, and theirs. *Journal of Family Issues* 6:451–81.

COX, S., ED. 1976. *Female Psychology: The Emerging Self.* Chicago: Science Research Associates.

CRISP, A. H. 1967. Anorexia nervosa. *Hospital Medicine* 1:713–18.

———. 1980. *Anorexia Nervosa: Let Me Be.* London: Academic Press.

CRISP, A. H., R. L. PALMER, AND R. S. KALUCY. 1976. How common is anorexia nervosa? A prevalence study. *British Journal of Psychiatry* 128 (June): 549–54.

CROSBY, F. J., ED. 1987. *Spouse, Parent, Worker: On Gender and Multiple Roles.* New Haven: Yale University Press.

CROSS, J. F., AND J. CROSS. 1971. Age, sex, race, and the perception of facial beauty. *Developmental Psychology* 5:433–39.

CUSHMAN, P. 1990. Why the self is empty: Toward a historically situated psychology. *American Psychologist* 45(5):599–611.

DALLY, P., AND J. GOMEZ. 1979. *Anorexia Nervosa.* London: Heinemann Medical.

DAVIDSON, M. 1983. *Uncommon Sense: The Life and Thought of Ludwig von Bertalanffy, Father of General Systems Theory.* Los Angeles: J. P. Tarcher.

DEAUX, K., AND T. EMSWILLER. 1974. Explanations for successful performance on sex-linked tasks: What is skill for the male is luck for the female. *Journal of Personality and Social Psychology* 29:80–85.

DE BEAUVOIR, S. 1968. *The Second Sex,* New York: Bantam.

DEITZ, S. R., M. LITTMAN, AND B. J. BENTLEY, 1984. Attribution of responsibility for rape: The influence of observer empathy, victim resistance, and victim attractiveness. *Sex Roles* 10(3/4):261–80.

DE LAURETIS, T., ED. 1986. *Feminist Studies and Critical Studies.* Bloomington: Indiana University Press.

DE PIZAN, C. 1982. *The Book of the City of Ladies.* New York: Persea Press.

DE RIVERA, J. 1989. Comparing experiences across cultures: Shame and guilt in America and Japan. Paper presented at the first annual conference of the American Psychological Society, Washington, DC, June.

DERMER, M., AND D. L. THIEL, 1975. When beauty may fail. *Journal of Personality and Social Psychology* 31:1168–76.

DEUTSCH, F. M., D. LEBARON, AND M. M. FRYER. 1987. What is in a smile? *Psychology of Women Quarterly* 11(3):341–51.

DEVILLERS, L. 1989. Building sexual confidence through exercise. Paper presented at the annual meeting of the Society for the Scientific Study of Sex, San Francisco, March.

DINNERSTEIN, D. 1976. *The Mermaid and the Minotaur*. New York: Harper & Row.

DOBASH, R. E., AND R. DOBASH. 1979. *Violence Against Wives: A Case Against the Patriarchy*. New York: Free Press.

DOUTY, H. I., J. B. MOORE, AND D. HARTFORD. 1974. Body characteristics in relation to life adjustment, body image, and attitudes of college females. *Perceptual and Motor Skills* 39:499–521.

DOUVAN, E. 1963. Employment and the adolescent. In *The Employed Mother in America*. Edited by F. I. Nye and L. W. Hoffman. Chicago: Rand McNally.

DOWNS, A. C., AND S. K. HARRISON. 1985. Embarrassing age spots or just plain ugly? Physical attractiveness stereotyping as an instrument of sexism on American television commercials. *Sex Roles* 13(1/2):9–19.

EDER, D. 1990. Serious and playful disputes: Variation in conflict talk among female adolescents. In *Conflict Talk*, pp. 67–84. Edited by Allen D. Grimshaw. Cambridge: Cambridge University Press.

EDNEY, J. J., AND N. L. JORDAN-EDNEY. 1974. Territorial spacing on a beach. *Sociometry* 37 (March): 92–104.

EHERNSAFT, D. 1984. When women and men mother. In *Mothering: Essays in Feminist Theory*. Edited by J. Trebilcot. Totowa, NJ: Rowman and Allanheld.

———. 1985. Dual parenting and the duel of intimacy. In *The Psychosocial Interior of the Family*. Edited by G. Handel. New York: Aldine.

EICHENBAUM, L., AND S. ORBACH. 1983. *Understanding Women: A Feminist Psychoanalytic Approach*. New York: Basic Books.

EISLER, R. 1988. *The Chalice and the Blade*. San Francisco: Harper & Row.

EKMAN, P., R. W. LEVENSON, AND W. V. FRIESEN. 1983. Autonomic nervous system activity distinguishes among emotions. *Science* 221(4616):1208–10.

ELIADE, M. 1959. *The Sacred and the Profane*. New York: Harcourt Brace.

EPSTEIN, C. F. 1988. *Deceptive Distinctions: Sex, Gender and the Social Order*. New Haven: Yale University Press.

ERIKSON, E. 1950. *Childhood and Society*. New York: Norton.

FAGOT, B. I. 1973. Sex-related stereotyping of toddlers' behaviors. *Developmental Psychology* 9:429.

FALLON, A. E., AND P. ROZIN. 1985. Sex differences in perceptions of desirable body shape. *Journal of Abnormal Psychology* 94:102–5.

FIERMAN, J. 1990. Why women still don't hit the top. *Fortune* (July 30): 40–62.

FINKELHOR, D., R. J. GELLES, G. T. HOTALING, AND M. A. STRAUS, EDS. 1986. *The Dark Side of Families and the Current Family Violence Research*. Beverly Hills, CA: Sage.

FINKELHOR, D., AND K. YLLO. 1985. *License to Rape: Sexual Abuse of Wives*. New York: Holt, Rinehart and Winston.

FISHER, S. 1973. *The Female Orgasm*. New York: Basic Books.

FLAX, J. 1981. The conflict between nurturance and autonomy in mother-daughter relationships and within feminism. In *Women and Mental Health*, pp. 51–69. Edited by E. Howell and M. Bayes. New York: Basic Books.

FLING, S., AND M. MANOSEVITZ. 1972. Sex typing in nursery school children's play interests. *Developmental Psychology* 7:146–52.

FODOR, I. G. 1974. The phobic syndrome in women. In *Women in Therapy*, pp. 132–68. Edited by V. Franks and V. Burtle.

———. 1977. Phobias in women. *Helping Women Change: A Guide for Professional Counseling*, New York: BMA Audio Cassette Program.

FONER, A. 1986. *Aging and Old Age: New Perspectives*. Englewood Cliffs, NJ: Prentice-Hall.

FOUCAULT, M. 1978. *The History of Sexuality*. New York: Pantheon.

FRANCES, A., AND P. DUNN. 1975. The attachment-autonomy conflict in agoraphobia. *International Journal of Psychoanalysis* 56:435–39.

FRANCES, J. 1979. Sex differences in nonverbal behavior. *Sex Roles* 5:519–35.

FRANK, P. 1990. Vanilla days/chocolate nights. *Contra Costa Woman* 3(6):6–7.

FREEMAN, H. R. 1985. Somatic attractiveness: As in other things, moderation is best. *Psychology of Women Quarterly* 9(3):311–22.

FREIRE, P. 1969. *Pedagogy of the Oppressed*, New York: Seabury Press.

FREUD, E. L., ED. 1975. *The Letters of Sigmund Freud*. New York: Basic Books.

FREUD, S. 1961. The dissolution of the Oedipus complex. In *The Standard Edition of the Complete Psychological Works of Sigmund Freud*. Vol. XIX, pp. 173–79. Edited and translated by J. Strachey. London: Hogarth Press. (Originally published 1924.)

FRIEDAN, B. 1963. *The Feminine Mystique*. New York: Norton.

FRIEDMAN, P. 1959. The phobias. In *American Handbook of Psychiatry*. Vol. I. Edited by S. Arieti. New York: Basic Books.

FRIES, H. 1977. Studies on secondary amenorrhea, anorectic behavior and body image perception: Importance for the early recognition of anorexia nervosa. In *Anorexia Nervosa*, pp. 163–76. Edited by R. Vigersky. New York: Raven.

FRIEZE, I. H., J. E. PARSONS, P. B. JOHNSON, D. N. RUBLE, AND G. L. ZELLMAN. 1978. *Women and Sex Roles*. New York: Norton (pp. 16–17).

FRYE, M. 1983. *The Politics of Reality: Essays in Feminist Theory*. Trumansburg, NY: Crossing Press.

GALDSTON, R. 1974. Mind over matter: Observations on 50 patients hospitalized with anorexia nervosa. *American Academy of Child Psychiatry Journal* 13:246–63.

GALLUP, G., JR., AND F. NEWPORT. 1990. The battle of the bulge: Americans continue to fight it. *Gallup Poll Monthly.* (December): 23–34.

GALTON, M., B. SIMON, AND S. CROLL. 1980. *Inside the Primary Classroom.* London: Routledge and Kegan Paul.

GANONG, L. H., AND M. COLEMAN. 1987. Effects of children on parental sex-role orientation. *Journal of Family Issues* 8(3):278–89.

GARDNER, C. B. 1980. Passing by: Street remarks, address rights, and the urban female. *Language and Social Interaction (Sociological Inquiry)* 50:328–56.

GARFINKEL, H. 1967. *Studies in Ethnomethodology.* Englewood Cliffs, NJ: Prentice-Hall.

GARFINKEL, P. E., AND D. M. GARNER. 1982. *Anorexia Nervosa: A Multi-dimensional Perspective.* New York: Brunner/Mazel.

GELLNER, E. 1974. *Legitimation of Belief.* Cambridge: Cambridge University Press.

GHENT, J. 1989. Older people get a wealth of new images. *Oakland Tribune,* April 2, D-1.

GILLIGAN, C. 1982. *In a Different Voice.* Cambridge: Harvard University Press.

GIRARD, R. 1972. *Violence and the Sacred.* Translated by P. Gregory, 1977. Baltimore: Johns Hopkins University Press.

GIRGUS, J. 1989. Body image in girls pushes rate of depression up. *APA Monitor,* October, Washington, DC.

GIRGUS, J., S. NOLEN-HOEKSEMA, AND M. E. P. SELIGMAN. 1989. Why do sex differences in depression emerge during adolescence? Paper presented at the annual convention of the American Psychological Association, New Orleans, August.

GLEASON, J. B. 1987. Sex differences in parent-child interaction. In *Language, Gender, and Sex in Comparative Perspective,* pp. 189–99. Edited by S. U. Philips, S. Steele, and C. Stanz. Cambridge: Cambridge University Press.

GOLD, D., AND D. ANDRES. 1978. Developmental comparisons between ten-year-old children with employed and unemployed mothers. *Child Development* 49:75–84.

GOLD, D., G. CROMBIE, AND S. NOBLE. 1987. Relations between teachers' judgments of girls' and boys' compliance and intellectual competence. *Sex Roles* 16(7/8):351–58.

GOLDBERG, P. 1968. Are women prejudiced against women? *Transaction* 5:28–30.

GOLDING, J. M. 1988. Gender differences in depressive symptoms: Statistical considerations. *Psychology of Women Quarterly* 12(1):61–74.

GOLDNER, V. 1985. Feminism and family therapy. *Family Process* 24:31–47.

GOLDSTEIN, R. 1983. *The Mind-Body Problem.* New York: Dell.

GOODENOUGH, E. W. 1957. Interest in persons as an aspect of sex difference in the early years. *Genetic Psychology Monographs* 55:287–323.

GORDON, C., E. BERESIN, AND D. B. HERZOG. 1989. The parents' relationship and the child's illness in anorexia nervosa. In *Psychoanalysis and Eating Disorders,* pp. 29–42. Edited by J. R. Bemporad and D. B. Herzog. New York: Guilford.

GORNICK, V. 1989. Twice an outsider: On being Jewish and a woman. *Utne Reader* (September/October): 95–96.

GOVE, W. R. 1972. The relationship between sex roles, marital status and mental illness. *Social Forces* 51:34–44.

GOVE, W. R., AND F. J. TUDOR. 1973. Adult sex roles and mental illness. *American Journal of Sociology* 79:45–67.

GRADY, K. 1984. Mainstreaming psychology into the curriculum. *XXI International Congress of Psychology,* Acapulco.

———. 1977. Sex as a social label: The illusion of sex differences. Ph.D. diss., City University, New York.

GRAY, S. H. 1977. Social aspects of body image: Perceptions of normalcy of weight and affect of college undergraduates. *Perceptual and Motor Skills* 45: 1035–40.

GRIFFIN, S. 1978. *Woman and Nature: The Roaring Inside Her.* New York: Harper & Row.

GURIN, P. 1985. Women's gender consciousness. *Public Opinion Quarterly* 49:143–63.

GUTEK, B. A. 1985. *Sex and the Workplace: Impact of Sexual Behavior and Harassment on Women, Men and Organizations.* San Francisco: Jossey-Bass.

HAGAN, R. L., AND A. KAHN. 1975. Discrimination against competent women. *Journal of Applied Social Psychology* 5(4):362–76.

HALEY, J. 1969. *The Power Tactics of Jesus Christ and Other Essays.* New York: Grossman.

HALMI, K. A., S. C. GOLDBERG, AND S. CUNNINGHAM. 1977. Perceptual distortion of body image in adolescence. *Psychological Medicine* 7:253–57.

HALPERT, F. E. 1988. You call this adorable? An open letter to the producer of NBC Sports. *Ms.* magazine (October): 36–39.

HAMILTON, J. A. 1984. Psychobiology in context: Reproductive-related events in men's and women's lives (review of *Motherhood and Mental Illness*). *Contemporary Psychiatry* 3:12–16.

HARBISON, G., AND J. C. SIMPSON. 1981. Modeling the '80s look. *Time* magazine (February 9): 82–88.

HARDING, S. 1987. *Feminism and Methodology.* Bloomington and Indianapolis: Indiana University Press.

HARE-MUSTIN, R. T. 1978. A feminist approach to family therapy. *Family Process* 17:181–94.

———. 1987. The problem of gender in family therapy. *Family Process* 26:15–27.

HARE-MUSTIN, R. T., AND J. MARACEK. 1986. Autonomy and gender: Some questions for therapists. *Psychotherapy* 23(2):205–12.

HARPER, L. V., AND K. M. SANDERS. 1975. Pre-school children's use of space: Sex differences in outdoor play. *Developmental Psychology* 11:119.

HASSETT, J. 1984. *Psychology in Perspective.* New York: Harper & Row (p. 14).

HAUG, M. R., AND FOLMAR, S. J. 1986. Longevity, gender, and life quality. *Journal of Health and Social Behavior* 27:332–45.

HAWKINS, R. C., S. TYRELL, AND L. J. JACKSON. 1983. Desirable and undesirable masculine and feminine traits in relation to students' dietary tendencies and body image dissatisfaction. *Sex Roles* 9(6):705–24.

HEGEL, G. W. F. 1807. *The Phenomenology of the Mind*. Translated by J. B. Baille, 1967. New York: Harper Torchbooks.

HEIDEGGER, M. 1979. *The Will to Power as Art, Nietszche*. New York: Harper & Row.

HEILBRUN, C. G. 1988. *Writing a Woman's Life*. New York: Ballantine.

HEISE, L. 1989. Abuse. *This World* (Sunday supplement). *San Francisco Chronicle*, July 2, p. 12.

———. 1989. Crimes of gender. *National Coalition Against Domestic Violence*. Washington, DC.

HENLEY, N. M. 1977. *Body Politics: Power, Sex and Nonverbal Communication*. Englewood Cliffs, NJ: Prentice-Hall.

HERMAN, J. 1981. *Father-Daughter Incest*. Cambridge: Harvard University Press.

HEWES, G. W. 1957. The anthropology of gesture. *Scientific American* (February): 123–32.

HEYN, D. 1989. Body hate. *Ms.* magazine (July/August).

HILDEBRANDT, K. 1980. Parents' perceptions of their infants' physical attractiveness. Paper presented at the International Conference on Infant Studies, New Haven, CT.

HILL, J. P., AND G. N. HOLMBECK. 1987. Familial adaption to biological change during adolescence. In *Biological-psychosocial Interactions in Early Adolescence*, pp. 207–33. Edited by R. M. Lerner and T. T. Foch. Hillsdale, NJ: Lawrence Erlbaum.

HITE, S. 1976. *The Hite Report*. New York: Macmillan.

HOFFMAN, L. 1972. Early childhood experiences and women's achievement motives. *Journal of Social Issues* 28(2):129–55.

———. 1974. Effects of maternal employment on the child: A review of the research. *Developmental Psychology* 10:204–28.

———. 1977. Changes in family roles, socialization, and sex differences. *American Psychologist* 32:644–58.

HOFFMAN, M. L. 1977. Sex differences in empathy and related behaviors. *Psychological Bulletin* 84(4):712–22.

HOLLINGSHEAD, A. B., AND F. C. REDLICH. 1958. *Social Class and Mental Illness: A Community Study*. New York: Wiley.

HOLLON, W.E. 1974. *Frontier Violence: Another Look*. New York: Oxford University Press (pp. 194–216).

HOLZER, C. E., B. M. SHEA, J. W. SWANSON, P. J. LEAF, J. K. MYERS, L. GEORGE, M. M. WEISSMAN, AND P. BEDNARSKI. 1986. The increased risk for specific psychiatric disorders among persons of low socioeconomic status: Evidence from the epidemiological catchment area surveys. *American Journal of Social Psychiatry* 6(4):259–70.

Hsu, F. L. K. 1971. Psychological homeostasis and *jen* conceptual tools for advancing psychological anthropology. *American Anthropologist* 73:23–44.

Hsu, L. K. G. 1987. Are the eating disorders becoming more common in blacks? *International Journal of Eating Disorders* 6:113–23.

Huenemann, R., L. Shapiro, M. Hampton, and B. Mitchell. 1966. A longitudinal study of gross body composition and body conformity and their association with food and activity in a teenage population. *American Journal of Clinical Nutrition* 18:325–38.

Ickes, W., and M. Turner. 1983. On the social advantages of having an older, opposite-sex sibling: Birth order influences in mixed-sex dyads. *Journal of Personality and Social Psychology* 45:210–22.

Irigaray, L. 1985. *This Sex Which Is Not One.* Translated by C. Porter with C. Burke. Ithaca, NY: Cornell University Press.

James, W. 1890. *Principles of Psychology.* 2 vols. New York: Holt.

Jayne, C. 1981. A two-dimensional model of female sexual response. *Journal of Sex and Marital Therapy* 7(1):3–30.

Joffe, C. 1971. Sex role socialization and the nursery school: As the twig is bent. *Journal of Marriage and the Family* 33:467–75.

Jordan, J. V., and J. L. Surrey. 1986. The self-in-relation: Empathy and the mother-daughter relationship. In *The Psychology of Today's Woman: New Psychoanalytic Visions.* Edited by T. Bernay and D. W. Cantor. Hillsdale, NJ: Analytic Press.

Jourard, S., and P. Secord. 1955. Body cathexis and the ideal female figure. *Journal of Abnormal and Social Psychology* 50:243–46.

Kabatznick, R. 1984. Nurture/nature. *Ms.* magazine: 76–102.

Kagan, J. 1984. *The Nature of the Child.* New York: Basic Books.

———. 1989. *Unstable Ideas: Temperament, Cognition and Self.* Cambridge: Harvard University Press.

Kanter, E. 1977. Sex differences in cue observations and inferences in person perception. Paper presented at the annual meeting of the Eastern Psychological Association, Boston.

Kappel, B. E., and R. D. Lambert. 1972. Self-worth among children of working mothers. Typescript, University of Waterloo.

Kaschak, E. 1976. Sociotherapy: An ecological model for psychotherapy with women. *Psychotherapy: Theory, Research and Practice* (Spring): 61–63.

———. 1978. Sex bias in students' evaluations of professors' teaching methods. *Psychology of Women Quarterly* 2(3):235–43.

———. 1981. Another look at sex bias in students' evaluations of professors: Do winners get the recognition that they have been given? *Psychology of Women Quarterly* 5(5):767–72.

———. 1990. How to be a failure as a family therapist. In *Handbook of Feminist Ethics*. Edited by H. Lerman and N. Porter. New York: Springer.

KASCHAK, E., AND S. SHARRATT. 1989. Gender roles in Costa Rica: The effect of the presence of males or females. *InterAmerican Journal of Psychology* (Winter).

———. 1989. Gender roles in the U. S.: The effect of the presence of males or females. Typescript, San Jose State University.

KELLER, E. F. 1985. *Reflections on Gender and Science*. New Haven: Yale University Press (p. 4).

KESSLER, R. C., AND J. A. MACRAE. 1982. The effect of wives' employment on the mental health of married men and women. *American Sociological Review* 47:216–27.

KESSLER, R. C., AND H. W. NEIGHBORS. 1986. A new perspective on the relationships among race, social class, and psychological distress. *Journal of Health and Social Behavior* 27:107–15.

KESSLER, S. J., AND W. MCKENNA. 1978. *Gender: An Ethnomethodological Approach*. New York: Wiley.

KINGSTON, M. H. 1977. *The Woman Warrior*. New York: Vintage (p. 35).

KINNEY, J., AND G. LEATON. 1978. *Loosening the Grip*. St. Louis: Mosby.

KINSEY, A., W. POMEROY, C. MARTIN, AND P. GEBHARD. 1953. *Sexual Behavior in the Human Female*. Philadelphia: Saunders.

KINZEL, A. S. 1970. Body-buffer zone in violent prisoners. *American Journal of Psychiatry* 127:59–64.

KITTAY, E. F. 1984. Womb envy: An explanatory concept. In *Mothering: Essays in Feminist Theory*, pp. 94–128. Edited by J. Trebilcot. Totowa, NJ: Rowman and Allenheld.

KLUFT, R. P. 1987. An update on multiple personality disorder. *Hospital and Community Psychiatry* 38(4):363–73.

KOEDT, A. 1976. The myth of the vaginal orgasm. In *Female Psychology: The Emerging Self*. Edited by S. Cox. Chicago: Science Research Associates.

KOHUT, H. 1968. The psychoanalytic treatment of the narcissistic personality disorder. *Psychoanalytic Study of the Child* 23:86–113.

———. 1971. *The Analysis of the Self: A Systematic Approach to the Treatment of Narcissistic Personality Disorders*. New York: International Universities Press.

———. 1977. *The Restoration of the Self*. New York: International Universities Press.

KOHUT, H., AND E. WOLF. 1978. The disorders of the self and their treatment: An outline. *International Journal of Psychoanalysis* 59:413–25.

KOJIMA, H. 1984. A significant stride toward the comparative study of control. *American Psychologist* 39:972–73.

KONNER, M. 1988. *This World* (Sunday supplement). *San Francisco Chronicle*, April 10, p. 14.

KOTELCHUCK, M. 1976. The infant's relationship to the father: Experimental evidence. In *The Role of the Father in Child Development*. Edited by M. E. Lamb. New York: Wiley

KRAMARAE, C., B. THORNE, AND N. HENLEY. 1978. Review essay: Perspectives on language and communication. *Signs* 3(3):638–51.

KRISTEVA, J. 1982. Women's time. In *Feminist Theory: A Critique of Ideology*, pp. 31–53. Edited by N. O. Keohane, M. Z. Rosaldo, and B. C. Gelpi. Translated by A. Jardine and H. Blake. Chicago: University of Chicago Press.

KÜBLER-ROSS, E. 1969. *On Death and Dying*. New York: Macmillan.

LABALME, P. H. 1984. *Beyond Their Sex: Learned Women of the European Past*. New York: New York University Press.

LA FRANCE, M., AND B. CARMEN. 1980. The nonverbal display of psychological androgyny. *Journal of Personality and Social Psychology* 38:36–49.

LAMB, M. E. 1976. Interactions between 8-month-old children and their fathers and mothers. In *The Role of the Father in Child Development*. Edited by M. E. Lamb. New York: Wiley.

———. 1977a. The development of mother-infant and father-infant attachments in the second year of life. *Developmental Psychology* 13:637–48.

———. 1977b. Father-infant and mother-infant interaction in the first year of life. *Child Development* 48:167–81.

LAMM, M. 1980. *The Jewish Way in Love and Marriage*. San Francisco: Harper & Row.

LANGE, C. G., AND W. JAMES. 1967. *The Emotions*. New York: Hafner.

LANGLOIS, J. H., AND A. C. DOWNS. 1980. Mothers, fathers and peers as socialization agents of sex-typed play behaviors in young children. *Child Development* 51:1217–47.

LATANE, B., AND J. M. DABBS. 1975. Sex. group size and helping in 3 cities. *Sociometry* 38:180–94.

LATANE, B., AND J. DARLEY. 1970. *The Unresponsive Bystander: Why Doesn't He Help?* Englewood Cliffs, NJ: Prentice-Hall.

LAUTER, E., AND C. S. RUPPRECHT. 1985. *Feminist Archetypal Theory*. Knoxville: University of Tennessee Press.

LAWS, J. L. 1979. *The Second X: Sex Role and Social Role*. New York: Elsevier.

LAWSON, C. 1989. In age of feminism, girls' toys are still sugar and spice. *San Jose Mercury News*, June 25, p. 5L.

LEE, R. B. 1979. *The !Kung San*. New York: Cambridge University Press.

LEE, V. E., AND A. S. BRYK. 1986. Effects of single-sex secondary schools on student achievement and attitudes. *Journal of Educational Psychology* 78(5): 381–95.

LEHMAN, P. 1979. Your choice: Breast reshaping. *Vogue* (July).

LEONARD, L. S. 1983. *The Wounded Woman: Healing the Father-Daughter Relationship*. Boulder, CO: Shambhala.

LERMAN, H. 1986. *A Mote in Freud's Eye: From Psychoanalysis to the Psychology of Women.* New York: Springer.

————. 1989. Theoretical and practical implications of the post-traumatic stress disorder diagnosis for women. Paper presented at the annual convention of the American Psychological Association, New Orleans, August.

LERNER, H. G. 1985. *The Dance of Anger.* New York: Harper & Row.

————. 1988. *Women in Therapy.* New York: Harper & Row.

LERNER, R., J. ORLOS, AND J. KNAPP. 1976. Physical attractiveness, physical effectiveness and self-concept in late adolescents. *Adolescence* 11:313–26.

LERNER, R. M. 1969. The development of stereotype expectancies of body build behavior relations. *Child Development* 40:137–41.

LERNER, R. M., AND S. A. KARABENICK. 1974. Physical attractiveness, body attitudes and self-concept in late adolescents. *Journal of Youth and Adolescents* 3(4):307–16.

LEWIN, T. 1991. In crime, too, some gender-related inequities. *New York Times,* January 20.

LEWIS, M. 1972. Parents and children: Sex role development. *School Review* 80:229–40.

LEWIS, M., AND M. WEINTRAUB. 1981. The role of the father in cognitive, academic and intellectual development. In *The Role of the Father in Child Development.* 2nd ed. Edited by M. Lamb. New York: Wiley.

LINGEMAN, R. 1980. *Small Town America.* New York: Putnam.

LORDE, A. 1984. Uses of the erotic: The erotic as power. *Sister Outsider.* Freedom, CA: Crossing Press (pp. 53–59).

LOTT, D. F., AND R. SOMMER. 1967. Seating arrangements and status. *Journal of Personality and Social Psychology* 7:90–95.

LOWE, D. 1982. *History of Bourgeois Perception.* Chicago: University of Chicago Press.

LUEPNITZ, D. A. 1988. *The Family Interpreted: Feminist Theory in Clinical Practice.* New York: Basic Books.

LURIA, Z. 1986. A methodological critique. *Signs* (Winter): 316–21.

LYELL, R. G. 1973. Adolescent and adult self-esteem as related to cultural values. *Adolescence* 8:85–92.

MACCOBY, E. E., AND C. N. JACKLIN. 1974. *The Psychology of Sex Differences.* Stanford: Stanford University Press.

McGOLDRICK, M., C. M. ANDERSON, AND F. WALSH. 1989. *Women in Families: A Framework for Family Therapy.* New York: Norton.

McGRATH, E., G. P. KEITA, B. R. STRICKLAND, AND N. F. RUSSO. 1990. *Women and Depression: Risk Factors and Treatment Issues.* Washington, DC: American Psychological Association.

MACKEY, W. C. 1976. Parameters of the smile as a social signal. *Journal of Genetic Psychology* 129:125–30.

241

MacKinnon, R. A., and R. Michels. 1971. *The Psychiatric Interview*. Philadelphia: Saunders.

Mahler, M. 1968. *On Human Symbiosis and the Vicissitudes of Individuation*. New York: International Universities Press.

Mahoney, E. R. 1974. Compensatory reactions to spatial immediacy. *Sociometry* 37:423–31.

Malamuth, N. M. 1981. Rape proclivity among males. *Journal of Social Issues* 37(4):138–57.

Malamuth, N. M., S. Haber, and S. Feshbach. 1980. Testing hypotheses regarding rape: Exposure to sexual violence, sex differences, and the "normality" of rapists. *Journal of Research in Personality* 14:121–37.

Marks, E. 1980. Breaking the bread: Gestures toward other structures, other discourses. *Bulletin of the MMLA* 13, no. 1 (Spring).

Marks, E., and I. de Courtivron, eds. 1981. *New French Feminisms*. New York: Schocken Books.

Marks, I. M. 1969. *Fears and Phobias*. London: Heinemann.

Marks, I. M., and E. R. Herst. 1970. A survey of 1,200 agoraphobics in Britain. *Social Psychiatry* 5:16–24.

Marks, S. R. 1977. Multiple roles and role strain: Some notes on human energy, time and commitment. *American Sociological Review* 42(6):921–36.

Maslow, A. H. 1970. *Motivation and Personality*. New York: Harper & Row.

Masson, J. 1984. *The Assault on Truth: Freud's Suppression of the Seduction Theory*. New York: Farrar, Straus and Giroux.

Masters, W., and V. Johnson. 1966. *Human Sexual Response*. Boston: Little, Brown.

Masterson, J. F. 1985. *The Real Self: A Developmental, Self and Object Relations Approach*. New York: Brunner/Mazel.

Matthews, A. M., M. G. Gelder, and D. W. Johnston. 1981. *Agoraphobia: Nature and Treatment*. New York: Guilford.

May, R. 1989. The birth and the collapse of the Western idea of the self. In *The World and I: A Chronicle of Our Changing Era*, pp. 515–25. Edited by M. Kaplan. Washington, DC: New World Communications.

Mazur, A. 1986. U.S. trends in feminine beauty and overadaptation. *Journal of Sex Research* 22(3):281–303.

Mead, M. 1949. *Male and Female: A Study of the Sexes in a Changing World*. New York: Laurel Editions, Bell Publishing.

Mehrabian, A. 1968. Relationship of attitude to seated posture, orientation, and distance. *Journal of Personality and Social Psychology* 10:26–30.

Merikangas, K. R., B. Prusoff, D. Kupfer, and E. Frank. 1985. Marital adjustment in major depression. *Journal of Affective Disorder* 9:5–11.

Merton, R. K. 1949. *Social Theory and Social Structure: Toward the Codification of Theory and Research*. Glencoe, IL: Free Press.

Miller, A. 1981. *Prisoners of Childhood*. New York: Basic Books.

References

MILLER, C., AND K. SWIFT. 1976. *Words and Women: New Language in New Times.* New York: Anchor Books.

MILLER, J. B. 1973. *Psychoanalysis and Women: Contributions to New Theory and Therapy.* New York: Brunner/Mazel.

———. 1976. *Toward a New Psychology of Women.* Boston: Beacon Press.

———. 1984. The development of women's sense of self. Work in Progress. Stone Center for Developmental Services and Studies, Wellesley, MA.

MILLER, S. D. 1989. Optical differences in cases of multiple personality disorder. *Journal of Nervous and Mental Disease* 177(8):480–86.

MILLER, T., J. COFFMAN, AND R. LINKE. 1980. Survey on body image, weight, and diet of college students. *Journal of the American Dietetic Association* 77:-561–66.

MILLETT, K. 1970. *Sexual Politics.* New York: Doubleday.

MILLMAN, M. 1980. *Such a Pretty Face: Being Fat in America.* New York: Norton.

MINTURN, L., AND W. W. LAMBERT. 1974. *Mothers of Six Cultures: Antecedents of Child Rearing.* New York: Wiley.

MINTZ, L. B., AND N. E. BETZ. 1986. Sex differences in the nature, realism, and correlates of body image. *Sex Roles* 15(3/4):185–95.

MISCHEL, H. N. 1974. Sex bias in the evaluation of professional achievements. *Journal of Educational Psychology* 66:157–66.

MISCHEL, W. 1984. Convergence and challenges in the search for consistency. *American Psychologist* 39:351–64.

MITCHELL, J. 1974. *Psychoanalysis and Feminism.* New York: Random House.

MOLDAWSKY, S. 1986. When men are therapists to women. In *The Psychology of Today's Woman,* pp. 291–303. Edited by T. Bernay and D. W. Cantor. Hillsdale, NJ: Analytic Press.

MONEY, J. 1973. Gender role, gender identity, core gender identity: Usage and definition of terms. *Journal of the American Academy of Psychoanalysis* 1:397–402.

MONEY, J., AND A. A. ERHARDT. 1972. *Man and Woman, Boy and Girl.* Baltimore: Johns Hopkins University Press.

MONEY, J., AND P. TUCKER. 1975. *Sexual Signatures.* Boston: Little, Brown.

MORAGA, C. 1983. Later, she met Joyce. In *Loving in the War Years,* p. 19. Boston: South End Press.

MORGAN, R. 1972. The invisible woman. *Monster.* New York: Vintage Books.

———. 1984. *Sisterhood Is Global.* New York: Anchor Books.

MORRISON, T. 1970. *The Bluest Eye.* New York: Washington Square Press.

MUSA, K. E., AND M. E. ROACH. 1973. Adolescent appearance and self-concept. *Adolescence* 8:385–94.

MUSSEN, P., AND E. RUTHERFORD. 1963. Parent-child relations and parental personality in relation to young children's sex-role preferences. *Child Development* 34:589–607.

NATHAN, S. G. 1981. Cross-cultural perspectives on penis envy. *Psychiatry* 41:39–44.

NEUGEBAUER, D. D., B. P. DOHRENWEND, AND B. S. DOHRENWEND. 1980. The formulation of hypotheses about the true prevalence of functional psychiatric disorders among adults in the United States. In *Mental Illness in the United States*. Edited by B. P. Dohrenwend, B. S. Dohrenwend, M. S. Gould, B. Link, R. Neugebauer, and R. Wunsch-Hitzig. New York: Praeger.

NEVO, S. 1985. Bulimic symptoms: Prevalence and ethnic differences among college women. *International Journal of Eating Disorders* 4(2):151–68.

NEW YORK TIMES. 1984. Violent death rate cited as U.S. health concern. November 28, p. A-14.

NIEVA, V. 1981. The perceptions of and reactions to female competence. Paper presented at the meeting of the American Psychological Association, Los Angeles.

NOLEN-HOEKSEMA, S. 1987. Sex differences in unipolar depression: Evidence and theory. *Psychological Bulletin* 101:259–82.

———. 1990. *Sex Differences in Depression*. Stanford: Stanford University Press.

NOYES, D. D., AND P. MELLODY. 1989. *Beauty and Cancer: A Woman's Guide to Looking Great While Experiencing the Side Effects of Cancer Therapy*. Los Angeles: AC Press.

NYLANDER, J. 1971. The feeling of being fat and dieting in a school population: Epidemiologic interview investigation. *Acta Sociomedica Scandinavica* 3:17–26.

OLOWU, A. A. 1988. The self-concept in cross-cultural studies. Paper presented at the International Congress of Psychology, Sydney, Australia.

OSGOOD, C. E., G. J. SUCI, AND P. H. TANENBAUM. 1957. *The Measurement of Meaning*. Urbana: University of Illinois Press.

OSOFSKY, J. D., AND E. J. O'CONNELL. 1972. Parent-child interaction: Daughters' effects upon mothers' and fathers' behaviors. *Developmental Psychology* 7:157–68.

PAGE, J. A. 1991. *Black Olympian Medalists*. Englewood, CO: Libraries Unlimited.

PAGELS, H. 1988. *The Dreams of Reason*. New York: Simon & Schuster.

PEDERSEN, F., AND K. ROBSON. 1969. Father participation in infancy. *American Journal of Orthopsychiatry* 39(3):466–72.

PELKA, F. 1989. Sexual malpractice: Therapists who seduce their patients. *On the Issues* 12:7–9, 30–31.

PERSON, E. S. 1983. Women in therapy. *International Review of Psychoanalysis* 10:193–204.

PERSON, E. S., AND L. OVESEY. 1983. Psychoanalytic theories of gender identity disorder. *Journal of the American Academy of Psychoanalysis* 11(2):203–26.

PILKONIS, P. A. 1977. The behavioral consequences of shyness. *Journal of Personality* 45:596–611.

PLATO. 1951. *Dialogues*. Edited by J. D. Kaplan. Translated by B. Jowett. New York: Pocket Books (p. 213).

POLIVY, J., D. M. GARNER. AND P. E. GARFINKEL. 1986. Causes and consequences of the current preference for thin female physiques. In *Physical Appearance, Stigma and Social Behavior: The Third Ontario Symposium in Personality and Social Psychology*, pp. 89–112. Edited by C. P. Herman, M. P. Zanna, and E. T. Higgins. Hillsdale, NJ: Erlbaum.

POLIVY, J., AND C. P. HERMAN. 1983. *Breaking the Diet Habit*. New York: Basic Books.

POLLACK, S., AND C. GILLIGAN. 1982. Images of violence in Thematic Apperception Test stories. *Journal of Personality and Social Psychology* 42(1):159–67.

PROBERT, C. 1981. *Lingerie in Vogue Since 1910*. New York: Abbeville Press.

PROPPER, A. M. 1972. The relationship of maternal employment to adolescent role activities and parental relationships. *Journal of Marriage and the Family* 34:417–21.

RADIN, N. 1981. The role of the father in cognitive, academic and intellectual development. In *The Role of the Father in Child Development*. 2nd ed. Edited by M. Lamb. New York: Wiley.

———. 1982. Primary caregiving and role-sharing fathers. In *Non-traditional Families: Parenting and Child Development*. Edited by M. E. Lamb. Hillsdale, NJ: Lawrence Erlbaum.

RAGAN, J. M. 1982. Gender displays in portrait photographs. *Sex Roles* 9:33–43.

RANK, O. 1909. *The Myth of the Birth of the Hero: A Psychological Interpretation of Mythology*. Translated by F. Robbins and S. E. Jelliffe (1914). New York: Journal of Nervous and Mental Disease Publishing Co.

RAY, R. 1990. Revolution in Romanian women's magazine. *San Jose Mercury News*, February 28, p. 2A.

RAYNOR, R., AND J. B. WATSON. 1921. The case of little Albert. *Scientific Monthly*, p. 493.

RICH, A. 1979. When we dead awaken. *On Lies, Secrets, and Silence*. New York: Norton (p. 48).

———. 1980. Compulsory heterosexuality and lesbian existence. In *Blood, Bread and Poetry*, pp. 23–75. Edited by A. Rich (1986). New York: Norton.

ROCHE, P. 1958. *The Oedipus Plays of Sophocles*. New York: Mentor.

RODIN, J., L. R. SILBERSTEIN, AND R. H. STREIGEL-MOORE. 1985. Women and weight: A normative discontent. In *Nebraska Symposium on Motivation*, pp. 267–307. Edited by T. B. Sonderegger. Vol. 32, *Psychology and Gender*. Lincoln: University of Nebraska Press.

ROIPHE, H., AND E. GALENSON. 1981. *Infantile Origins of Sexual Identity*. New York: International Universities Press.

ROLAND, A. 1988. *In Search of Self in India and Japan: Toward a Cross-Cultural Psychology*. Princeton: Princeton University Press.

ROMANO, D. L. 1980. Eating our hearts out. *Mother Jones* (June): 20–24.

ROMER, N. 1981. *The Sex-Role Cycle: Socialization from Infancy to Old Age*. New York: McGraw-Hill.

Romer, N., and D. Cherry. 1978. Developmental effects of preschool and school age maternal employment on children's sex-role concepts. Typescript, Brooklyn College.

Rosenberg, M. 1979. *Conceiving the Self*. New York: Basic Books.

Rosenthal, R., and L. Jacobson. 1968. *Pygmalion in the Classroom*. New York: Holt, Rinehart and Winston.

Rosewater, L. B. 1987. Personality disorders: The dinosaur of the DSM-III? Paper presented at the annual convention of the American Psychological Association, New York, August.

Ross, C. E., and J. Mirowsky. 1988. Child care and emotional adjustment to wives' employment. *Journal of Health and Social Behavior* 29:127–38.

Ross, C. E., J. Mirowsky, and J. Huber. 1983. Dividing work, sharing work, and in-between: Marriage patterns and depression. *American Sociological Review* 48:809–23.

Rotter, J. B. 1966. Generalized expectancies for internal vs. external control of reinforcement. *Psychological Monographs* 80(1, no. 609).

Rowbotham, S. 1973. *Woman's Consciousness, Man's World*. Baltimore: Penguin Books.

Rubin, G. 1975. The traffic in women: Notes on the "political economy" of sex. In *Toward an Anthropology of Women*. Edited by R. R. Reiter. New York: Monthly Review Press.

Rubin, J., F. Provenzano, and Z. Luria. 1974. The eye of the beholder: Parents' views on sex of newborns. *American Journal of Orthopsychiatry* 44:512–19.

Rudnytsky, P. L. 1987. *Freud and Oedipus,* New York: Columbia University Press.

Russell, D. 1982. *Rape in Marriage*. New York: Macmillan.

———. 1983. The incidence and prevalence of intrafamilial and extrafamilial sexual abuse of female children. *Child Abuse and Neglect: The International Journal* 7:133.

Russett, C. E. 1989. *Sexual Science: The Victorian Construction of Womanhood*. Cambridge: Harvard University Press.

Russo, N. F., H. Amaro, and M. Winter. 1987. The use of inpatient mental health services by Hispanic women. *Psychology of Women Quarterly* 11:427–42.

Russo, N. F., and S. B. Sobel. 1981. Sex differences in the utilization of mental health facilities. *Professional Psychology* 12:7–19.

Sadker, M., and D. Sadker. 1985. Sexism in the schoolroom of the '80's. *Psychology Today* (March): 54–57.

Salaam, K. Y. 1980. Searching for the mother tongue: An interview with Toni Cade Bambara. *First World* 2(4):48.

San Francisco Chronicle. 1989. *This World* (Sunday supplement). April 23, p. 17.

Scarf, M. 1980. *Unfinished Business: Pressure Points in the Lives of Women*. New York: Doubleday.

Schaefers, J. 1989. *Seventeen* magazine (July): 68.

Schofield, J. 1982. *Black and White in School*. New York: Praeger.

SCHULMAN, G. I., AND M. HOSKINS. 1986. Perceiving the male versus the female face. *Psychology of Women Quarterly* 10:141–54.

SCHULMAN, J. 1980. The marital rape exemption in the criminal law. *Clearinghouse Review* 14(6):538–40.

SCHWARTZ, P., AND D. STROM. 1978. A social psychology of female sexuality. In *The Psychology of Women: Future Directions in Research,* pp. 149–78. Edited by J. A. Sherman and F. L. Denmark. New York: Psychological Dimensions.

SCOTT, V. 1989. McGillis looms over most leading men. *San Francisco Chronicle,* April 20, p. E3.

SEARLES, H. 1965. *Collected Papers on Schizophrenia and Related Subjects.* New York: International Universities Press (p. 296).

———. 1979. *Countertransference and Related Subjects: Selected Papers.* New York: International Universities Press.

SEARS, P. S., AND A. II. BARBEE. 1977. Career and life satisfaction among Terman's gifted women. In *The Gifted and the Creative: Fifty-Year Perspective.* Edited by J. Stanley, W. George, and C. Solano. Baltimore: Johns Hopkins University Press.

SEARS, R., E. MACCOBY, AND H. LEVIN. 1957. *Patterns of Childrearing.* Evanston, IL: Row, Peterson.

SECORD, P. F., AND S. M. JOURARD. 1953. The appraisal of body cathexis: Body-cathexis and the self. *Journal of Consulting Psychology* 17:343–47.

SELIGMAN, C., J. BRICKMAN, AND D. KOULACK. 1977. Rape and physical attractiveness: Assigning responsibility to victims. *Journal of Personality* 45:554–63.

SELIGMAN, M. E. P. 1975. *Helplessness. On Depression, Development and Death,* San Francisco: Freeman.

SELYE, H. 1978. *The Stress of Life.* New York: McGraw-Hill.

SERBIN, L. A., K. D. O'LEARY, R. N. KENT, AND I. J. TONICK. 1973. A comparison of teacher response to the preacademic and problem behavior of boys and girls. *Child Development* 44:796–804.

SHAINESS, N. 1982. Antigone: The neglected daughter of Oedipus. *Journal of the American Academy of Psychoanalysis* 10(3):443–56.

———. 1986. Antigone: Symbol of autonomy and women's moral dilemmas. In *The Psychology of Today's Woman: New Psychoanalytic Visions,* pp. 105–20. Edited by T. Bernay and D. W. Cantor. Hillsdale, NJ: Analytic Press.

SHEA-BUCKLEY, F. 1989. *Oakland Tribune.* June 25, p. A-2.

SHEEHY, G. 1989. The blooming of Margaret Thatcher. *Vanity Fair* (June): 102–12, 164–74.

SILVERSTEIN, B., AND L. PERDUE. 1988. The relationship between role concerns, preference for slimness, and symptoms of eating problems among college women. *Sex Roles* 18(1/2):101–5.

SILVERSTEIN, B., B. PETERSON, AND E. KELLEY. 1986. The role of the mass media in promoting a thin standard of bodily attractiveness for women. *Sex Roles* 14(9/10):519–32.

SIMMONS, R. G., AND F. ROSENBERG. 1975. Sex, sex roles and self image. *Journal of Youth and Adolescence* 4:229–58.

SMITH, D. E. 1975. The statistics on mental illness: What they will not tell us about women and why. In *Women Look at Psychiatry*, p. 97. Edited by D. E. Smith and S. David. Vancouver: Press Gang.

SMITH, G. J. 1985. Facial and full-length ratings of attractiveness related to the social interactions of young children. *Sex Roles* 12(3/4):287–93.

SOMMER, R. 1969. *Personal Space*. Englewood Cliffs, NJ: Prentice-Hall.

SONTAG, S. 1973. The third world of women. *Partisan Review* 40:188.

SPIELER, S. 1986. The gendered self: A lost maternal legacy. In *Psychoanalysis and Women: Contemporary Reappraisals*, p. 36. Edited by J. L. Alpert. Hillsdale, NJ: Analytic Press.

STACK, C. B. 1986. The culture of gender: Women and men of color. *Signs* 11(2):321–24.

STAFFIERI, J. R. 1967. A study of social stereotype of body image in children. *Journal of Personality and Social Psychology* 7(1):101–4.

STAKE, J., AND M. L. LAUER. 1987. The consequences of being overweight: A controlled study of gender differences. *Sex Roles* 17(1/2):31–47.

STANKO, B. 1988. No safe space. *Women's Review of Books* (November).

STANWORTH, M. 1981. *Gender and Schooling: A Study of Sexual Divisions in the Classroom*. London: Women's Research and Resources Center.

STAPLEY, J. C., AND J. M. HAVILAND. 1989. Beyond depression: Gender differences in normal adolescents' emotional experience. *Sex Roles* 20(5/6):295–308.

STERN, D. 1985. *The Interpersonal World of the Infant*. New York: Basic Books.

STEVENSON, M. H. 1989. Review of M. Waring, *If Women Counted*. *New York Times*, October 29, p. 36.

STOLLER, R. 1968. *Sex and Gender*. New York: Science House.

———. 1973a. The "bedrock" of masculinity and femininity: Bisexuality. In *Psychoanalysis and Women: Contributions to New Theory and Therapy*, pp. 245–58. Edited by J. B. Miller. New York: Brunner/Mazel.

———. 1973b. Overview: The impact of new advances in sex research on psychoanalytic theory. *American Journal of Psychiatry* 130:241–51.

STONE, M. 1976. *When God Was a Woman*. New York: Harcourt Brace Jovanovich.

STRACHEY, J. 1953–74. *The Standard Edition of the Complete Psychological Works of Sigmund Freud*. London: Hogarth Press (pp. 228–29).

STREIGEL-MOORE, R. H., L. R. SILBERSTEIN, AND J. RODIN. 1986. Toward an understanding of risk factors for bulimia. *American Psychologist* 41:246–63.

STYCZYNSI, L., AND J. H. LANGLOIS. 1977. The effects of familiarity on behavioral stereotypes associated with physical attractiveness in young children. *Child Development* 48:1137–41.

SUEMATSU, H., H. ISHIKAWA, T. KUBOKI, AND T. ITO. 1985. Statistical studies on anorexia nervosa in Japan: Detailed clinical data on 1,011 patients. *Psychotherapy Psychosomatic* 43:96–103.

SULEIMAN, S. R. 1986. *The Female Body in Western Culture: Contemporary Perspectives*. Cambridge: Harvard University Press.

TACHE, J., AND H. SELYE. 1985. On stress and coping mechanisms. Special issue: Stress and anxiety. *Issues in Mental Health Nursing* 7(1–4):3–24.

TAGGART, M. 1985. The feminist critique in epistemological perspective: Questions of context in family therapy. *Journal of Marital and Family Therapy* 11(2):113–26.

TASCH, R. 1952. The role of the father in the family. *Journal of Experimental Education* 20:319–61.

THOITS, P. A. 1986. Multiple identities: Examining gender and marital status differences in distress. *American Sociological Review* 51:259–72.

THOMAS, A., AND S. CHESS. 1977. *Temperament and Development.* New York: Brunner/Mazel.

THOMAS, A., S. CHESS, H. G. BIRCH, M. E. HERTZIG, AND S. KORN. 1963. *Behavioral Individuality in Early Childhood.* New York: New York University Press.

THOMPSON, J. K. 1986. Larger than life. *Psychology Today* (April): 39–44.

THOMPSON, S. K., AND P. M. BENTLER. 1971. The priority of cues in sex discrimination by children and adults. *Developmental Psychology* 5:181–85.

THOMSON, C. 1942. Cultural pressures in the psychology of women. *Psychiatry* 5:331–39.

THORNE, B., C. KRAMARAE, AND N. HENLEY, EDS. 1983. *Language, Gender, and Society.* Rowley, MA: Newbury House.

THORNE, B., AND Z. LURIA. 1986. Sexuality and gender in children's daily worlds. *Social Problems* 33(3):176–90.

THORNTON, B., AND R. M. RYCKMAN. 1983. The influence of a rape victim's physical attractiveness on observer's attributions of responsibility. *Human Relations* 36(6):549–62.

TIEGER, T. 1981. Self-rated likelihood of raping and the social perception of rape. *Journal of Research in Personality* 15:147–58.

TIME MAGAZINE. 1989. February 9: 85–111.

TOBIN-RICHARDS, M. H., A. M. BOXER, AND A. C. PETERSON. 1983. The psychological significance of pubertal change. Sex differences in perceptions of self during early adolescence. In *Girls at Puberty*, pp. 127–54. Edited by J. Brooks-Gunn and A. C. Peterson. New York: Plenum Press.

TOUFEXIS, A. 1990. Sex and the sporting life. *Time* magazine (August 6): 76–77.

UNGER, R. K. 1976. Male is greater than female: The socialization of inequality. *Counseling Psychologist* 6:2–9.

———. 1979. *Female and Male: Psychological Perspectives.* New York: Harper & Row.

———. 1983. Through the looking glass: No wonderland yet! (The reciprocal relationship between methodology and models of reality). *Psychology of Women Quarterly* 8:1.

VANCE, C. S. 1984. *Pleasure and Danger: Exploring Female Sexuality.* Boston: Routledge & Kegan Paul.

VANFOSSEN, B. 1981. Sex differences in the mental health effects of spouse support and equity. *Journal of Health and Social Behavior* 22:130–43.

VAN WORMER, K. 1989. Co-dependency: Implications for women and therapy. *Women and Therapy* 8(4):51–64.

VEITH, I. 1965. *Hysteria: The History of a Disease.* Chicago: University of Chicago Press.

VEROFF, J. 1983. Contextual determinants of personality. *Personality and Social Psychology Bulletin* 9(3):331–43.

VEROFF, J., E. DOUVAN, AND R. KULKA. 1981. *The Inner American: A Self-Portrait from 1957 to 1976.* New York: Basic Books.

VIETS, E. 1989. Granny Fannies get big exposure. *St. Louis Post-Dispatch,* March 7, p. 3D.

VILLIMEZ, C., N. EISENBERG, AND J. L. CARROLL. 1986. Sex differences in the relation of children's height and weight to academic performance and others' attributions of competence. *Sex Roles* 15(11/12):667–81.

WALKER, L. 1979. *The Battered Woman.* New York: Harper & Row.

WALSTER, E., V. ARONSON, D. ABRAHAMS, AND L. ROTTMAN. 1966. Importance of physical attractiveness in dating behavior. *Journal of Personality and Social Psychology* 4(5):508–16.

WALTERS, M., B. CARTER, P. PAPP, AND O. SILVERSTEIN. 1988. *The Invisible Web: Gender Patterns in Family Relationships.* New York: Guilford.

WARDLE, J., AND S. BEALES. 1986. Restraint, body image, and food attitudes in children from 12 to 18 years. *Appetite* 7:209–17.

WARING, M. 1988. *If Women Counted: A New Feminist Economics.* New York: Harper & Row.

WARREN, L. W., AND L. McEACHREN. 1985. Derived identity and depressive symptomatology in women differing in marital and employment status. *Psychology of Women Quarterly* 9(1):133–44.

WARSHAW, R. 1988. *I Never Called It Rape: The Ms. Report on Recognizing, Fighting and Surviving Date and Acquaintance Rape.* New York: Harper & Row.

WATTENBERG, E., AND H. REINHARDT. 1981. Female-headed families. In *Women and Mental Health,* pp. 357–72. Edited by E. Howell and M. Bayes. New York: Basic Books.

WATZLAWICK, P., J. H. BEAVIN, AND D. D. JACKSON. 1967. *Pragmatics of Human Communication,* New York: Norton.

WEI-MING, TU. 1989. Embodying the universe: A note on Confucian self-realization. In *The World and I: A Chronicle of Our Changing Era,* pp. 475–85. Edited by M. Kaplan. Washington, DC: New World Communications.

WEINRAUB, M., AND J. FRANKEL. 1977. Sex differences in parent-infant interaction during free play, departure, and separation. *Child Development* 48:1240–49.

WEISSMAN, M. M. 1987. Advances in psychiatric epidemiology: Rates and risks for major depression. *American Journal of Public Health* 77:445–51.

WEISSMAN, M. M., AND G. L. KLERMAN. 1977. Gender and depression. *Trends in Neurosciences* 8:416–20.

———. 1985. Sex differences in the epidemiology of depression. *Archives of General Psychiatry* 34:98–111.

WELLS, L. 1989. *New York Times Magazine*. Cited in *On the Issues* 12:6.

WESTKOTT, M. 1986. *The Feminist Legacy of Karen Horney*. New Haven: Yale University Press.

WESTPHAL, C. 1871. Die Agoraphobie: Eine Neuropathische Erscheinung. *Arch für Psychiatrie und Nervenkrankheiten* 3:138–61.

WHITE, T. H. *The Once and Future King*. New York: Berkley (p. 122).

WINNICOTT, D. W. 1960. The theory of parent-infant relationship. *International Journal of Psychoanalysis* 41:585–95.

———. 1964. *The Child, the Family and the Outside World*. New York: Penguin.

———. 1965. *Maturational Processes and the Facilitating Environment: Studies in the Theory of Emotional Development*. New York: International Universities Press.

———. 1969. The use of an object. *International Journal of Psychoanalysis* 50:700–716.

WOLMAN, C., AND H. FRANK. 1975. The solo woman in a professional peer group. *American Journal of Orthopsychiatry* 45:164–71.

WOLOWITZ, H. M. 1972. Hysterical character and feminine identity. In *Readings on the Psychology of Women*. Edited by J. M. Bardwick. New York: Harper & Row.

WOLPE, J. 1958. *Psychotherapy by Reciprocal Inhibition*. Stanford: Stanford University Press.

———. 1970. Identifying the antecedents of an agoraphobic reaction: A transcript. *Journal of Behavior Therapy and Experimental Psychiatry* 1:299–304.

WOOLEY, O., S. WOOLEY, AND S. DYRENFORTH. 1979. Obesity and women—II. A neglected feminist topic. *Women's Studies Institute Quarterly* 2:81–92.

YAGER, J. 1989. The ideal body: Gay vs. straight. *Psychology Today* (August): 67.

YALOM, I. 1989. *Love's Executioner*. New York: Basic Books.

YANG, C. F., AND C. C. CHIU. 1988. Exploratory studies on measuring the Chinese concept of self-esteem. Paper presented at the International Congress of Psychology, Sydney, Australia.

Z MAGAZINE. 1989. Crimes of gender. July/August: 61.

ZILBOORG, G. 1944. Masculine and Feminine: Some biological and cultural aspects. *Psychiatry* 7:257–96.

ZIVNEY, O. A., M. R. NASH, AND T. L. HULSEY. 1989. Sexual abuse in early versus late childhood: Differing patterns of pathology as revealed on the Rorschach. *Psychotherapy* 25(1):99–106.

ZUK, G. R. 1972. Family therapy: Clinical hodgepodge or clinical science? *Journal of Marriage and Family Counseling* 2:229–304.

Index

A

Abortion, 142, 162

Abrahams, Marianne, 110

Adler, Alfred, 150

Adolescence: depression in, 176; dieting in, 192–93; importance of attractiveness in, 90–91; magazines and, 109; physically based self-concept in, 90–91

Advertising, 107–8, 113, 181, 194, 199–200

Aggression, 108, 123–28

Agoraphobia, 17, 186–87

Al-Issa, Ihsan, 186

Allport, Gordon, 149

American Medical Association, 168

American Psychiatric Association, 166, 168

Amnesia, 187

Androgyny, 43, 163

Anger, 102, 139, 222–23

Anhedonia, 171

Anorexia nervosa, 190–92, 196, 208

Antecedents of Self-Esteem, The (Coopersmith), 159–60

Antigonal psychology, 75–86; assessment and, 215–16; awareness of, in therapy, 210–25; phases of development in, 83–85; resolution in, 76–77, 84–88, 223

Antigone, 57–60, 62, 64–65, 72, 75–79, 81–83, 86, 88, 94, 126, 223

Antigone (Sophocles), 58, 59, 60

Anxiety, 183–87; castration, 20–21, 63, 65–67, 69

Aristotle, 82

Arnold, Karen, 162

Assertiveness, 12, 157, 177, 182

Assessment: in feminist therapy, 215–19; language of, 165–70; of women's disorders, 165–70

Athletes, female, 109–10, 201

Athletic programs, 156–57, 200–201

Attractiveness, female: advertisements and, 107–8, 113; body as combat zone and, 195–97; body as presentation in, 193–95; dieting and, 197–201; eating

Attractiveness, female *(continued)*
  disorders and, 192; focus on, 181–82;
  hypervisibility and, 99–100; importance of, 55, 56, 70–71, 76, 81, 84,
  90–91, 96–97, 103–11, 144–45, 178,
  179, 192–93, 216–17; life or death
  and, 201–2; parts vs. whole and, 202,
  203–4; rape and, 146; self-esteem and,
  159, 160, 191–93; self-evaluation of,
  100, 112; toys and, 108; training for,
  90–91, 94–95, 194–95; vulnerability
  and, 97–98, 104–5
Attractiveness, male, 93; self-esteem
  and, 160; self-evaluation of, 112
Attribution, 158
Australia, 135–36

Body image, 176
Bonding: female, 94–95; male, 224
Borderline Personality Disorders, 187
Boundaries: definition of, 93; lack of
  male, 61–67, 70–74, 132–37; limits
  vs., 131; permeable, of women, 125,
  137–47
Bozarth, Glenn, 108
Branch, C. H. Hardin, 191
Breasts, 79, 100, 112, 145, 153, 198, 206
Brickman, J., 146
Brodsky, Annette, 3
Broverman, I. K., 21
Brown, Laura, 168
Bruch, Hilde, 208
Bulimarexia, 190
Bulimia, 190, 192
Burton, Gabrielle, 89, 112
Bush, George, 40

B

Balmary, M., 60
Bambara, Toni Cade, 7–8
Barbie dolls, 108
Bargaining, 222
Barr, Roseanne, 96
Barry, Rick, 136
Bart, Pauline, 3, 137
Bateson, Gregory, 23–24, 29, 69
Bateson, Mary Catherine, 69
Becker, Ernest, 30, 135, 153
Behaviorism, 12–14
Behavior modification, 12–14
Belk, Russell, 109, 113
Betz, Nancy, 176
Blindness, oedipal, 63, 64, 75, 159,
  162
Bodichon, Barbara, 62
Body building, 198

C

Caplan, Paula, 168
Careers: dress-for-success concept and,
  103–4; of mothers, 34
Carli, Linda, 157
Castration anxiety, 20–21, 63, 65–67,
  79
Celibacy, 81, 143
Chaiken, Shelly, 110
Chalice and the Blade, The (Eisler), 96*n*
Chassegeut-Smirgel, Janine, 107
Chernin, Kim, 203, 204, 207
Chesler, Phyllis, 3
Chicago, Judy, 138, 208–9
Child-rearing arrangements: in the colo-
  nial U.S., 117; gender training in,

120–25; male attitudes to, 135, 136; in nuclear family, 115–17, 128–30; other types of, 117; parenting by men, 121–23, 128–29, 135, 157–58; shift in, 119

China, 151

Chocolate, 207

Chodorow, Nancy, 16, 26–27, 61, 114, 116–20, 122, 123, 127, 129, 154

Circumcision, 135–36

Classical conditioning, 12–14

Class identity, 50, 155, 170, 174

Clinical psychology, 19–22

Clitoridectomy, 79

Clitoris, 3, 79

Clothing, 94, 103–6, 109, 181, 194

Clotilde, 100

Co-dependency, 29, 161, 181

Cognitive therapy, 28

Cohen, Richard, 80

Competency: of men, 194; of women, 157, 158, 179

Conscious, 15, 214–15

Consciousness raising, 3, 25, 214–15, 222–23

Contempt, of men for women, 40–41

Control: anorexia nervosa and, 191, 192; of body, 194–95; depression and, 218–19; eating disorders and, 205–6; locus of, 97–98; responsibility and, 161, 218

Coopersmith, Stanley, 155, 159–60

Cosby, Bill, 136

Cosmetics, 104, 194

Cosmetic surgery, 104, 194, 195, 206

Countertransference, 16

Couples therapy, 136–37, 216–17

Creon, 58–59, 63, 64, 77

Crombie, Gail, 124

Crying, 105

Culture: as context, 30–32; defined, 30; psychology of the body and, 48–54

D

Dally, Peter, 196

d'Andrea, Novella, 70

Daughters: antigonal psychology of, 75–86; eating disorders of, 204–6; father-daughter incest, 58–61, 62–63, 65–67, 75–77, 142–43, 144; fathers and development of, 92–94; sexualization by father, 58–61, 65–69. *See also* Women

de Beauvoir, Simone, 31

de Lauretis, Teresa, 215

Denial, 71, 222

Denial of Death (Becker), 30

Dependency, 29, 161, 181, 186

Depression, 113, 171–83; control and, 218–19; disconnection and detachment in, 175–79; false responsibility and, 180–81; gender identity and, 173–74; loss and, 182–83; mastery and, 176, 178–79; negative evaluations of women and, 179–80; shame and, 181–82; social inequities and, 174–75; symptoms of, 171, 177

Descartes, René, 19, 149, 153

Desensitization, 12

Detachment, 175–79

Deutsch, Francine, 158

Diagnostic and Statistical Manual (DSM): DSM-II, 166; DSM-III, 168; DSM-IIIR, 166, 168, 184, 186–87

Dickinson, Janice, 100

Dieting, 192–94; mother-daughter relationship and, 204–6; as normal eating for women, 197–201; "thin within" approach to, 203–4

Dimen, Muriel, 107

"Dinner Party, The" (Chicago), 208–9

Dinnerstein, Dorothy, 114

Diotima of Mantineia, 82

Disconnection, 175–79

Dissociation, 187–80

Double description, 53–54

Downs, A. Chris, 107

Dreams, 149

Dress-for-success concept, 103–4

DSM-IIIR (Diagnostic and Statistical Manual), 166, 168, 184, 186–87

ing of meaning and, 10, 23–24; prefeminist, 10–23

Erhardt, Anke, 38

Erikson, Erik, 137

Esquire, 109

Eteocles, 58

Ethnic identity, 85, 101, 104

Eurman, Linda J., 191

Exercise, 87–88, 156–57, 194, 198, 199–201

Eyes, 113

E

Eating: dieting as normal, 197–201; female obsession with, 197

Eating disorders, 83, 84, 113; anorexia nervosa, 190–92, 196, 208; bulima-rexia, 190; bulimia, 190, 192; disowning of physical and, 203; mother-daughter relationship and, 204–6

Eder, Donna, 157

Education, 150; academic achievement and, 196; female mastery and, 162–63; women and, 177, 178

Eichenbaum, Luise, 82, 154

Eisler, Riane, 96*n*

Ekman, Paul, 47

Electra complex, 61

Emotion, psychology of the body and, 46–54

Enmeshment, 2, 17–18, 129–30

Entitlement, 62, 67, 70–73, 84, 87, 93; of fathers, 196; male fear of loss of, 140; male lack of boundaries and, 61–67, 70–74, 132–37; rape as, 65–66, 81; relinquishment of, 73–75

Epistemology: defined, 10; feminist, 24–36, 210; masculinist, 10, 11–23; mean-

F

Facial expression, 47, 158, 178

Fallon, April, 112

False self, 153

Family therapy, 2, 16–18, 21–22; active role of father and, 129; relationship role of women and, 126–27

Family Therapy Networker, 105–6

Fathers: anorexogenic, 196; as child-rearing experts, 17–18, 129; development of daughters and, 92–94; entitlement of, 196; gender stereotypes and, 45; incest with daughters, 58–61, 62–63, 65–67, 75–77, 142–43, 144; jealousy of children and, 116; mirroring by, 107; oedipal psychology and, 61–75; parenting by, 121–23, 128–29, 135, 157–58; sexualization of women by, 58–61, 65–69. *See also* Men

Fear: anxiety and, 183–85; phobias and, 185–86

Female bonding, 94–95

Feminist epistemology, 24–36, 210

Feminist psychology: clinical psychology and, 19–22; context and, 30–32; critique of feminist epistemology and, 24–27; critique of masculinist epistemology and, 10–23; meaning-symbolism and, 32–36, 211; object-relations approach, 16, 26–27, 56–57, 61, 106–7, 114, 153, 204; oedipal psychology and, 61–75; toward a feminist epistemology in, 27–36

Feminist therapy, 26–27, 210–25; artificial separation of mind and body and, 219–21; assessment in, 215–19; behaviorism and, 12–14; consciousness in, 214–15; invisibility of women and, 211–12; lost sense of self and esteem and, 221–23; meaning in, 32–36, 211, 212–14; model for, 211–12; origins of, 3–4; patient-therapist relationship in, 212; psychoanalysis and, 14–16, 153

Feminist Therapy Institute, 4

Fetishistic male desire, 56

Fodor, Iris, 186

Food, 157; female obsession with, 197; gender identity and, 107, 110–11; sex and, 207–9. *See also* Eating disorders

Freire, Paulo, 214

Freud, Anna, 60, 77, 101

Freud, Mathilde, 60

Freud, Sigmund, 3, 20–21, 30, 60–61, 62, 63, 65, 67, 70, 101, 150, 223; on anatomy as destiny, 42, 54; antigonal psychology and, 75, 76; female orgasm and, 80; on female superego, 180; oedipal conflict and, 57–61, 62, 63, 65, 67, 70; psychoanalysis and, 14–16

Frieze, I. H., 22

Frigidity, 3–4, 80, 166–67

Frye, Marilyn, 224

Fryer, Maury, 158

Fugue state, 187

G

Galenson, Eleanor, 79

Gardner, Carol Brooks, 138

Garfinkel, Harold, 38*n*, 112

Gellner, Ernest, 24

Gender identity, 26–27; anatomy as destiny and, 42–46, 54; dichotomy in, 38–42, 107, 168; enforcement of, 39–42; establishment of, 42 13; food and, 107, 110–11; magazines and, 109; nature of, 43; in preverbal period, 120–21; psychoanalysis and, 15–16; psychology of the body and, 46–54; self and, 149–52; self-esteem and, 155–64; sexuality and, 55–57; sex vs., 38, 41; stereotyping of, 45, 121–22, 155; television and, 107–8, 117; toys and, 108; training for, 120–25

Gender identity, female: appearance as basis of, 90–91; depression and, 173–74; fragmented sense of, 187–89; hypervisibility and, 87, 99–100; invisibility and, 87, 100–102; mourning losses and, 222; permeability of boundaries and, 137–47; prism of self-image and, 106–11; seeing self from outside in, 103–6

Gender identity, male, 39–40; lack of boundaries and, 61–67, 70–74, 132–37

General systems theory, 34

Genitalia, 3, 38–39, 79, 101, 135–36

Gestalt psychology, 28, 204

Gilligan, Carol, 114, 125–26, 154

Girard, René, 66

Girgus, Joan, 176

Gold, Dolores, 124

Goldman, Emma, 85

Goldstein, Rebecca, 152

Gomez, Joan, 196

Gondolf, Edward, 81

Gornick, Vivian, 138

Gossip, 178

Grandiosity, infantile, 62–65, 71–75, 93, 221

Grief, 222

Griffin, Susan, 37

Griffith-Joyner, Florence, 109–10, 201

Gurin, Patricia, 154

H

Haemon, 59

Hair, 94, 103, 104, 108, 113

Haley, Jay, 17–18

Halpert, F. E., 109–10

Hansen, Patti, 100

Harrison, Sheila K., 107

Heartbreak Hotel (Burton), 89, 112

Heightened vigilance, 139, 183–87

Heilbrun, Carolyn, 88

Heisenberg Uncertainty Principle, 9

Herman, Judith, 101, 126

High-heeled shoes, 56, 97–98, 103

Hoffman, Lynn, 186

Homosexuality, 101, 168; eating disorders and, 191; parenting and, 119.
See also Lesbianism

Horney, Karen, 68, 101

Humiliation, 202; eating and, 191; gender identity and, 41, 123–24. *See also*
Shame

Humor, 158

Hypervisibility, 87, 99–100, 202, 203

Hysteria, 169

I

If Women Counted (Waring), 164n, 223

Impotence, 80, 166–67

Incest: father-daughter, 58–63, 65–67,
75–77, 142–43, 144; sensitivity to aggressor and, 126

Indeterminate observer, 82, 108, 112,
175, 176, 178, 188, 210, 212, 214,
220

India, 151

Individuality, 136, 149–51

Infibulation, 79

Initiation rites: female, 142–45; male,
135–36

Intimacy: orgasm vs., 145; violence and,
126

Invisibility, of women, 19, 31–32, 76–
77, 80–81, 87–88, 100–102, 134, 138,
176, 177, 189, 211–12

"Invisible Woman, The" (Morgan),
101–2

Islam, 69

Ismene, 59, 88

Isolation, 150

J

Jacklin, Carol, 178
James, William, 159–60
James-Lange theory of emotion, 47–48
Japan, 133, 151, 191
Jewelry, 104
Jocasta, 58, 62, 63, 64, 65, 75–76, 78, 82, 86, 88, 116, 205, 208, 221
Johnson, Virginia, 3
Jordan, Judith, 154
Judaism, 69
Jung, Emma, 77

K

Kagan, Jerome, 155
Keller, Evelyn Fox, 13, 19
Kennedy, John F., 85
Kessler, Ronald, 174
Klein, Melanie, 101, 153
Koedt, Anne, 3
Kohut, Heinz, 153
Kovlack, D., 146
Kübler-Ross, Elizabeth, 222

L

Laius, King, 58, 59, 60, 64, 66, 75
Language, limits of, 6–8, 29, 45, 166–70
LeBaron, Dorothy, 158

Legs, 113
Lerman, Hannah, 3, 187
Lesbianism, 81, 101, 119, 139. *See also* Homosexuality
Lewis, Helen Block, 101
Limits, 131, 137–38
Lincoln, Abraham, 29, 33
Locus of control, 97–98
Logical empiricism, 23
Logical positivism, 13, 14
Lorde, Audre, 87
Loss: depression and, 182–83; male fear of, 140; mourning and, 222
Love's Executioner (Yalom), 70 71
Luria, Zella, 45

M

Maccoby, Eleanor, 178
Mademoiselle magazine, 109
Magazines, 2, 72, 109, 195
Mahler, Margaret, 106
Makeup, 100, 103–6, 108, 109
Male bonding, 224
Manic depression, 174
Marriage, 149; depression and, 182–83; female preference for, 161; protection of, in cohabitation, 141; rape in, 132–33, 141, 143, 144
Mascara, 105
Masculinist epistemology, 11–23; clinical theories and methods of, 11–22; defined, 10
Maslow, Abraham, 153
Masters, William, 3
Masterson, James, 153

Mastery, 162–64, 176, 178–79

Masturbation, 145, 207

Matriarchy, 224

Mattering maps, 152, 163, 178, 192, 211

McGrath, Ellen, 174

McLuhan, Marshall, 31

Mead, Margaret, 80

Meaning, 210; of experience in therapy, 212–14; in feminist psychology, 32–36, 211, 212–14; of meaning, 10, 23–24

Men: attitude toward physical space, 50–52, 132, 133; bonding of, 224; competency of, 194; eating disorders of, 191; grandiosity of, 62–65, 71–75, 93, 221; initiation rites of, 135–36; lack of boundaries and, 61–67, 70–74, 132–37; magazines for, 109; multiple roles and, 163; nature of, 19, 20–22; oedipal psychology and, 61–75; parenting by, impact of, 121–23, 128–29, 135, 157–58; relatedness of, 115–20, 127; self-esteem of, 155–56; sense of self and, 149–51; separation and individuation by, 136; sexualization of women by, 62, 63, 68–69; violence and, 66–67. *See also* Attractiveness, male; Fathers; Gender identity, male; Sexuality, male

Menstruation, 135–36

Meta-communication, 23–24

Miller, Alice, 106, 153

Miller, Jean Baker, 91, 127, 154

Millman, Marcia, 203

Mills College, 163

Mind-Body Problem, The (Goldstein), 152

Mintz, Laurie, 176

Minuchin, Salvador, 17–18

Mirroring, 106–7

Mischel, Walter, 154

Misogyny, 17, 26–27, 38, 40, 70–71, 79, 208

Models, fashion, 2, 100

Moldawsky, Stanley, 111

Molestation, 81–82, 142–45; identification with aggressor and, 126; multiple-personality disorder and, 188; in nuclear family, 118; shame and, 105

Money, John, 38, 41

Morgan, Robin, 101–2, 133

Mother-child relationship: adult men and, 115–16; in nuclear families, 115–17

Mothers: antigonal psychology of, 75–86; eating disorders of daughters and, 204–6; employment of, 34; enmeshed, 2, 17–18, 129–30; female separation from, 82; gender stereotypes and, 45; mirroring by, 106–7; oedipal conflict and, 57–58, 61–67, 204–6; relationship with daughters, 64–65, 75–86, 95, 204–6; role of, 115–17; schizophrenogenic, 2. *See also* Women

Mourning, 222

Multiple-personality disorder, 47, 113, 187–89

Musa, Kathleen, 112, 160

N

Names, women and, 101, 138, 161, 177

Nathan, Sharon G., 67

Neighbors, Harold, 174

New Guinea, 135

Noble, Sally, 124
Nose jobs, 104
Nuclear family, 115–17, 128–30, 223; father as primary caregiver in, 122; sexual assault in, 58–61, 62–63, 65–67, 75–77, 118, 142–43, 144. *See also* Fathers; Mothers; Parenting

O

Obesity, 71, 96, 206
Objectification, of women by men, 62, 63, 68–69, 85–86
Object-relations psychology, 26–27, 61; female vs. male, 114; feminist psychology and, 16; fragmentation of self and, 204; mirroring in, 106–7; self in, 153; sexuality and, 56–57
Obscene phone calls, 93
Oedipal psychology: awareness of, in therapy, 210–25; blindness and, 63, 64, 75, 159, 162; feminist psychology and, 61–75; Freud's view of, 57–63, 65, 67, 70; mothering in, 204–6; phases of development and, 72–73; psychoanalysis and, 15–16; resolution of, 62, 74–76, 87, 221, 223–24; of women, 76
Oedipus, 57–79, 83, 94, 116
Oedipus at Colonus (Sophocles), 58–59
Oedipus Rex (Sophocles), 58
Operant conditioning, 12–14
Orbach, Susie, 82, 154
Orgasm, 109, 145, 166–67; faking of, 80; female, 79–81; types of, 3, 80

P

Pagels, Heinz, 49
Parenting: depression and, 183; homosexual, 119; male vs. female, 121–25, 128–29. *See also* Fathers; Mothers
Pelops, King, 59
Penis, 3, 79, 101, 135–36
Penis envy, 15, 67
Perpetual vigilance, 139, 183–87
Person, Ethel, 111
Personality: changes in, 155; multiple, 47, 113, 187–89
Phallic symbols, 79
Phallocentrism, 15
Phenomenology, 52–54
Phobias, 186–87; behaviorism and, 12; family therapy and, 18; psychoanalysis and, 15–16
Physical abuse: multiple-personality disorder and, 188, 189. *See also* Rape
Playboy magazine, 2, 109
Pliner, Patricia, 110
Pollack, Susan, 125–26
Polynices, 58, 59
Pornography, 181
Post-Traumatic Stress Disorder (PTSD), 184–85, 187
Power: differential, male vs. female, 39–40; gender differences and, 17–18; of male therapist over female patient, 3; sex and, 65, 66, 71–72, 73, 80, 146–47
Prefeminist epistemology, 10–23
Pre-oedipal period, 61, 76
Pre-orgasmic therapy, 3–4, 79–80
Preverbal period, 120–21
Projective identification, 16
Provenzano, Frank, 45
Psychoanalysis, 14–16, 153
Psychoneuroimmunology, 9, 47

Psychopathology, in women, 3–4, 5, 165–70

Psychosexual development, 15–16

Rozin, Raul, 112

Rubin, Gayle, 38, 41

Rubin, Jeffrey, 45

Rudnytsky, P. L., 58

Russell, Bertrand, 20

R

Racial identity, 34, 50, 85, 104, 155, 174

Rank, Otto, 75

Rape, 21, 53, 65, 66, 81, 180, 184–85, 212–13; attractiveness of women and, 146; gang bang, 143–44, 219; as male fantasy, 146; marital, 132–33, 141, 143, 144; shame and, 105

Rational-emotive therapy, 28

Reagan, Ronald, 85

Rebellion, adolescent, 91

Rejection, male fear of, 140

Relatedness: depression and loss of, 181; of men and women, 115–20, 127; need for, and depression, 176–77; as safety for women, 138–40; self-concept and, 119–20; self-esteem and, 160–62

Repression, 30–31. *See also* Oedipal psychology

Responsibility: control and, 161, 218; false, 180–81

Rich, Adrienne, 88

Rivera, Geraldo, 100

Roach, Mary, 112, 160

Rogers, Carl, 153

Roiphe, Herman, 79

Romania, 110

Rosewater, Lynne, 168

S

Safety, female concern for, 124–25, 127–28, 138–40

Satir, Virginia, 17

Schizophrenia, 170

Schizophrenogenic mothers, 2

Schulman, Joan, 141

Searles, Harold, 16, 92–93

Seduction hypothesis, 59–60

Self, 149–54; in context, 154–55; as feminine construct, 151–52; interrelation of, 151; lost sense of, 221–23; as masculine construct, 149–51; psychological approach to, 152–53; as separate and individual, 149–51

Self-actualization, 153

Self-concept: self-esteem vs., 156; separateness and individuality of, 149–51

Self-concept, female, 95–111; central components of, 98; fragmentation of, 111–13; male vs., 123–24; personal control and, 97–98; physical appearance and, 90–99; relatedness and, 119–20

Self-esteem: defined, 155; feminist therapy and, 221–22; male vs. female, 119–20; masculinity as norm in, 155–

56, 158–59; paradox of women's, 156–62; physical attractiveness and, 159, 160, 191–93; primacy of relationships and, 126–27

Self-hatred, of women, 67, 84

Self-in-context, 154–55

Self-mutilation, 63

Seligman, C., 146

Seligman, Martin E. P., 180

Separation, sense of self and, 82, 136, 149–51

Seventeen magazine, 109

Sex: anatomy as destiny and, 42–46; food and, 207–9; gender vs., 38; and power, 65, 66, 71–72, 73, 80, 146–47; psychology of the body and, 46–54

Sexual abuse, 207–8; multiple-personality disorder and, 188, 189. *See also* Rape

Sexual harassment, 142

Sexual intercourse: intimacy and, 145; orgasm in, 3–4

Sexuality, female, 87–88; body as combat zone and, 195–97; denial of, 79; fragmentation of, 82; incest and, 58–61, 62–63, 65–67, 75–77, 142–43, 144; initiation and, 142–45; life cycle of, 81; male lack of boundaries and, 141–47; male vs., 56–57, 68, 146; from masculine perspective, 55–57; mutilation and, 79; orgasm in, 79–81; shame and, 68–69, 81–82, 85. *See also* Rape

Sexuality, male: dominance and power in, 66–67; female sexuality vs., 56–57, 68, 146; fetishism, 56; oedipal conflict and, 57–75

Shainess, Natalie, 85–86

Shame, 42, 105, 189; depression and, 181–82; female sexuality and, 68–69, 81–82, 85; gender identity and, 41, 123–24; hypervisibility of women and, 202, 203

Shea-Buckley, Frances, 184

Shoes: of men, 104; of women, 56, 97–98, 103

Shopping, 94, 105–6, 181, 220

Single parenting, 119

Sisterhood Is Global (Morgan), 133

Sitting position, 134

Skin, 113

Skinner, B. F., 12

Slate, Kenneth R., 123

Smiling, 47, 158, 178

Smith, Dorothy, 167

Smoking, 198, 201

Social context: behaviorism and, 13–14; causality and, 38, 40; culture as, 30–32; family therapy and, 18; feminist psychology and, 30–32; gender identity and, 38, 40, 45–46; mothering in, 204–6; self in, 154–55

Socrates, 82

Sontag, Susan, 147

Sophocles, 57, 58, 59, 60

Standing position, 134

Stereotypes, gender role, 45, 121–22, 155

Stoller, Robert, 38

Stone, Merlin, 96n

Stress, 47; chronic, 184–85; of parenting, 183; perpetual vigilance and, 139, 183–87

Subincision, 135–36

Sullivan, Harry Stack, 150

Superego, 180

Surnames, 101, 138, 161, 177

Surrey, Janet, 154

Symposium (Socrates), 82

T

Taggart, Morris, 27
Television, 56, 81, 107–8, 113, 117, 194–95
Thatcher, Margaret, 110
Thematic Apperception Test (TAT), 125–26
Thomson, Clara, 91
Tiresias, 63
Toys, mirroring and, 108
Transsexuals, 38, 41

U

Unconscious, 15, 30. *See also* Oedipal psychology
Unger, Rhoda, 27

V

Vagina, 3, 79, 101
Values, 34–35
Vance, Carole, 49, 141
Veith, Ilza, 169
Veroff, Joseph, 154
Veterans, women as, 184
Violence, 65–67, 124–25, 184; female fear of, 139; male vs. female attitudes to, 125–26; against women, 180. *See also* Rape
Vulnerability, attractiveness and, 97–98, 104–5

W

Walker, Lenore, 168
Walking shoes, 103
Waring, Marilyn, 164*n*, 223
Watson, John, 12
Weisstein, Naomi, 3
Westphal, Carl Otto, 186
When God Was a Woman (Stone), 96*n*
When Harry Met Sally (film), 80
Whitehead, Alfred North, 20
Winfrey, Oprah, 204
Winnicott, D. W., 106, 153
With a Daughter's Eye (Bateson), 69
Wolpe, J., 12
Women: appropriately feminine behaviors and, 157–58; attitude toward physical space, 49–50, 53, 133–34, 137; bonding of, 224; castration anxiety of men and, 66–67; competence of, 158, 159, 179; definition of disorders of, 165–70; height of, 137; hypervisibility of, 87, 99–100; initiation rites of, 142–45; initiative in psychological development and, 74–75; invisibility of, 19, 31–32, 76–77, 80–81, 87–88, 100–102, 134, 138, 176, 177, 189, 211–12; magazines for, 109; mastery and, 162–64, 176, 178–79; mother-daughter relationship and, 64–65, 75–86; multiple roles and, 163; nature of, 19, 20–22; obese, 71, 96, 206; oedipal psychology and, 61–75; permeable boundaries of, 125, 137–47; relatedness of, 115–20; relationships to men, 62, 64, 75–79; responsibility and, 180–81; safety and, 124–25, 127–28, 138–40; self-esteem of, 156–62; self-hatred of, 67, 84;

sense of self and, 151–52; sensitivity
of, to aggressor, 125–28, 184–85, 187–
89; sexualization of, 62, 63, 68–69,
85–86; size of, 200; surnames of, 101,
138, 161, 177. *See also* Attractiveness,
female; Daughters; Feminist psychology; Gender identity, female; Mothers; Self-concept, female; Sexuality,
female
Women and Madness (Chesler), 3
Women's Counseling Service, 4
Women's movement, 1–2
Working Girl (film), 103

Y

Yager, Joel, 191
Yalom, Irvin, 70–71

Z

Zilboorg, Gregory, 39, 62
Zuk, Gerald, 125